Ceramic Art

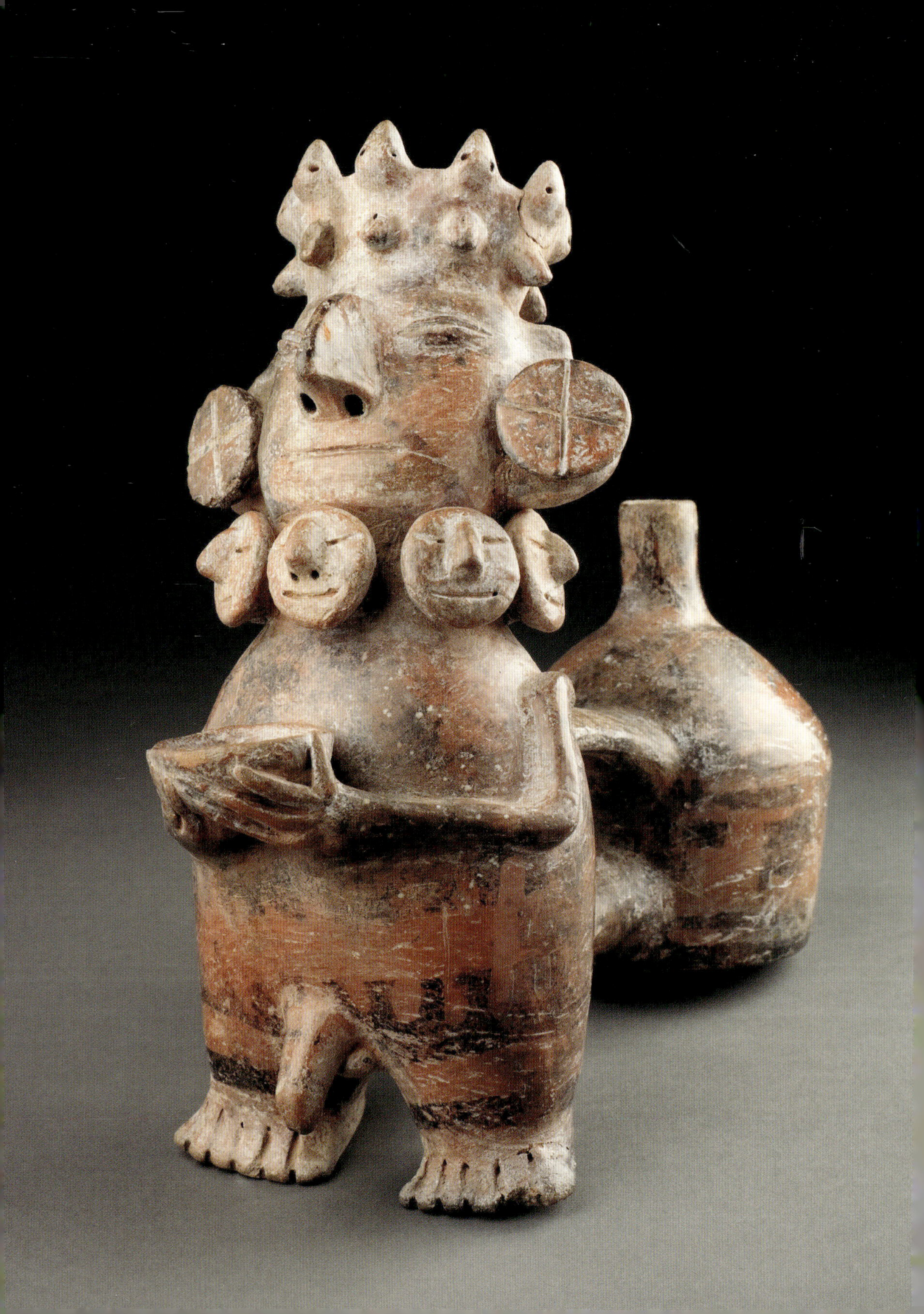

ART/WORK Edited by Caroline Fowler and Ittai Weinryb

Ceramic Art

Margaret S. Graves
Sequoia Miller
Magdalene Odundo
Vicki Parry

Princeton University Press
Princeton and Oxford

Published by
Princeton University Press
41 William Street
Princeton, New Jersey 08540

In the United Kingdom
Princeton University Press
99 Banbury Road
Oxford OX2 6JX

press.princeton.edu

Printed on acid-free paper. ∞

Library of Congress Cataloging-in-Publication Data

Names: Weinryb, Ittai, editor. | Fowler, Caroline O., editor. | Graves, Margaret S. | Miller, Sequoia. | Odundo, Magdalene. | Parry, Vicki.

Title: Ceramic art / Margaret S. Graves, Sequoia Miller, Magdalene Odundo, and Vicki Parry ; edited by Caroline Fowler and Ittai Weinryb.

Other titles: Ceramic art (Princeton University Press)

Description: Princeton : Princeton University Press, [2023] | Series: Art/Work | Includes bibliographical references and index.

Identifiers: LCCN 2022029524 (print) | LCCN 2022029525 (ebook) | ISBN 9780691226637 (paperback) | ISBN 9780691247434 (ebook)

Subjects: LCSH: Pottery—Conservation and restoration.

Classification: LCC NK4233 .C47 2023 (print) | LCC NK4233 (ebook) | DDC 738.1/8—dc23/eng/20220706

LC record available at https://lccn.loc.gov/2022029524

LC ebook record available at https://lccn.loc.gov/2022029525

British Library Cataloging-in-Publication Data is available

Design and composition: Binocular, New York

This book has been composed in Sole Serif and Sole Sans.

Page ii : Ancestor. Vicus ceramic whistling vessel. Northern coast, 500 BCE–200 CE. Museo Larco, Lima, Peru, ML031834 (see fig. 35).

Front cover images, left to right: Bowl with lotus, Thailand, 15–16th centuries (detail of fig. 18); Sacrifice and presentation of the goblet (Mochica ceramic, northern coast, 100–800 CE) (detail of fig. 37); A Meissen porcelain bowl after the 2019 conservation (detail of fig. 44).

Back cover images, left to right: Shaman drum (Nazca ceramic, southern coast of Peru, 100–600 CE) (detail of fig. 33); Cycladic bird jug found at Knossos (detail of fig. 38d).

Printed in China
10 9 8 7 6 5 4 3 2 1

Contents

Foreword

This series maintains that the history of art is about not only the moment of making but also the periods of care, preservation, and decomposition. In this volume, the history of art is a narrative about conservation, preservation, and loss as much as artistic production. This series tells these stories, making accessible how material knowledge impacts the writing and methods of art history.

Ceramic Art is the first volume in the Art/Work series, which aims to make histories of conservation accessible beyond specialist journals and publications. Many of the authors in this volume make explicit their background, and the tools and methods that they use to make, conserve, research, and study ceramics. While these essays are grounded in the understanding that materials matter, the authors remain focused on care, conservation, and how works of art age, change, and metamorphosize over time. In his introduction, Sequoia Miller provides the reader with a brief overview of the history of ceramics to introduce key terms and methods of making. Following Miller's essay, the volume is structured around two essays, one by an art historian—Margaret Graves—and the other by a conservator—Vicki Parry. Both are specialists in ceramics, and both have a deep knowledge of how vessels, pots, sculptures, and all things clay are formed, fired, and glazed. Yet methodologically, they approach their material with a different set of training and tools. These two authors demonstrate how conservation, science, and art history are all dependent on one another as disciplines yet also remain radically distinct methods. These essays are complemented by a variety of perspectives, from that of the maker—Magdalene Odundo—to specialists in a variety of fields who offer brief studies on ceramics from archaeology, conservation, and museum practice. Certain authors, such as Yao-Fen You, also address the limits of technical art history and the field of conservation to provide historical context.

In bringing together these multiple perspectives—from the practitioner to the scholar, from the ancient to the contemporary—we are modeling the necessity of collaboration and conversation to tell stories that encompass geographic and historical range. We are not telling the entire history of ceramic art. Instead, this volume is an introduction as well as a provocation for further reading, looking, and—as Miller suggests in his introduction—holding a vessel in our hands to contemplate how the raw materials of earth and clay transform into an artwork.

Caroline Fowler
Williamstown, MA

Ittai Weinryb
New York, NY

Ceramic Art

Ceramic Art: An Introduction

Sequoia Miller

You are likely more familiar with ceramic than you think. Most of us have an intimate, often daily connection to the material through dishes, sanitary ware, tiles, bricks, and countless other sources. Ceramic art, a subset of the broader field of ceramics, frequently infuses our domestic lives through the vessels, vases, figurines, and many ceramic keepsakes sprinkled throughout the modern, and ancient, worlds.

This volume aims to transform the reader's casual familiarity with ceramic art into a deeper appreciation and understanding. It focuses on the material history of the art form, considering how ceramic expression is both bound and enhanced by the physical properties of clay itself. While art history as a discipline has long analyzed style, expression, and, more recently, the social context that gave rise to various art forms, this study centers the material history of art, which accounts for how the physical characteristics of a medium impact how artworks communicate. Ceramics is an ideal case study because the materiality of clay is never far from our experience of ceramic objects. These objects retain a strong sense of the earth, a kind of insistent *ceramicness*, which keeps us particularly aware of them as material objects. A greater understanding of clay and ceramic enables us to bring our haptic knowledge—a material fluency we have built up through repeated, intimate exposure to ceramics—into the realm of consciousness. From here, we can begin to unfold the stories these objects hold about the past, present, and ourselves. Ceramic art, both global and ancient, is unfathomable in its totality. So how to approach the subject in a volume of this scale?

Rather than a sprawling overview, this book offers individual episodes written from multiple points of view. The contributors write from the perspectives of art history, archaeology, material culture, conservation, museology, studio practice, and material science. We preserve the individuality of voices contained here to point toward the range of possible interpretative strategies. The first three essays anchor the text through a close consideration of how histories of ceramics can be built out of global traditions, conservation, and the individual studio practice of a renowned contemporary artist. Four case studies follow, all of which focus on individual ceramic objects (or groups). While they can be read in any order, collectively the essays demonstrate the particular ways that ceramic art illuminates aspects of the past and the human condition. For the purposes of this book, ceramic art includes objects made with aesthetic, expressive, or artistic intent. The borders of this category are broad, somewhat porous, and not at all policed, yet we do intentionally set aside purely industrial applications (crucibles, insulators, etc.), high-tech ceramics (bullet-proofing, space shuttles, etc.), and architectural applications beyond tile.

This introduction will first describe the core materials and traditions of ceramics, followed by a consideration of the key themes of production and consumption. I will define the terms of the medium (clay, glaze, kiln, etc.), while pointing toward ways that specific materials, technologies, and human need gave rise to multiple traditions. The second section looks at cultural rather than material definitions of ceramics to offer ways of thinking about the broader forces that have shaped its histories. Taken together, this chapter argues that ceramic art has an internal logic bound by both its material and cultural histories. This logic informs how we understand and relate to the medium, at both a deeply human level and within the disciplines of art history and visual culture. Ceramic art—materially insistent, deeply human, and ubiquitous—meets us in the present moment with renewed complexity and relevance.

The power of a ceramic object to open questions about the world occurred vividly for me with a particular eighteenth-century jar [FIG. 1]. I was near the beginning of my training as a historian and curator when a mentor organized a handling session including the jar. I had been a professional studio potter for many years, so I knew clay well, but at the time I carried certain biases against eighteenth-century European ceramics as being overly decorative and fussy. When I held this jar as I would a pot on the potter's wheel, one hand on the inside and one on the outside, I was jolted by feeling finger grooves on the interior created when the potter made the form. Ceramic objects like this one are so highly finished, it is almost impossible to imagine how they come into being. Yet suddenly I found direct traces of the potter's hand, feeling how his fingers had made the grooves that my own fingers fit into so well. The whole object shifted at that moment, becoming something that had been wrought, or fabricated, rather than simply present. I could shift away from my preconceptions about style, and see how the pot was the result of certain decisions made by the makers and designers (objects like this were seldom made by one individual). The decisions embedded in the physical object—for example, that it had been wheel-thrown instead of cast in

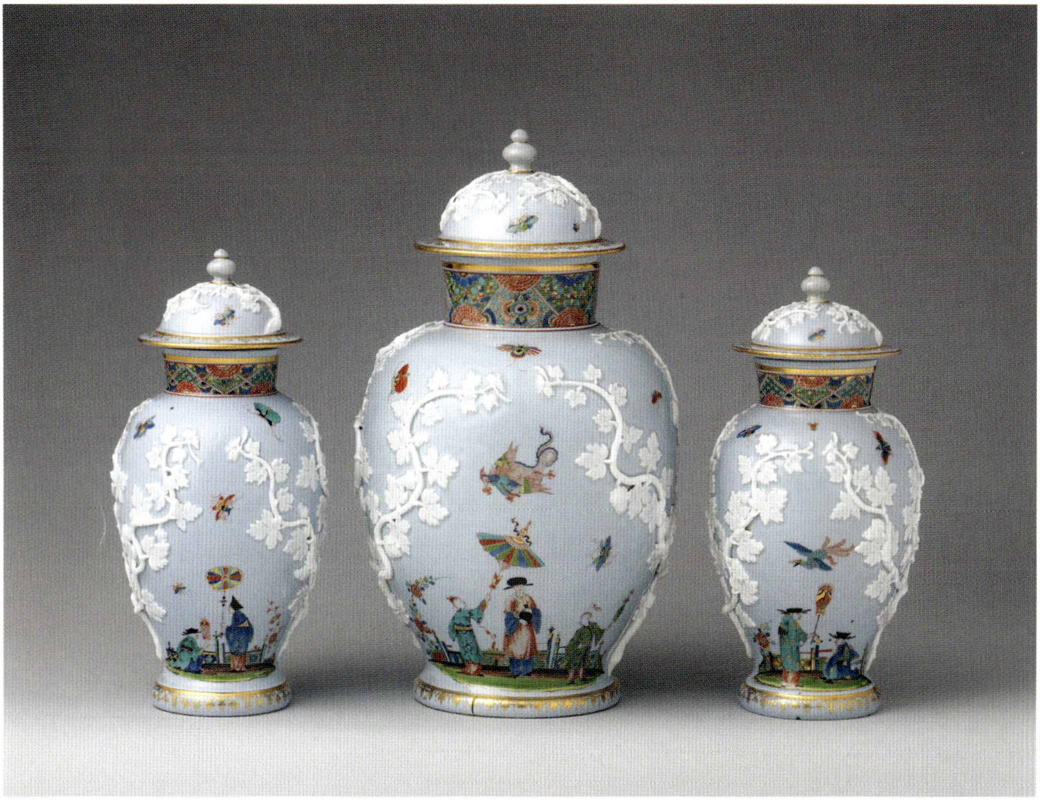

[FIG. 1]
Garniture of three vases, ca. 1725–30. Meissen Porcelain Manufactory (Germany). Metropolitan Museum of Art, New York, 64.101.155a, b.

a mold, or had a tinted clay body as opposed to a colored glaze—soon opened onto broader, complex questions about the myriad social, political, and economic forces that went into an object such as this being created in Germany in the 1730s. How did they develop the technology to make it? Why did light blue semi-Chinese-looking objects become popular? Who would have bought this, and how did that person live with it? How did it help visualize a materialist and expansionist Europe? What was the value of the labor that went into it, and how was that labor organized?

This Meissen jar opened multiple lines of inquiry about how it came into being and the society that created it. Undergirding these questions is a materially based logic for constructing meaning through ceramics. Through both this chapter and those that follow, this book will acquaint the reader with the overall scope of expression in ceramic art, while enhancing perception of the nuances of the medium.

Materials and Traditions of Ceramics: What Is Ceramic?

At its core, ceramic consists of clay that has been transformed by heat into a dense, rocklike material. The heating up of clay, called firing, can occur in an open setting like a pit or in an enclosure, known as a kiln. The clays that go into ceramics are naturally occurring in the earth's crust and common enough that they generally have little commercial value in themselves. The cost of clay is connected more to its extraction, processing, and transportation rather than with the material itself. In fact, clay is often the waste material of other mining processes.

A wide variety of clays occur in the earth. They are composed of rock that has been broken down through geological processes such as erosion into small particles that are sticky and mud-like when wet. Other key physical characteristics of clay include plasticity, meaning it is bendable when wet and can hold its shape when dry. Chemically, clay is composed of silica and alumina, along with trace minerals such as iron and manganese. Unfired clay can always be wetted down (slaked) and returned to a plastic state, whereas fired ceramic will not become workable again. Clays differ from each other based on the composition of originating rock or rocks, the trace minerals, and the particle size and shape resulting from being worn down. Each of these factors, along with the inclusion of any organic material, impacts the clay's workability, firing temperature, and final appearance. While some clays are workable on their own, it is far more frequent that naturally occurring clays are combined to offer the particular characteristics needed. These combinations are called clay bodies.

Firing chemically transforms clay into ceramic. Heat melts some of the molecules so that they create a dense wall suspended in a lattice-like matrix, while the rest of the molecules create the matrix itself. This partial melting process is called vitrification, and when fully vitrified, clay becomes relatively strong and absorbs little moisture—important for storing and serving liquids, especially in preindustrial times. Not all vitrified ceramic is fully impervious to liquid. Some objects are instead designed to absorb water into the clay wall, which can be useful; water storage jars often absorb and "sweat" a bit of water, keeping the contents cool.

Humans have been firing clay for at least twenty-eight thousand years. The earliest ceramics were fired in the open, likely near the fuel used for the firing itself, such as wood, brush, or dung. Eventually, people built enclosures out of clay for firing, which allowed for greater heat retention and higher firing temperatures, creating more durable and watertight ware. These enclosures became kilns, built out of more refractory (heat-resistant) clays. Kiln technology varied throughout the world, but for millennia potters in China had the most sophisticated kilns, able to reach the highest temperatures and exert control over the results. Kilns were fueled with wood or other plants, and later with coal, oil, or gas. Combustible fuels can have a dramatic impact on the appearance of ceramics. A kiln starved of oxygen gets smoky, and that excess carbon can infuse the clay with a variegated blackish surface at lower temperatures. At higher temperatures, the excess carbon actually draws oxygen molecules out of the ceramic matrix in order to burn, changing the material chemically and radically altering the surface of the ware. This process is called reduction and has the strongest impact on the glaze, as discussed below. The red and black of classical Greek vases, rich greens of Chinese celadons, and luscious metallic lusters of Islamic ceramics all depend on the deft manipulation not just of heat but also the kiln atmosphere.

Many of the approaches to firing developed over the course of human history are still in use today. Pit firing, smoke firing, and wood and coal kilns all occur in numerous traditional, workshop, studio, and academic contexts. Makers today often investigate how different firing approaches enhance their work. The majority of contemporary kilns, however, are powered by electricity, which creates a constant, radiant heat. Electric kilns can be highly sophisticated, with sensors and computers adjusting to the slightest variations in atmosphere or temperature. These kilns, alongside highly refined materials, can help deliver a stunning range of bold, vivid colors and elaborate surfaces for artists, smaller-scale manufacturers, and high-volume industrial producers alike. Even with the high degree of control available, firing ceramic art is inherently unpredictable. Materials melt and combine in unexpected ways; small variations of thickness and heat can yield new and surprising results. The materials in the unfired state rarely appear as they will when fired, so the artist must imagine how the work will look. Many makers minimize this aspect of ceramics through training, skill, and experience, while others embrace it fully. Ceramics is not a medium of total control: all makers collaborate with materials and kilns, turning their work over to the elemental process of transformation through fire.

The Ceramic Surface

Part of what makes ceramics so engaging is the interaction of form and surface. As many commentators have remarked, ceramic combines attributes of painting and sculpture (and chemistry). Ceramic surfaces vary to a seemingly infinite degree in color, texture, character, and ornament, sometimes becoming a mass or entity unto themselves. The earliest ceramic surfaces were clay based, comprised of special, usually contrasting colored clays (called slips) that were watered down and brushed onto the surface. The meanings of these early patterns are obscure to us now, but archaeologists and art historians typically link them to ritual functions. This applied surface ornament frequently interacts in dynamic ways with an object's form, as with Neolithic Chinese Banshan ware, or variations in the surface from firing. Applied clay ornament that rises up from the skin of the form can also complement brushed-on slip, or stand on its own as a form of decoration or elaboration.

What Is Glaze?

Encountering ceramic art, we often see a surface made of glaze rather than clay. Glaze is glass formulated to melt onto and fuse with ceramic. Like clay, glass is comprised mainly of silica, which with the addition of alumina or clay can melt onto and shrink with a ceramic body in the kiln (all clays shrink a bit when fired). In addition to silica and clay, glazes have a fluxing agent, which lowers the melting temperature of the silica and other ingredients, and colorants such as iron, cobalt, chrome, or copper. Glazes are formulated to melt at specific temperatures, typically forming a hard surface impervious to liquids. If a glaze is overfired, it can melt off the side of an object; if underfired, it can remain pasty or dry.

Glazed ceramic surfaces originated thousands of years ago, but are not as old as ceramic itself. The earliest glaze-like material is called Egyptian paste or faience, which was developed from around the year 4000 BCE. Egyptian paste is unusual in combining the glaze-forming materials with the body rather than coating the surface. The process yielded hard, brightly colored objects that evoke precious stones and likely carried magical meanings. The earliest applied glazes were developed in China during the Shang dynasty (ca. 1600–1046 BCE). Translucent gray, brown, and greenish in tone, they appeared on or in early high-fired (so-called proto-porcelain) vessels. The glazes were made of clay, limestone, and plant ash, and offered a smooth glossy surface that was more impervious to liquid than the already hard body. Lead-based glazes, which melt at a low temperature and thus are inexpensive to produce, came into broad use in the first century BCE in both the Roman Empire and China. Lead glazes can be clear or honey colored, or with the addition of minerals like copper and iron, take on a bright green, yellow, or blue hue. Many additional glazes now confront the ceramic artist, with a vast palette of colors and surface qualities.

Surface Ornament, Mimicry, and Medium Specificity

While the character of a glaze can be the dominant ornament in ceramic art, applied decoration also often appears. Contrasting glazes can be layered or put on side by side, creating elaborate patterns as seen on the ornamental tiles from Iznik, a pottery-producing town in Turkey. Cobalt, iron, and other metallic oxides can be applied under or on top of glazes, creating detailed imagery or patterns, as in the many examples of blue-and-white ceramics found globally. Similar to metallic oxides, enamels (or china paints) can be applied onto an already fired glaze surface, allowing for brightly colored and highly controlled imagery, as seen on many European porcelain figurines from the eighteenth century and later, and discussed further by Yao-Fen You in this volume. Transfer printing offers yet another source of imagery, mechanically reproducing scenery, portraits, and patterns ad infinitum for large-scale production and consumption; this technique is used not only for tablewares but also as a tool of social critique in the work of contemporary artists such as Paul Scott, explored in the chapter by Margaret Graves. While these and numerous other surface approaches cannot be exhaustively considered here, the sheer range points toward a key aspect of the medium: its ability to embrace and mimic an incredibly wide variety of forms and surfaces.

The imitation of other materials has long been central to the language of ceramics. The plasticity of clay—which can take on nearly any shape—and truly astounding range of surfaces combine to make ceramic a primary medium of trompe l'oeil, or fooling the eye. From Chinese teapots shaped like bundles of bamboo to European vessels in the shape of boar heads and leather suitcases, ceramic arts have a deep catalog of portraying other materials. This chameleon aspect plays with the gap between what we see and what we know, inviting us to touch the objects to reconcile, or perhaps relish, the cognitive dissonance. Adjacent to mimicry intended to fool the eye, makers of ceramics have long looked to other media, particularly glass and fine metals, to make copies. In most historical periods, ceramic art has conveyed less status and prestige than have objects made in more expensive materials. Goblets, ewers, chargers, and numerous other forms appear in ceramic, echoing the formal and decorative properties of, say, raised silver. While a healthy exchange of influence has often prevailed, most scholars understand ceramics to be more frequently in the position of replicating the characteristics of other, more expensive media, rather than the reverse.

Ceramic as a medium of mimicry stands alongside an equally (if not more) complex history of emphasizing the unique character of the medium. Across the globe, makers of ceramics have long cultivated the aesthetic properties of the material itself, stressing forms and surfaces that look like fired clay and glaze. Perhaps the most vivid example of this approach in this volume is Magdalene Odundo's work, which evokes vegetable gourds, leather, and even human flesh, but is clearly and could only be fired clay. Similarly, blue-and-white porcelain has been prized for centuries in part because the hardness, tone, translucency, and vivid blue is a combination unique to the medium. Finally, several types of revered Japanese ceramics highlight the craggy and irregular surfaces that could only be ceramic [FIG. 2]. Taken together, mimicry and medium specificity can be considered horizons of ceramic aesthetics.

In the modern context, commercially available materials and the spread of digital computing are altering the historic balance of extrinsic versus intrinsic aesthetics in ceramics. Before the mid-nineteenth century, ceramic materials were generally processed by or directly for those who used them. Materials typically did not travel far, unless they were exceptionally rare, as with cobalt in the early years of porcelain manufacture. From the third quarter of the nineteenth century onward, though, ceramic supply companies have emerged that sell premixed clays, prepared glazes, portable kilns, and the like. These suppliers have progressively lowered the barriers of entry to ceramics, especially supporting hobby and part-time practitioners, academic studios, and individual workshops. This process has in particular opened the field to generations of women ceramists, many of whom entered as hobbyist decorators and have come to represent a significant proportion of the field. Such industrially processed materials are widely available, reducing the natural variation seen earlier in ceramics while also expanding the material palette dramatically. The possibilities available to makers for the last fifty or so years differ phenomenally from those in the past.

In tandem with a broader material palette, changes wrought by the digital revolution of society are impacting ceramics too. Many kilns, both electric and gas powered, are now controlled by computers, allowing for the precise modulation of surface effects even at a student level. Glaze calculation software helps artists develop entirely new materials that had not existed previously. And perhaps more than anything, the increased velocity of digital images has profoundly impacted the volume and perception of historical and contemporary objects. Ceramic history, long

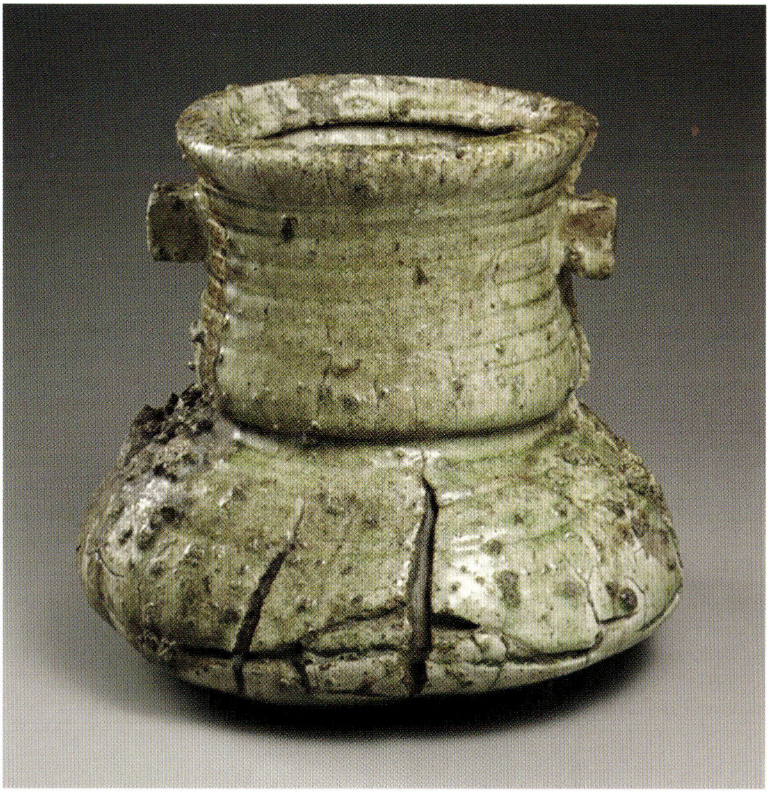

[FIG. 2]
Water jar, named Yabure-bukuro (burst pouch), Iga ware. Japan, Momoyama period, ca. 1550–1600 CE. 24.1 × 11.6 × 11.9 cm. Gotoh Art Museum, Tokyo.

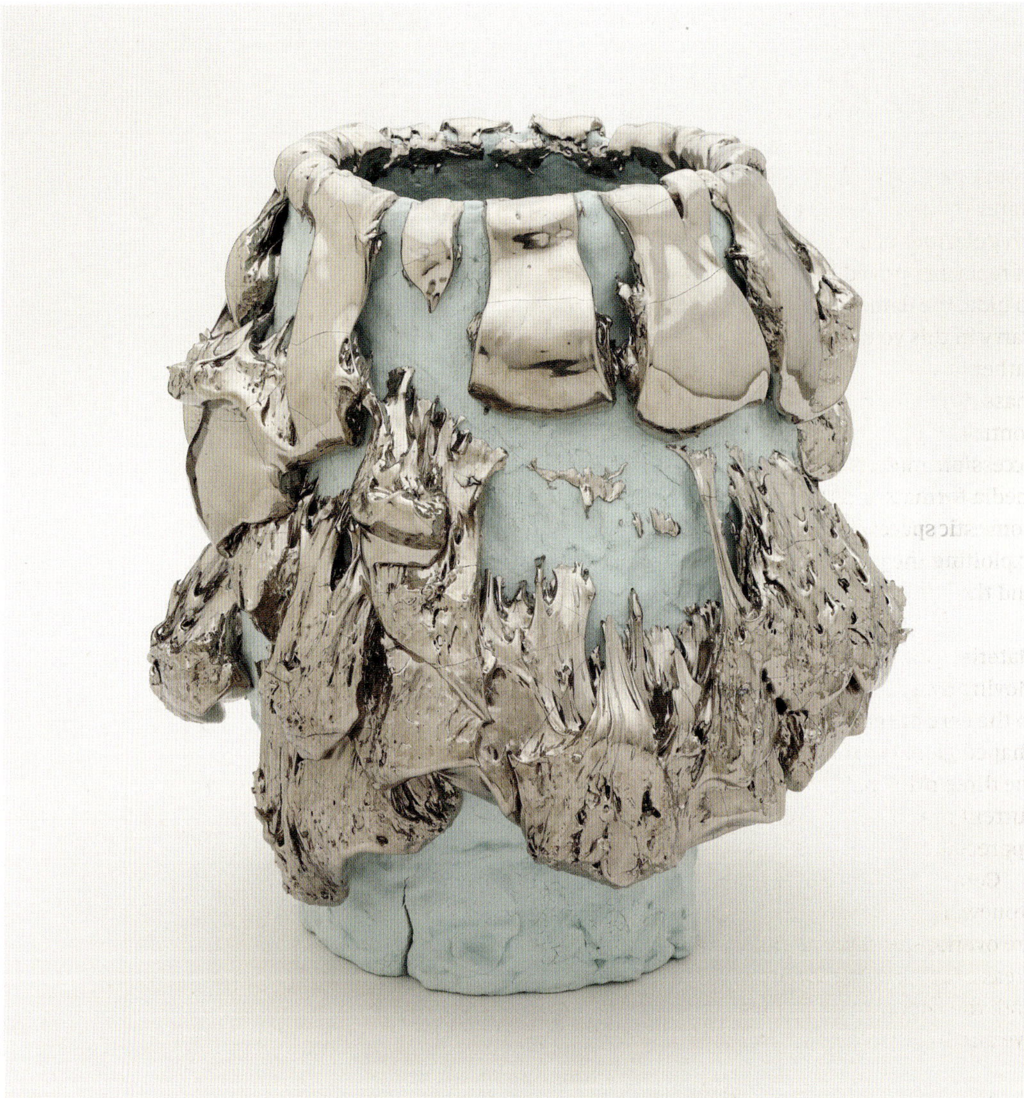

[FIG. 3]
Tea bowl. Takuro Kuwata (b. 1981). Japan, 2021. 54.9 × 53.5 × 51 cm. Salon 94, New York.

a lodestone for artists, is now widely accessible to anyone with an internet connection.

While these shifts are almost too large to grasp, one artist who embodies many of them is Takuro Kuwata (b. 1981), a young Japanese ceramist and international phenomenon [FIG. 3]. Kuwata's work draws from Japanese ceramic history, emulating forms seen in tea ceremony wares of the sixteenth and seventeenth centuries and cherished for their irregularities and rough surfaces. He also references *kintsugi*, the practice of repairing prized historical ceramics with gold to highlight, as opposed to hide, the damage. Like *kintsugi*, a process examined further by Vicki Parry in this volume, his luxurious cakes of gold and silver showcase rather than conceal split surfaces. Kuwata's use of glaze as an oozing mass rather than just as a surface is achievable through multiple, tightly controlled firings. His saturated palette depends on highly refined and accessible materials, and the work as a whole is arguably keyed to social media formats and the globalized art market at least as much as it is to domestic spaces. Honoring and building on the past, while fearlessly exploiting the present, ceramic art works within both its material history and the broader cultural present.

Material Distinctions in Ceramic Art and History

Moving away from the present and a focus on surface, I will now return to the core of ceramics—clay—to discuss how material distinctions have shaped global traditions. The aim here is to familiarize the reader with the three principal types of historical ceramics as well as their impact on current practice. These distinctions can lay the groundwork for further appreciation of the incredible variety within the medium.

Ceramic bodies divide into three main categories: earthenware, stoneware, and porcelain. While the three types are not absolute—there are overlaps, exceptions, and combinations—they do indicate the primary areas of global production. Distinctions between the three emerge from both the chemical properties of the materials and how they appear to the eye and hand of the end user.

Earthenware

Earthenware is the most common clay type and appears in (or as) the ground virtually all over the world. Many people are familiar with it through planters, pipes, tiles, and innumerable other objects produced widely. Others will know it from the red dirt of many deserts and exposed ridges. Also called common clay, the category refers to almost any clay that matures or becomes ceramic at around 750 to 900 degrees Celsius, or red heat. Earthenware clay typically has a red, yellow, or buff tinge caused by traces of iron and other minerals, but sometimes can be a milky white.

The final tone of an earthenware ceramic depends on both the clay itself and the firing process, with a cleaner-burning flame typically resulting in red or lighter-toned ware. Earthenware vessels, devotional figures, and funerary markers were among the earliest ceramics made by humans on account of the relatively low maturation temperature of the material.

Earthenware is closely tied with traditions of food and water storage, cooking, and housing—the vessels for the essentials of life. In these contexts, clay was dug, processed, formed, and fired usually within one locality, resulting in many discrete traditions. While the objects are utilitarian in origin, many have since been recategorized as art. Widely celebrated earthenware traditions include the many classical Greek vases that line the shelves of Western art museums; Chinese funerary figures, including the terracotta army of Emperor Qin Shi Huang (259–210 BCE); beer and water jars from southern Africa; elaborately and exquisitely ornamented vessels from Indigenous communities in the American Southwest; and the figurative, often narrative vessels from Mesoamerican and South American cultures, considered in this volume by Ulla Holmquist Pachas. In the classical Mediterranean, earthenware amphorae served as the shipping barrels of their day, used for transporting olive oil, fish sauce, and other liquids by water, like the vessels described in the case study by Carl Knappett. All of these traditions rely on clay and clay-based materials for both their form and surface.

Glazed earthenware traditions are equally vast and notable for their vibrant color palettes and luscious surfaces. Early lead glazing elevated earthenware by transforming it from being dirt-like to appearing vibrant and glossy, as in the glorious funerary horses and camels from Tang dynasty (618–907 CE) China. Later, these rich surfaces would animate the lifelike swamp tableaux of French Renaissance ceramist Bernard Palissy (d. 1589). Lead-based glazes were adopted into many folk traditions, such as those from Portugal and Mexico, and in some cases are still in use today. They were also integral to the global ceramics industry that emerged in England in the eighteenth century. Manufacturers such as Wedgwood used lead-based glazes on their early emulations of porcelain, while in the nineteenth century, Minton and other companies redefined the ceramic palette with brightly colored majolica, keyed to the new era of electrification.

A type of opaque-glazed earthenware originally emulating Chinese porcelain has had global impact too. Typically called faience or delftware, this type of ceramic was developed in the Middle East in the ninth or tenth century and consists of an earthenware body, which is often tan or buff, coated by a glaze opacified with tin oxide. This flat white surface echoed the whiteness of porcelain, becoming a clean ground on which to add ornament. Faience spread across North Africa and into Islamic Spain by the fourteenth century, then into Italy and across Europe from the fifteenth century onward. Its ornament included highly reflective metallic lusters such as those made in Valencia; the richly painted polychrome *istoriato* of Renaissance Italy; and the blue-and-white wares of the Netherlands and elsewhere known as delftware. Faience continues as a global tradition, anchored by the ubiquity of earthenware clay and appeal of brightly ornamented surfaces in our daily lives.

Stoneware

Stoneware, the second principal type of ceramic, is distinct from earthenware in being harder and more durable. It is fired to a higher temperature than earthenware—around a thousand degrees Celsius—creating a fully vitrified, stonelike body that is virtually impervious to liquids. Stoneware developed first in China and later in other parts of the world as kiln technology improved. It tends to be tan, buff, or brown, and often somewhat gritty or rough. It occurs naturally in the ground, but is most frequently combined into clay bodies to achieve specific working properties, including maturation temperature, color, and toothiness. Most stonewares are glazed, such as the greenish Yue and brown-black Tenmoku wares of China, Oribe-type wares of Japan, or myriad twentieth-century studio ceramics inspired by them.

Stoneware tends to be impenetrable to liquids, and so has long been used for food storage and presentation. Examples include the early Chinese celadons that were developed on stoneware clays and have earned the appreciation of connoisseurs for over a thousand years, as well as the large kimchi jars of Korea dating back hundreds of years. The vast numbers of crocks, churns, and other storage vessels produced from the eighteenth to the early twentieth centuries in manufactories in the United States and elsewhere constitute another dimension of stoneware. Many of these containers—utilitarian in their day yet now considered art—were in fact glazed through the addition of salt to the kiln during the firing versus being applied individually to the pots. Salt vaporizes at high temperatures, forming a glaze with the surface of the pots as the sodium from the salt and silica from the clay bond. This process was initially discovered in Germany in the fourteenth century and is used now in artistic more than industrial production.

Porcelain

Porcelain is white, hard, cold, and impervious. Of all types of ceramic, porcelain has perhaps the most complex layering of cultural meanings, from imperial China to hotel china. Porcelain is ubiquitous today, yet it retains an association with elite status in part because of its relatively high cost of production and history of exclusivity. Porcelain also participates in discourses of whiteness and purity, giving the material racialized connotations in some contexts.

Porcelain is a dense, fully crystallized ceramic. The body is typically translucent when thin and makes a ring when tapped as opposed to a "thunk" like many earthenwares. Materially, porcelain consists of china clay, or kaolin, and petuntse, a type of limestone also called china or porcelain stone, fired to about fourteen hundred degrees Celsius. Both kaolin and petuntse are notable for having few trace minerals, like iron, which accounts for the whiteness of the resulting ceramic. Kaolin is uncommon relative to other clays and requires greater processing than, say, earthenware. Examples of fired kaolin survive from Neolithic China, although porcelain as a material is generally considered to have originated in the seventh century, and then spread in the eighth and ninth centuries. Production in the famed city of Jingdezhen, China's porcelain capital, began in the tenth century and was soon highly sophisticated. Porcelain was exported from about the ninth century on, reaching South Asia, the Middle East, and the east coast of Africa. The porcelain trade increased sharply from the fourteenth century with the advent of blue-and-white porcelain ornamented by cobalt applied underneath a clear glaze.

Chinese porcelain has long been avidly and even obsessively collected. Imperial kilns produced literally hundreds of thousands of objects for Chinese emperors of all dynasties. Porcelain abounds in royal collections from the South Asian subcontinent to Central Asia and the Near East. European elites prized the material from the fifteenth century onward, and it became a cornerstone of Enlightenment visual culture throughout the eighteenth century. While early Islamic and later European potters emulated the look of porcelain with faience, it was chemists (actually, alchemists) sponsored by Elector of Saxony Augustus the Strong (1670–1733) who first created a true or hard-paste porcelain using kaolin in 1709–10. A lower-firing alternative, so-called soft-paste porcelain, had been developed in the sixteenth century, but was successfully produced only from the early 1700s on. By the mid-1700s, now well-known names such as Sèvres and Worcester began producing additional varieties of soft—or slightly later, hard—paste porcelain for elite and then mass markets. The artistic production of porcelain continues alongside mass-market and utilitarian ware in highly skilled manufacturing centers like Jingdezhen, legacy manufactories of Europe including Meissen and Sèvres, and academic and studio contexts, principally in Europe, North America, and East Asia.

Fritware

Early efforts by Middle Eastern potters to replicate porcelain gave rise to faience, as discussed above, and a ceramic body called fritware, also known as stonepaste, developed around the eleventh century. In the absence of kaolin, or a hard-firing white clay, these early potters substituted ground sand and glass, with a little bit of clay to form a moldable body. The material has the same basic ingredients as clay (silica and alumina), but is closer to glass or glaze in its composition. Fritware paste can be formed into tiles and smaller vessels; larger and more elaborate forms are exceedingly difficult, so most works are of domestic scale. Its particular luminosity echoes the glassiness and translucency of true porcelain, serving as an ideal ground for colorful and delicate surface ornament, such as that seen on ware from Iznik. In twelfth-century Iran fritware potters borrowed a glass-ornamenting technique, first used on ceramics in ninth-century Iraq, to develop fine lusterware, whose thin sheens of luminous gold and silver have often been revived and elaborated by subsequent potters.

Key Themes of Production and Consumption

The differences between clays, glaze types, and firing traditions are grounded in the material properties of ceramics, yet have a deeply cultural function as well. As with hard- and soft-paste porcelain, definitions are not grounded entirely in chemistry or geology. Rather, they emerge also from how objects function socially—what discourses they participate in, and how they connect to patterns of production, consumption, and meaning making. Ceramic art has been studied, collected, preserved, modified, and handed down for generations. The meanings that ceramic objects accord often far exceed their material parameters, yet what they are made of and how they are made impact our readings of the objects. The next section considers cultural as opposed to material ways of understanding ceramics, focusing on the broad issues of production and consumption specific to the medium.

Production

A key aspect of ceramic is its ubiquity. Ceramics have been made in nearly every culture across the globe as one of the earliest human technologies. At times, individual types of ceramic art are highly valued, yet far more frequently it is relatively accessible—sometimes extremely so. The ubiquity of ceramic is reinforced by its persistence: while it can be easy to break, it is almost impossible to degrade. Sherds of ceramic objects remain intact for millennia, allowing for the extensive study of the deep historical past and long-dead cultures. Ceramic art historically was made in multiples, with individual objects being the exception and variations of an object type being the norm. There is not one Neolithic Chinese jar, Zulu beer pot, or commedia dell'arte figurine but rather hundreds or possibly thousands of each. Collectively, the accessibility, durability, and seriality of ceramics have impacted how we perceive the value of individual objects along with the interpretative strategies we use to unpack them.

The character and scale of the workshop is a second theme related to production that impacts how we understand ceramics. As historian Paul Greenhalgh recently demonstrated, ceramic production has long thrived at the amateur, workshop, manufactory, and, more recently, individual artist levels. Amateur production can encompass local potters who were primarily farmers and made pots in the off-season. Similarly, it can include the legion hobbyist potters working in community centers and home studios today. Objects from these settings tend to be for immediate, local use in the historical context, and leisure consumption and individual expression in the modern. Workshop settings are often communal, based on family units or village structures, and comprising around ten or fewer workers. They also tend to produce more regularized forms frequently identified with a particular locality, such as the Renaissance potteries of Deruta, Italy, with their signature scallop-patterned edges. Workshop settings relied on specialized labor for different stages of manufacturing, and the wares met a regional and sometimes broader market. Making processes in workshops are often based on hand techniques, such as wheel throwing and press molding, yet as described above, involve repetition and seriality more frequently than one-off items.

Manufactories typically have over ten workers and sometimes thousands, and consistently produce high volumes of wares for regional and distant markets. The objects produced by manufactories tend to be extremely consistent and consumer oriented; they are made to be sold. In the preindustrial era, examples included the porcelain factories of Jingdezhen as well as European producers like Sèvres, whose royal patronage ensured a steady, elite clientele. With industrialization and the further development of global capitalism, brands like Minton in the nineteenth century and Homer Laughlin (makers of Fiestaware) in the twentieth became large-scale producers, often working at the intersection of ceramic art and product design. Manufactories lend name recognition to ceramics, especially collectibles, while also indicating a level of economic organization and market appeal.

Individual artist production is a relatively recent phenomenon. Around the turn of the twentieth century, ceramic artists mainly in France and the United Kingdom began working in individual studios, where one person, sometimes with the help of an assistant, was newly responsible for all stages of production. The rise in commercially available materials and equipment supported this transition, and the growth of what became the studio ceramics movement continued throughout the twentieth century, yielding many individually named, well-known artists, including Adelaide Alsop Robineau (d. 1929) and Peter Voulkos (d. 2002) in the

United States. From the late 1950s, studio ceramics in the West dovetailed (albeit problematically) with sculpture, so that contemporary ceramic art overlaps to some degree with the mainstream fine art world. In studio production, the individuality of the object and expressive force of the maker are at the fore. Whether manufactured through contracted specialists (as in the case of Jeff Koons) or made entirely through the artist's handwork (as in the case of Simone Leigh), contemporary ceramic sculpture emphasizes originality and vision. All types of ceramic production imply certain economic and social conditions, such as family-based labor, immigrant economic opportunity, access to export markets, industrial infrastructure, a developed fine art market, and the like. The other chapters in this book exemplify the ways that some of these stories embedded in ceramic objects can be revealed, drawing connections to many aspects of life in the past as well as present.

Consumption

How ceramics are consumed—used, repaired, maintained, and preserved—is equally important to the meanings they can hold. The paradigmatic functions of the medium are sustenance and ritual. Since time immemorial, ceramics have helped keep humans alive by holding and offering nourishment and refreshment. We touch ceramics to our lips billions of times a day. We have long created ritual objects out of clay, from the enigmatic earthenware figures of the Nok culture in Nigeria to the Roman ancestor effigies and the tomb figures of ancient China.

Related to symbolic meanings, yet more concrete, is the relationship between the haptic and optic in ceramics. Long a liability within modernist ideologies of art, ceramics has a deep association with the haptic, or tactile. As so many humans routinely handle ceramics, when we look at ceramic art, whether based on a utilitarian form or not, we can imagine (and perhaps cannot help ourselves from imagining) touching it. Most ceramic surfaces we know as well through touch as sight. The repeated physical handling of ceramics creates what we can call a haptic sympathy, such that when we view a ceramic object, we conceptually enact touching it: the surfaces feel to us rather than only look. While this material literacy may often go unrecognized, it contributes to how we perceive ceramic objects, creating a conceptual stickiness wherein we are less able to retreat to the purely optical in the work. Perceiving in our mind the feel of a ceramic work ties us to its material presence. An encounter with ceramics is never purely visual but instead carries with it what critic Philip Rawson called "memory traces" that are distinctly physical.

From about 1860 to 1960, mainstream modernism and its emphasis on opticality dominated ideas about art in the West, leaving ceramics with a contested status at best. Long relegated to the subaltern realms of the manual, decorative, and applied, the insistent materiality of ceramic—rooted in our haptic sympathy—kept it tethered to the world and earth, unable to generate the autonomous aesthetic contemplation envisioned by Western philosophers like Immanuel Kant. Ceramic was not easily understood as a medium of fine art, in part because it so often kept one foot (or hand) in the realm of the physical.

In recent decades, we have witnessed the steady reappraisal of these long-standing ideological and material hierarchies. That insistent materiality of ceramic, so long a liability, is now becoming a locus of wonder and meaning. The elaborate histories, sheer physical ubiquity of the material, unstable distinctions between art and nonart, symbolic resonances with the core experience of being human, and haptic sympathy—all of these attributes that have made ceramics sing to a narrow band of advocates now resonate with emerging ideas about value and meaning in art as well as what roots us to being human. The very realness of ceramic is part of what we celebrate today, as many of our lives and relationships become dominated by screens. Ceramic art tethers us to our bodies and the earth, reminding us of the messy as well as glorious parts of being human. Hopefully, the individual objects considered in this book open further questions and a deeper exploration of ceramic art for you, the reader.

Ceramics: The Art of Being Human

Margaret S. Graves

Studying ceramics is an inherently collaborative venture. The subject touches on so many different fields of research and practice that no one person could possibly attain complete expertise in all of them. Only when potters, archaeologists, conservators, curators, archaeometrists, anthropologists, and art historians work in dialogue with each other can there be a holistic understanding of the ceramic object as physical material, social and economic artifact, and aesthetic choice.

Ceramics also require the engagement of all the senses. The prime role of touch in the creation and use of ceramics gives them a complicated status within art history—a discipline that has long privileged the visual aspects of artworks above all else. Ceramics can be decorated with all kinds of designs as well as painted or transfer-printed pictures, but their insistent material presence makes them much more than just vehicles for imagery. The feel of a glazed surface, its reflectivity, the weight of a piece in your hands, and the traces of the potter's wheel or mold—all of these are experienced both visually and tactilely through what Sequoia Miller describes as "haptic sympathy," meaning the human capacity to imagine feeling (and making) through looking and vice versa. Nor should the other senses be forgotten. Hearing can be a guide in the firing process, and with the finished object sound is critical in the so-called tap test: When you tap the surface of a bowl or jar, do you hear the true ring of an intact glazed vessel—bell-like in the case of porcelain, or more of a short "ping" for other types of ceramic body? Or is your tap answered by the dry "clonk" (or unhealthier still, a dismal rattling sound) that tells of a piece that has been broken or reconstructed from fragments? With archaeological material, smell is also part of the sensory data used to identify types or sources of ceramic bodies along with processes of degradation. Even taste has a role. More than one expert has told me, off-the-record, that they have been known to lick ceramic samples, using the taste of mineral salts in the clay body as a diagnostic aid.

This chapter does not set out to survey the history of ceramics—an impossible task—but instead will explore three different ways to formulate an art history of ceramics. Each of its three sections responds to a different set of considerations arising directly from the material itself. The first explores ceramics as a form of documentary evidence of human actions, not only in archaeological contexts but also in the setting of the museum, where the filtering mechanisms of aesthetic selection have brought some forms of ceramic production to center stage while obscuring others. The second section looks at the ceramic object as an artistic medium defined by movement, at both the microlevel of individual acts of making and handling, and the macroscale of global trade networks and economies of labor. The third part of the chapter investigates ceramic arts as a form of world making, a practice through which humans have continually created objects to represent, order, and make sense of the world they live in—at the same time that the medium itself has impacted human conceptualization of the world.

The Imperishable Pot

Wherever human civilization has been, there will be potsherds. Fragments of fired clay vessels, broken, abandoned, buried, and lost, only to be raised again one day by the digging of farmers or archaeologists: potsherds are history's most enduring material testament to human existence. As English traveler and sometime archaeologist Gertrude Bell (d. 1926) wrote in a letter sent from Baghdad in 1917,

> The immortal baked clay preserves the trace of human habitation when all else has returned to the dust it was; as soon as the canal dries up and the village is deserted, the roaming Arab pulls out the roof beams and breaks up the doors for firewood, the mud walls disintegrate, and nothing remains but the imperishable pot. You may break him up as much as you choose, but unless you take a hammer to him and reduce him systematically to powder, he will continue to bear witness to the household which he served.[1]

Bell presumably didn't perform any such experiments with hammers herself, and her casual characterization of the "roaming Arab" as a faceless scavenger may give us pause, but she is certainly right about the extraordinary material durability of fired clay. Unlike wood, textile fibers, metals, and bone, artifacts made from fired clay are largely resistant to decay and corrosion. Only carved hardstone can really be said to surpass them in terms of durability. Pots break, certainly, and if the pieces end up buried in the ground then mineral salts can leach into them from the soil; glazes may degrade—sometimes with quite attractive and interesting results—and certain clay bodies can eventually disintegrate if enough moisture is present for sustained periods. But for the most part, ceramics endure even on the seabed, and their primary component, clay, is almost universally available. The record of human civilization contains exponentially more potsherds than anything else. Every one of those millions of broken pieces of ceramic bears witness, in Bell's words, to the hands that once shaped and used it, to vessels made and food eaten and lives lived, hundreds and even thousands of years ago.

For these reasons, the archaeologist and historian of the premodern world can track many things through the ceramic fragments found in sherd deposits. In a *longue durée* vision of history, pottery becomes a proxy not only for human presence but also for more complex flows and trade networks between settlements, as people moved and took both tangible objects and intangible technical knowledge with them. Although unglazed earthenwares of various kinds make up the bulk of ceramic production throughout much of history, the development of more refined recipes, glazing techniques, and decorative practices have meant that not only technologies but also tastes can be tracked through sherd distribution. Highly specialized forms of production, like fine porcelain or the prized iridescent metallic surfaces of luster overglaze decoration, tend to be localized; both the raw materials and technical know-how need to be available for potters to become skilled in these difficult techniques. As production gains sufficient traction it gives rise to a local industry, where craft knowledge thrives and techniques can be refined through experimentation; eventually certain places attain wide renown for particular types of ceramics. When fragments of ceramics that are incontrovertibly linked with one site or region turn up in other places, we can begin to reconstruct trade routes, tastes for the exotic, and regional responses to objects from elsewhere.

In the most obvious example—which will appear again in this chapter—the pan-Eurasian regard for Chinese ceramists as the preeminent masters of the craft has carried Chinese ceramics around the globe for many centuries. The fragments excavated at the ninth-century caliphal palace city of Samarra in Iraq attest to both the scale and impact of Chinese ceramic imports in the capital of the Abbasid Empire (750–1258 CE). A museum tray of sherd samples from Samarra, laid out like gems in a jeweler's display, showcases the cosmopolitan consumption of ceramics at the site [FIG. 4]. Fragments of white-slipped, clear-glazed stonewares imported from the Tang-era Gongxian kilns in northern China (center) are mimicked in local earthenware production with a glaze made opaque and white by the addition of tin (top right). Iraqi earthenware imitations of Chinese green-splashed whiteware (lower center) lie alongside a stoneware bowl base from the Changsha kilns in Hunan

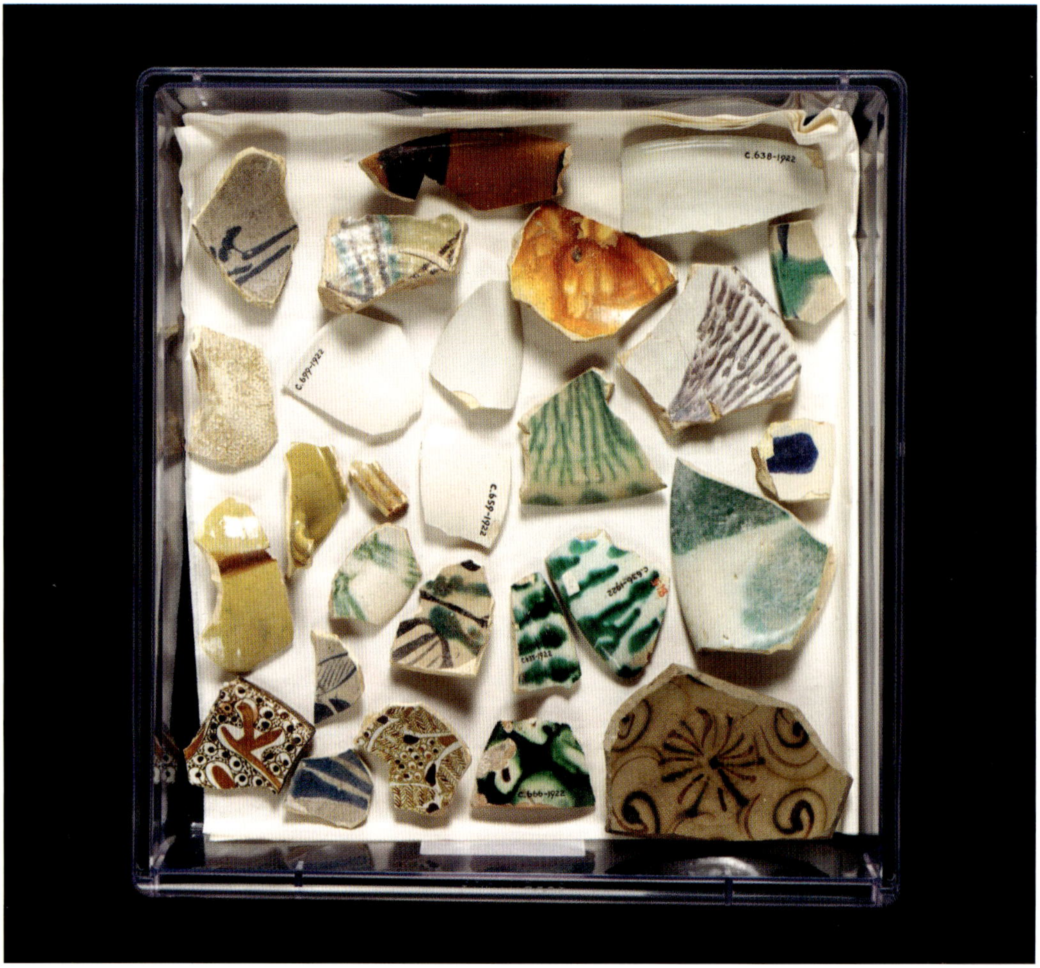

[FIG. 4]
Tray with ninth-century CE ceramic sherds from vessels created in China and Iraq, reportedly found at Samarra, Iraq. Victoria and Albert Museum, London.

Province, with its characteristic green-and-brown palette (bottom right). Finally, the three great technological advances of the ninth-century Iraqi potters—fired overglaze decoration in multiple shades of metallic luster, in-glaze painting in cobalt blue, and the creamy white tin glaze—are on display in the lower-left corner of the tray.

The entangled, global nature of ceramics by the ninth century is amply borne out by the fragments found at Samarra. Moreover, the evidence of the Belitung shipwreck, recovered from the seabed in 1998, has deepened our understanding of the ceramic dialogue that took place between the great medieval empires of the Abbasid Middle East and Tang China. This dhow (a type of seafaring boat used in the Arabian Peninsula), which sank off the coast of Belitung Island near Sumatra in the ninth century, was making its return journey from China loaded with approximately sixty thousand glazed vessels destined for the Middle Eastern market. Among these thousands were three dishes decorated with cobalt blue on a white ground—a color combination now strongly associated with Chinese ceramics, but once found in widespread use in Iraq, close to the Middle Eastern sources of high-quality cobalt, around the same time as its early use on high-fire whitewares in China. The idiosyncratic Chinese blue-on-white wares found in the Belitung wreck use palmette patterns of fronds radiating from central lozenges; the best preserved of the three gives the distinct impression of rapid, somewhat experimental execution [FIG. 5]. Most strikingly, it has much more in common with the decoration found on the contemporaneous blue-and-white bowls of Iraq than it does with anything seen on other ceramics being made in China, strongly suggesting Iraqi wares as the major source of inspiration. The three blue-and-white bowls on the shipwreck might even have been samples intended to gauge potential interest in a Chinese product that mimicked Iraqi blue-and-white wares, sent by an enterprising businessman to test the market. Recent analysis suggests that one of the main sites for luxury pottery production in ninth-century Iraq was the port city of Basra—where Chinese ceramics would have been unloaded in their thousands from trade ships, illuminating the networks that kept information moving between ceramics makers and transregional traders. It is common to imagine the medieval era as a time when individual horizons were narrow, but the picture that emerges from the archaeological and economic evidence of ceramics across Asia is quite the opposite, with multidirectional exchange through ocean and overland trade, and industries producing at scale for local, regional, and global markets.

The tray of Samarra sherds provides us with a sumptuous illustration of the transregional flow of ceramics in the ninth century. But what are we actually looking at? This is hardly unmediated historical matter. In the first place, no archaeological ceramic fragments come out of the ground

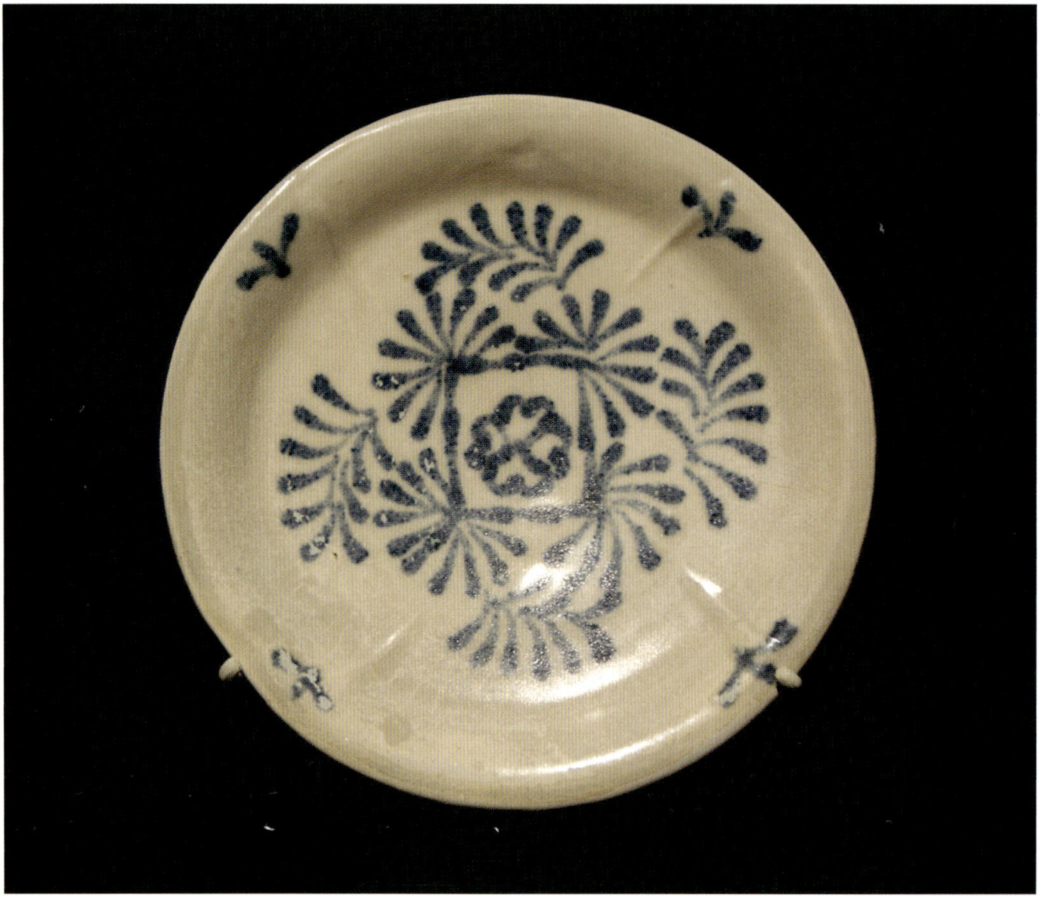

[FIG. 5]
Stoneware dish with white slip, cobalt, and clear glaze, recovered from the Belitung shipwreck. Tang China, possibly Gongxian kilns, ca. 830s CE. Diameter 23 cm. Asian Civilizations Museum, Singapore, 2005.1.00474.

looking so luscious and photogenic. These pieces were excavated in the early twentieth century, cleaned, sorted, selected, and categorized long before the museum's photographer arrived to document them. Artfully arranged on their white background, the fractured remains of bowls and dishes have been converted into a visual code of knowledge that favors tidy taxonomies, but is not afraid to bend the rules for the sake of aesthetic effects. Less appealing types of ceramic are left by the wayside, with the dull, plain, and workaday nowhere to be seen in this constellation of prized techniques arranged into color fields. A solitary fragment of unglazed ware has been included, yet it bears an intricate molded design to delight the eye and fingers. Ceramics are a near-universal medium of expression, but our knowledge of the history of ceramics has been mediated through the collecting practices of the European Enlightenment and the colonial project—endeavors that saw antiquities harvested on a grand scale to inform particular narratives of civilizational achievement. In this way, a large part of the total ceramic record has fallen quietly out of view. Just as the textual archives on which historians depend render certain voices mute, so too does the material archive of the museum—even the seemingly comprehensive drawers of potsherds brought back en masse from colonial excavations—exclude and erase practices deemed of lesser interest.

In point of fact, this chapter's first interlocutor, Bell, embodies the entanglement of premodern ceramics with modern geopolitics and the colonial-era rise of archaeology. Bell was writing to her parents about the "immortal baked clay" of the Fertile Crescent just a few months after the British had wrested control of Baghdad from the Ottoman Empire, during a time when her compatriots were consolidating what would soon be called the British Mandate of Iraq. The region has long attracted the interference of Western powers for several reasons, with oil reserves of course now chief among them. But for Bell and some others, the area's primary lure in the early twentieth century was the access they could gain to its deep history—not only its potsherds, but also its architectural remains in baked brick and ancient clay tablets bearing documents recorded in the world's oldest writing system, cuneiform. This system of wedge-shaped marks, incised into a pliant clay surface using an angled stick, was employed over many centuries to write documents in a range of ancient languages of the Near East and Egypt, including Akkadian, the lingua franca of the third and second millennia BCE. Nineteenth-century scholars in Europe, many of them searching for historical sources that would confirm the veracity of the Bible, competed to crack the cuneiform code and decipher the masses of tablets being excavated in Iraq. As translation skills accelerated, it became clear that the cuneiform tablets held a huge range of textual records, from the celebrated Epic of Gilgamesh to legal codes, medical and magical texts, temple accounts, and receipts from the sale of slaves. Humankind's first documents were written in clay.

Nor were humans the only species to leave their mark in the clay of the ancient Near East. Bricks from the Sumerian city of Ur in Iraq, datable to the reign of King Ur-Nammu in the twenty-first century BCE, also bear the accidental testimony of canine kind. One such brick from the site of the legendary ziggurat at Ur names Ur-Nammu in its stamped cuneiform inscription; beside the name of the king, two paw prints are sunk deep into the clay, recording the pressure of pads and claws as a dog stepped on, and pushed off from, the surface of the unfired, stamped brick [FIG. 6].

It is the plasticity of clay that makes it possible for a viewer in the twenty-first century CE to witness the actions of a dog in the twenty-first century BCE. There is something both wonderful and shocking about coming face-to-face with the momentary, incidental movement of a living animal that died thousands of years before one's own life began, unintentionally preserved through pure accident. Unfired clay's ability to take and retain the direct impression of movement is one of its unique material qualities; perhaps equally unique is our human ability to see those impressions and immediately, intuitively reconstruct the physical forces and motions that created them. This is another form of the haptic sympathy described in the introduction to this volume. Not only do we instinctively imagine what it would feel like to touch the indentations on the clay surface when we see the brick (even if we are only viewing it in a photograph, this response can still be felt if we pause over it) but our haptic sympathy also re-creates the actions that impacted that surface—the brief, forceful strike of paws and scampering away of a dog that got in somewhere it wasn't supposed to be, four thousand years ago.

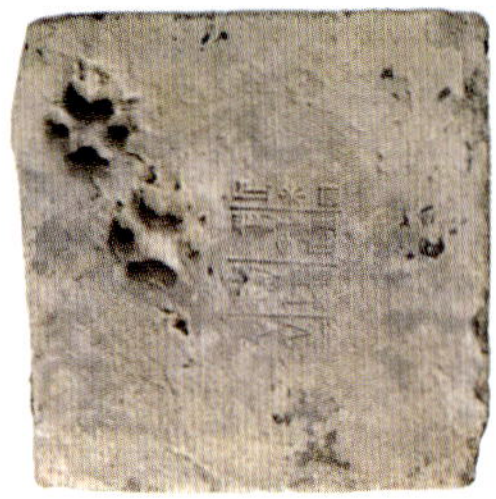

[FIG. 6]
Fired clay brick stamped with cuneiform inscription naming King Ur-Nammu (r. 2112–2095 BCE). Ur, Iraq, ca. 2100 BCE. Length 30 cm. British Museum, London, 1935,0112.116.

Moved by Hand and Sea

Unfired clay's uniquely immediate receptivity to impressions made by tools or fingers—or paws—is belied by the rigidity of fired ceramic products, especially when they have been covered with a glaze that gives a smooth, vitrified surface. Most of us are accustomed to eating and drinking from industrially produced ceramics that give almost nothing away about the touch they have received during production, yet when we stop to think we must realize that all of our teacups and saucers have been handled throughout their making. British artist Richard Wentworth draws quiet attention to this in his piece *Three Hundred and Sixty Degrees* (1999), a plate mass-produced by the Royal Doulton ceramics manufactory in Stoke-on-Trent in a project to support affordable art [FIG. 7]. Each of the dinner plates in this line is dead white, shiny, and perfectly plain—apart from the indented and gilded finger-and-thumb prints that make up the span of a human hand across the diameter of the surface, as if

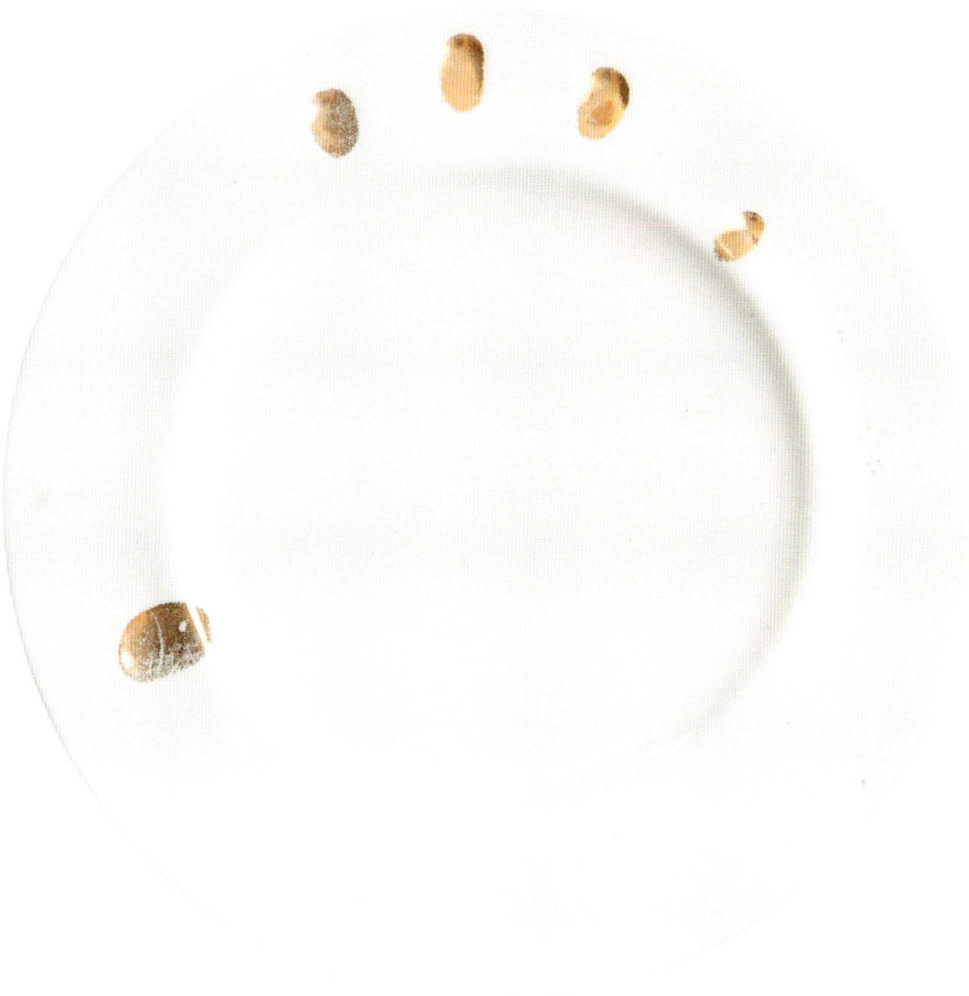

[FIG. 7]
Richard Wentworth (b. 1947), *Three Hundred and Sixty Degrees*, 1999. Glazed fine bone china with gilding. Diameter 27 cm.

the plate had been balanced facedown, while the glaze was still wet, on fingertips extended from an outstretched palm. On the back of the plate, in small capital letters encircling the manufacturer's logo, is the legend "A Royal Doulton Plate Is Touched More Than Twenty Times during Its Making." The otherwise invisible acts of touching and handling in industrial production are brought into abrupt—if intentionally artificial—focus on the surface of the plate by the artist's insertion of fingerprints made ostentatiously visible through gilding. Wentworth's factory piece subverts our preconceptions about the mutual exclusivity of the handmade and the industrial. His plate design invites meditation on the nature of modern production, contrasting the movements of making with the industrial erasure of touch, while simultaneously drawing attention to the particularities of ceramic as a medium that is both fingertip fashioned and industrially finished.

While Wentworth's Royal Doulton plate strives to render the maker's hand visible, other ceramists have sometimes left similar traces in spite of their best efforts not to. An extraordinary fifteenth-century earthenware bowl from Málaga, Spain, with a deep conical shape borrowed from North African ceramic traditions, discloses some of the difficulties its makers faced in handling such a large vessel through the complex processes of manufacture [FIG. 8]. At just over half a meter (1.65 feet) in diameter, it is both spectacular and somewhat hard to maneuver. The interior surface of the bowl is decorated with a large, detailed depiction of a ship sailing under the royal arms of Portugal, painted using overglaze luster—that complicated technique of ceramic decoration, pioneered in ninth-century Iraq, that requires a carefully controlled second firing to bond a microscopically thin layer of metal to the surface of the already fired glaze. Medieval authors referred to these Spanish wares as "gilded" because of the reflective, iridescent metallic sheen of their luster decoration, and they were prized as far away as Tabriz in Iran.

The picture on the interior of this bowl is famous and has often been published; less frequently seen, however, is the exterior surface. Here the difficulties of moving such a large and cumbersome vessel into the kiln become clear. Fingertips have landed in the luster paint while it was wet, smudging it and lifting it off in places, then redistributing it as lustered fingerprints at the rim of the bowl (just visible near the top and bottom of the circumference shown in this picture), where two or more hands struggled to lift it by the rim without destroying the exterior design. Glazed ceramics do not often offer such an intimate glimpse into workshop fumbles because glaze itself flows as it changes state in the kiln, covering the surface with a glassy layer that glosses over some of the potter's touchmarks. Here it is the paint-like substance of luster before firing—metal oxides mixed with clay or ocher and

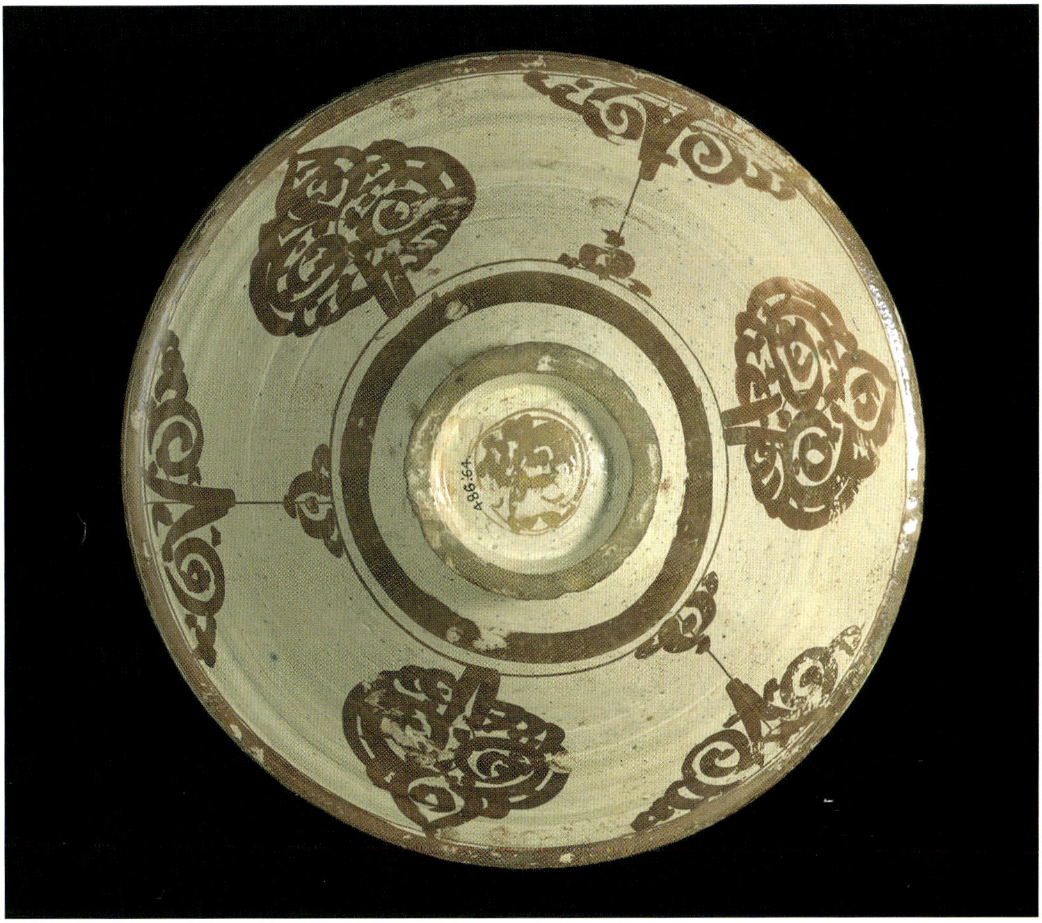

[FIG. 8]
Earthenware bowl with tin glaze and overglaze luster decoration (view of base showing fingerprints in luster at rim). Málaga, Spain, ca. 1425–50 CE. Diameter 51.2 cm. Victoria and Albert Museum, London, 486–1864.

other compounds—that has captured straining hand movements in the workshop. The difficulties of the luster technique, which is one of the least controllable in ceramics, mean that the bowl must have been regarded by its maker and patron as a spectacular success in spite of the fingerprints.

The Málaga bowl was an exceptional vessel in its own time, as it is now. It was almost certainly made on commission, perhaps for a successful Portuguese maritime trader, and represents the last period of output from the Málaga kilns as well as a monument to oceanic exploration at the dawn of the early modern period. In its detailed representation of an identifiable type of seafaring vessel used by the Christian traders of the Iberian Peninsula, it forecasts the tremendous importance of maritime shipping to the vast expansion of global trade that would occur over the next three centuries. Ceramic tablewares, already shown by the Belitung wreck to be a significant component of ocean trade in the medieval period, would become a supremely mobile form of export in the early modern era. The global reach of all of these seaborne dishes is attested in their sometime incorporation into architectural settings, rendering them immobile (and helpfully providing the art historian with fixed data points).

Ceramic vessels had been set into the facades of Italian churches as decoration from as early as the eleventh century, studding blind arcades and gable ends with inset bowls of jewel-like color that contrasted with stone walls. Most of these so-called *bacini* (Italian for "bowls") were imported to Italy from the Islamic lands around the Mediterranean, including Spain, North Africa, Syria, and the Levant. Still in situ today on Italian churches, they can be read as testaments to Mediterranean commerce as well as more complex Muslim-Christian political rivalries. A similar practice, albeit with a different set of meanings, was brought to bear on the interiors of some fourteenth- or fifteenth-century mosques on the Swahili coast of East Africa, where complete Chinese and Iranian ceramic vessels—as many as fifty of them—were set into niches arranged on the qibla wall around the mihrab (the arcuated niche that indicates the orientation toward Mecca). While only a few of the original ceramic vessels have survived in situ at the excavated Swahili mosques at Tundwa and Kua, some of the related mosques in Oman from the sixteenth and seventeenth centuries retain multiple vessels from contemporary China in the decoration of their qibla walls [FIG. 9]. The visual effect is overwhelming: Ming-era dishes, some of them decorated with dragons, birds, or flowers, are woven into a lacy network of deep knife-carved stucco, punctuating the framing band of interlaced circles or sometimes set above or even into the mihrab itself. The Great Mosque of Muqazzah has nineteen such dishes, the largest number of surviving ceramic vessels of any Omani mihrab. Forming a frame around the mihrab, they create an

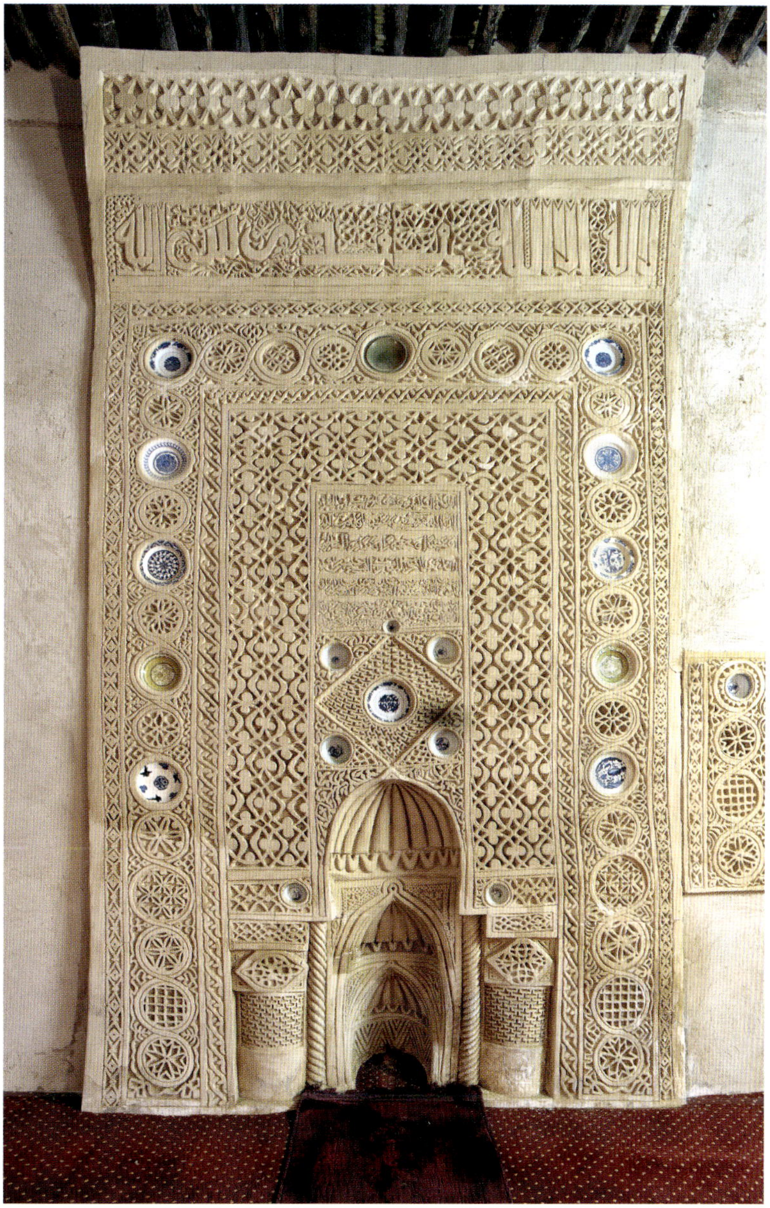

[FIG. 9]
Carved plaster mihrab in the Great Mosque of Muqazzah, Oman, dated 1029 H / 1619 CE, with inset ceramic vessels from Ming China, Wanli period (1563–1620 CE).

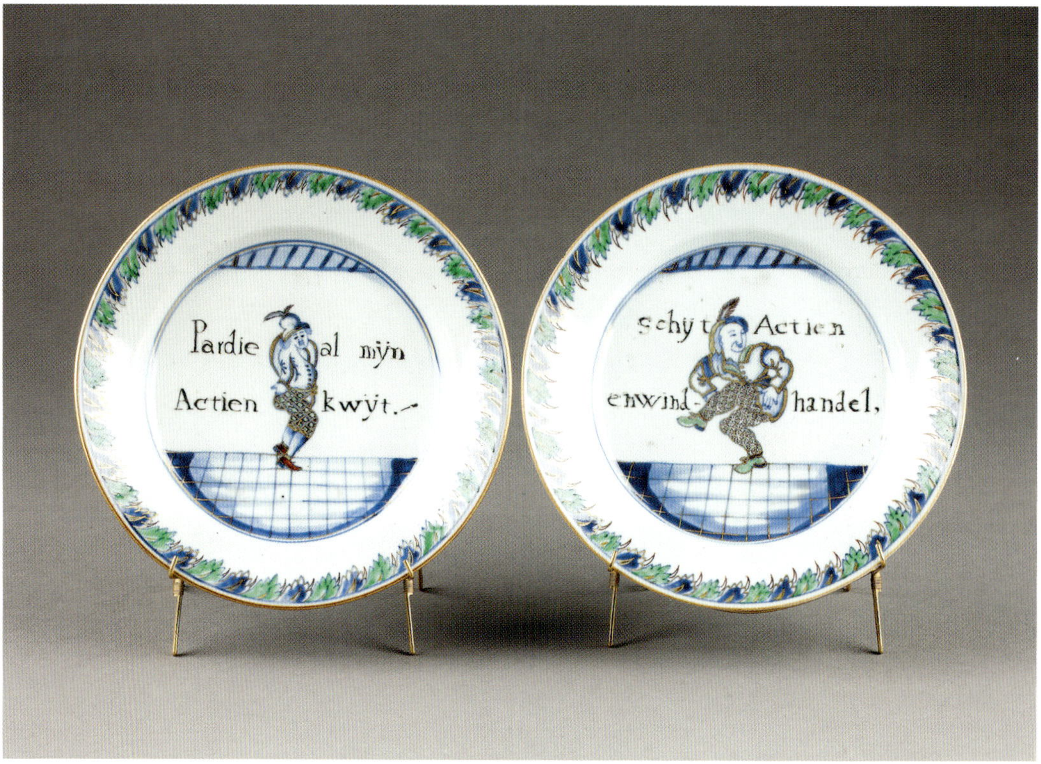

[FIG. 10]
Two porcelain plates decorated in underglaze blue, with overglaze colors and gilding. China, Qing dynasty (1644–1911 CE), made for the Netherlandish market, ca. 1720. Diameters 21 and 21.1 cm. Hallwyl Museum, Stockholm.

architectonic rhythm through color as well as the sharp contrast of glazed surface textures with the textile-like designs of the stucco. The result is a cosmopolitan idiom unique to the western Indian Ocean, with Chinese bowls caught in the net of a decorative language that links Oman, Yemen, and East Africa.

Many of the ceramics in the Omani mihrabs were likely produced at the famous kilns at Jingdezhen in Jiangxi Province, the largest single site of ceramic production in China for many centuries. Located near the region's best source of porcelain stone (petuntse)—a vital ingredient for the creation of porcelain's hard-paste body—the Jingdezhen potters brought blue-on-white porcelain to a high art by the end of the fourteenth century. Their early experiments with the palette were probably stimulated by the tastes of the Mongol Yuan emperors as well as material coming from the Middle East and Southeast Asia by sea and via the Mongol Empire's overland trade routes. It was during the Ming dynasty (1368–1644) and especially from the end of the fifteenth century onward that blue-on-white Chinese porcelain became a major global commodity. This was partly the result of stimulation from the Western markets through the rise of the European megacorporations. Already by the end of the sixteenth century Chinese ceramics were being transported by sea in two different directions, between them encircling the globe: the Portuguese moved them westward, through the Indian Ocean and around the Cape of Good Hope, while the Spanish sailed them eastward across the Pacific from the Philippines to Mexico, sometimes continuing them onward across the Atlantic. The establishment of Portuguese and Spanish trade in East Asia in the early sixteenth century was followed in the seventeenth century by the rise of the Dutch East India Company and an increasing focus on China from the British East India Company.

The preeminence of the Chinese kilns during the early modern period is legendary; this was the time when the ceramics of the Ming dynasty started to become proverbial in the Western imagination. Millions of pieces of Chinese ceramic moved around the globe, with the Dutch East India Company in particular flooding the Netherlands with imported porcelain throughout the seventeenth and eighteenth centuries. A taste for Chinese designs had long since arrived in the center of Europe, but as always, the flow was not monodirectional. European patrons sent designs to China from the sixteenth century onward, including coats of arms, family crests, and self-aggrandizing inscriptions, commissioning Chinese potters to produce porcelain wares to their specifications. Sometimes the instructions sent from Europe gave rise to unexpected transpositions, as when coats of arms or texts were applied upside down by painters unfamiliar with European armorial conventions or the script they were required to copy.

As satire flourished in this early modern world of international trade, vendors also began to request designs that punctured the gravitas of porcelain more intentionally. Two plates made in China (probably at Jingdezhen) circa 1720 for a commission from the Netherlands show grotesque, clownish male figures grimacing toward the viewer [FIG. 10]. One gestures helplessly, twisting over his exaggerated rump, while the other squats and raises his leg to break wind violently. Both men have been drawn from the stock of the commedia dell'arte—the inspiration, too, for many eighteenth-century European ceramic figurines of Harlequin, Pierrot, and so forth—and the perspectival checkered floors on which they stand indicate that prints were likely the original source for the imagery. The Dutch inscriptions have been written in black enamels by a slightly awkward hand, but they are nonetheless perfectly legible: "Pardie al mÿn Actien Kwÿt" (By God, I lost all of my shares) and "Schÿt Actien en Windhandel" (Shit shares and trade in wind). The targets of their mockery were financial speculators, particularly the shareholders of the Dutch East India Company who had fared badly when the world's first international financial bubble burst in 1720. Ceramics, as a highly adaptable and mobile status symbol in the eighteenth century, were emerging as a medium for the critique of modern capitalism as well as one of its prime sites of sensory pleasure and aesthetic enjoyment.

The global success of Chinese blue-on-white porcelain gave rise to many regional responses, although the porcelain body was not successfully replicated by any manufacturer outside China until the early eighteenth century. Instead, stoneware and earthenware produced from Vietnam to Mexico and Syria to the Netherlands sought to emulate the aesthetic of Chinese blue-on-white porcelain using cheaper materials for local markets, becoming highly successful industries in their own right. The next stage of imitation came with the industrialization of ceramic production in England and the advent of transfer printing in the mid-eighteenth century. This is a process that permits the mass production of standardized designs, whereby a monochrome print on tissue is taken from an inked engraved plate and laid over the surface of a biscuit-fired plate. With the ink transferred to the surface of the dish, the tissue can be floated off in water or left to burn off during firing. The transfer process can also be done over the glaze layer (requiring a second firing to melt the ink into the glaze). The technique lends itself particularly well to precise pictorial scenes, and by the nineteenth century it had become massively successful in the British and North American markets. The greatest success story of transfer-printed ceramics has to be the famous willow pattern, a blue-on-white chinoiserie fantasy synthesized at the end of the eighteenth century by British designers from various elements they encountered on Chinese ceramics: pagodas, figures

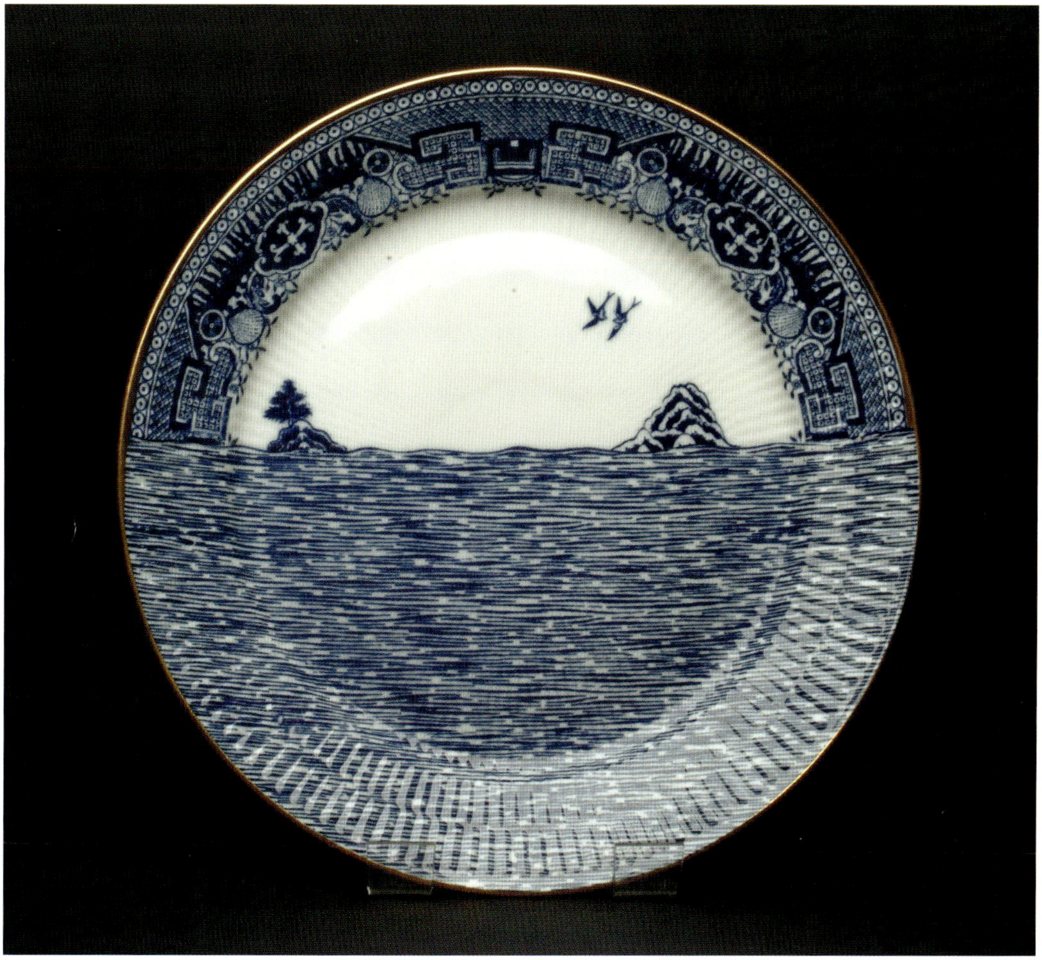

[FIG. 11]
Paul Scott (b. 1953), plate from *Cumbrian Blue(s), Cockle Pickers Tea Service*, 2007. Inglaze decal collage on Royal Copenhagen plate. Diameter 25 cm. Victoria and Albert Museum, London, C.77:10–2008.

crossing a bridge, ornate trees, water, and birds in flight. Versions of the design were produced on complete dining sets in their thousands by many manufacturers in nineteenth-century Britain—a quintessential work of mass production that continues to be sold today.

The ubiquitous willow pattern, with its layered resonances of domesticity, empire, and Orientalism, has recently been adapted and subverted by a number of artists. One of the most explicitly political reimaginings of the design is Paul Scott's 2007 *Cockle Pickers Tea Service* [FIG. 11]. In 2004, at least twenty-one trafficked Chinese people working as cockle pickers drowned in Morecambe Bay in northwest England when they were cut off by the incoming tide. Their deaths were a national scandal that exposed the plight of illegal migrant workers in the United Kingdom: the cockle pickers and unnumbered others like them were modern-day slave laborers, trafficked into the country in shipping containers in order to live and work in appalling conditions from which they had no real prospect of escape. Most of those who died at Morecambe Bay were from Fujian Province, famous for its production of oolong tea. Scott intended the *Cockle Pickers Tea Service* as both a memorial to those who died and a sardonic reflection on the self-congratulatory rhetoric surrounding the bicentennial of the 1807 British Slave Trade Act, which prohibited trade in enslaved people in the British Empire. Working with found pieces of crockery and transfer decals, he manipulated the design to flood most of the iconic pattern with a rising blue-and-white tide that obscures all but the hopelessly distant imagined hills. Around the edge of the plate, sections of geometric design have been subtly replaced with images of enslaved Africans taken from a famous abolitionist diagram illustrating the inhuman conditions aboard a slave ship. Bourgeois European tea things have been transformed into a bitter, if beautiful, lament for those enslaved and drowned by the global supply chains that put sugar, tea, and other delicacies—as well as ceramics—on bourgeois tables.

World Making and World Breaking

Clay's unique material qualities have given it a special place in the human imagination. Creation stories from around the world record the beginnings of humankind in figures fashioned from clay by a deity, from the Chinese goddess Nuwa, the Yoruba divinity Obatala, and the Inca god Viracocha, to the Hindu legend of Parvathi fashioning Ganesha from clay mixed with ghee and the Qur'anic genesis of man from potter's clay. Khnum, one of the oldest deities of ancient Egypt, was sometimes called the "divine potter" and is shown in temple carvings fashioning human figures with his hands at a carefully rendered potter's wheel. Genesis from clay is so deeply embedded in the human worldview that it seems almost unsurprising to encounter scientific proposals for the emergence of the

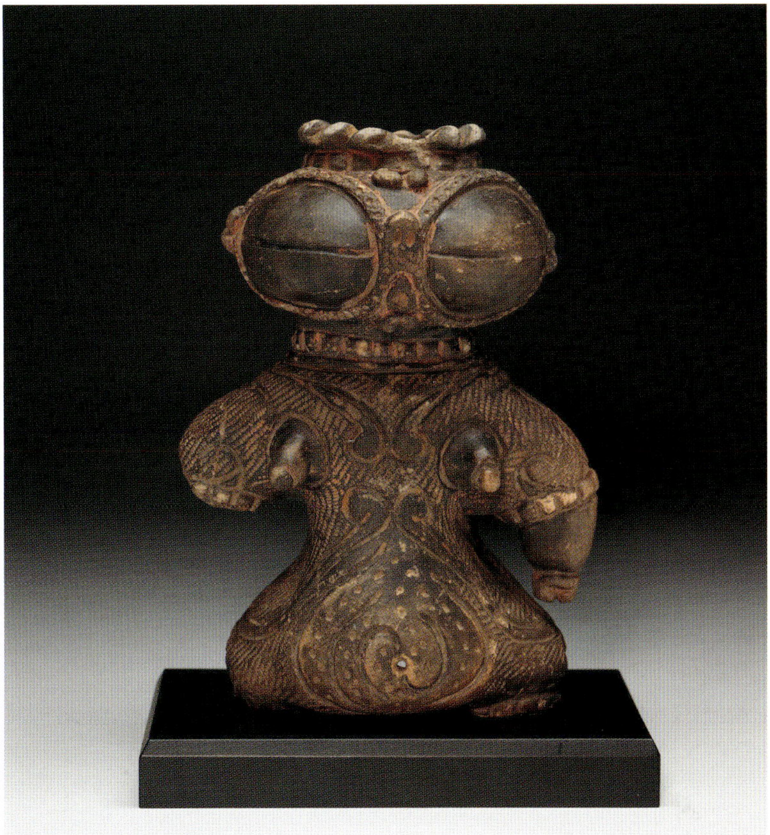

[FIG. 12]
Earthenware figurine.
Japan, ca. 1000–800 BCE.
Height 19.4 cm. Minneapolis
Institute of Art, 2016.46.

first organic life from clay (Graham Cairns-Smith's so-called clay theory of abiogenesis).

Not coincidentally, the earliest surviving representational artifacts created from fired clay are figurines in human form: the Paleolithic "Venus" figures depicting female bodies that have been found at sites across Eurasia. While debates about the meaning and function of these female figures continue, they attest to the ancient origins of ceramic as both a technology and an artistic medium that has developed in tandem with the human species. Human and animal figurines in clay represent some of the oldest surviving artworks from virtually every culture. To take just one exceptionally striking example, the final Jōmon period (ca. 1100–400 BCE) in prehistoric Japan has furnished some of the most compellingly enigmatic representations of the human form ever made [FIG. 12]. Huge, bisected eyes completely dominate the face of the earthenware figurine, above a body that presents a stylized female torso, with wide sloping hips and pointed breasts. The patterning of the body, once enhanced by the red pigment still visible in some areas, is made from incised and applied designs and impressions created by pressing twisted plant fibers into the unfired surface. In fact, it is this technique of decoration with cord impressions, found on the elaborate earthenware vessels of the period as well as its figurines, that has given the Jōmon (literally "cord-marked") period its name. Some excavated Jōmon figurines show breakages deliberately inflicted before scattering, leading to much speculation about their use and meaning. Some were placed alongside burials or enshrined in pits. Were they propitious agents? Were they fragmented during rituals? Were some of them broken up after they had brought about a hoped-for event, like the safe delivery of a baby or another form of prosperity for the community?

The artistry of the Jōmon figures delivers a jolt across the millennia. Curved, graspable, tactile surfaces invite the fingers to trace the lines of design and circle the enormous, insectoid eyes. We remain largely ignorant about their social roles, but we assume they were efficacious objects in some way. Why create things that are so human in their appeal to the hand and yet so uncanny in appearance, why break them on purpose, and why bury them in the ground, if not to bring about some wished-for thing in this life or the next? The efficacious function of the human figure in ceramic is a phenomenon that could fill volumes, from the most elemental Neolithic votive and commemorative figurines to the enormous terracotta funerary army that accompanied Qin Shi Huangdi (d. 210 BCE) to the afterlife. And while we are accustomed to thinking of the mantelpiece figurines of the more recent past (and their present-day descendants made by companies like Lladró) as a purely decorative phenomenon, it is worth pausing over the ways in which even the chintziest shepherds and shepherdesses model a desired world order for their owners. They perform a pastoral utopia for urban patrons, where the tinted high gloss of porcelain rebuffs all realities of decay, time, and work.

The porcelain figurines produced in large numbers in eighteenth-century Europe were long derided by modernist critics as the worst kind of knickknack. Close attention to the lustrous forms produced by such skilled modelers as the Meissen factory's virtuoso Johann Joachim Kändler (1706–75), however, often reveals a world that is as strange as it is appealing. An extraordinary set of five figurines designed by Kändler during the 1730s presents personifications of the five senses. The preexisting tradition of anthropomorphizing the senses—related to the personifications of the continents seen in Yao-Fen You's case study in this book, as well as the seasons, elements, and so forth also found in contemporary ceramic series—makes the embodiment of senses in the forms of women a natural choice for a figurine series. Still, representing sensory experience in porcelain poses a major challenge of synesthesia, and some of the means chosen for evoking the individual senses are rather alarming. Take the figure representing touch [FIG. 13]. Rather than pursuing any of the pleasurable sensuality seen in some of the other figures in the set, the designer has portrayed touch as a harried woman being pecked in the breast by a parrot, while putti have a fistfight beside her and a spaniel prepares to savage her foot. Completing the sense of disaster is the disembodied hand that ventures forth from the base of the figurine (the same position is occupied by a disembodied nose on the figure for smell, a disturbing porcelain mouth eating something that looks like an elongated slug on the one for taste, and so forth). The dainty fingers grope blindly, only to be met by the threatening raised pincer of a lobster emerging from another gilded curlicue of the base.

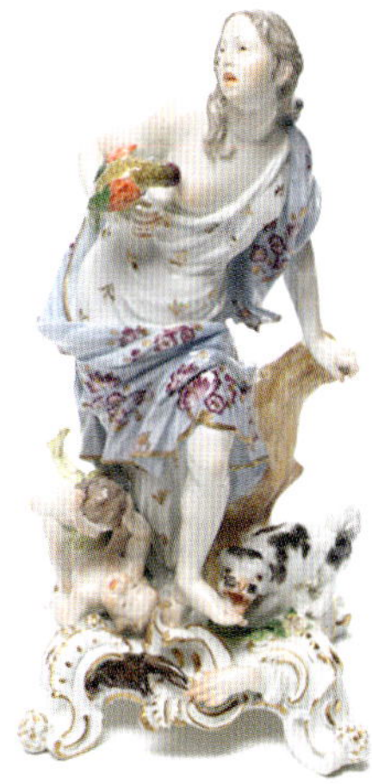

[FIG. 13]
Touch, from a series of figurines representing the five senses. Porcelain with polychrome painting, clear glaze, and gilding. Meissen Porcelain Manufactory (Germany), ca. 1733–40. Height 28.5 cm. Walters Art Museum, Baltimore, 48.932.

Kändler's design clearly expresses the perceived hierarchy of the senses in eighteenth-century Europe, in which sight was ranked top as the most "rational" sense. Tellingly, the serene figure representing sight in this set is looking through a telescope while being aided rather than harassed by her associates. The supposedly bestial sense of touch was relegated to the bottom—and in this case punished accordingly, albeit with some degree of humor. It is curious to witness this negative judgment of touch in such a tactile art as porcelain, but this is of course another form of world making: porcelain is here the medium of expression of a worldview, an Enlightenment model for understanding and mandating the human experience of sensory information and sensory compulsions. There is a sly—and surely intentional—irony to an object that proclaims the baseness of touch while making us desire so strongly to touch it.

Unsurprisingly, the porcelain figurine is also a prime site for accessing eighteenth-century European understandings of the wider world and their place within it in an era of imperial expansion. The recurrence of figures representing various kinds of "others"—a category defined by class and occupation as well as ethnicity and race—signals clearly the medium's role in articulating social curiosities, anxieties, and acquisitiveness toward human beings outside one's own circle. In some instances, the acquisitive urge intersected fully with the imperial project. One of the bluntest realizations of this is the series of seventy-four figurines known as the *Peoples of Russia*, initially commissioned by Catherine the Great and created at the Russian Imperial Porcelain Manufactory in Saint Petersburg between circa 1780 and 1800. The series was based on the illustrations to a landmark three-volume publication by a German botanist, *Description of All the Peoples Inhabiting the Russian State* (1776–77), one of the first comprehensive ethnographies of its kind. Designed in male-female pairs, prettified and dressed in picturesque ethnic costumes to maximize their differentiation from each other, the series was intended to represent every "people" of the vast, polyglot lands brought together under the Russian Empire, from Laplanders (Sámi), Samoyeds (Indigenous Siberians), and Armenians, to Kyrgyz, Kalmyk, and Manchurian subjects. Such was the success of the porcelain series that many figures from it were given as imperial and diplomatic gifts. The imperial urge to categorize and possess had found its ideal surrogate subject in the ceramic figurine.

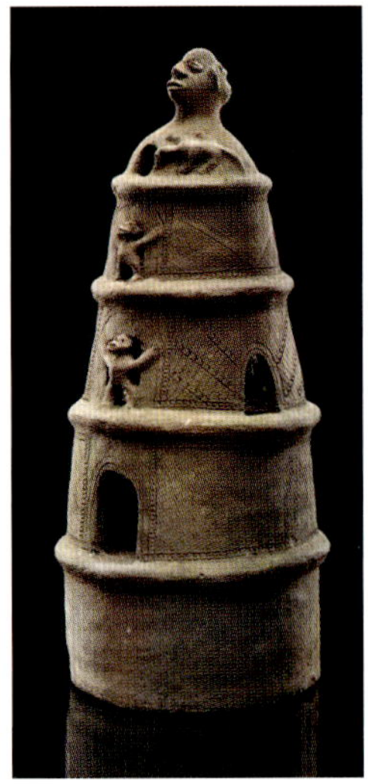

[FIG. 14]
Dibondo five-tiered funerary column. Terracotta. Bakongo Ba Mboma, Democratic Republic of Congo, early twentieth century. Height 67 cm. Musée Barbier-Mueller, Geneva, 1026–485.

After birth, sensation, and empire, what is left but death? Across the world, ceramics have played a central role in many funerary practices, whether as containers for remains, markers of burial sites, or objects accompanying the dead to the afterlife. The grave-marking vases of ancient Greece, architectonic ossuaries of the Sogdians in central Asia, and figural urns of the northern Andes all demarcate the end of life through ceramic containers. The imperishability of the medium fits it for endurance into eternity, and its plasticity lends itself to meaningful elaboration through three-dimensional modeling. A spectacular and rare instance of this kind of elaboration is the fired earthenware *dibondo* (pl. *mabondo*), a type of vessel used to mark the grave of important persons among the Bakongo people of Angola and the Democratic Republic of Congo [FIG. 14]. In the example pictured here, which probably dates from the early twentieth century, the five levels of ceramic construction embody the transformation of the dead man's physical form into spiritual manifestation. The language of gesture employed on the figures—who are visible on the outside as well as hidden on the inside of the central chambers—along with the double-faced bust and lizard modeled at the crown of the vessel, carry social and spiritual meanings particular to Bakongo cosmology. The monumental form of the *dibondo* and intricacies of its design attest to a sophisticated tradition of ritual pottery production that required careful preparation of the clay body as well as control of the firing conditions to produce such large and complex objects in earthenware. The practice seems to have disappeared by the 1930s.

The relationship between ceramics and death is not limited to the material's practical suitability for urns and memorial vessels. As with the beginning of life, so too may the end of life be conceptualized through the elemental material of ceramic. A Yoruba tradition holds that humans split on death into three forces, the last of which (*ori*, "destiny") needs help in its onward journey to avoid ending up in "the world of broken pots." The friability of fired ceramics is of course another of the unique properties of the medium; like the plasticity of unfired clay, the breakability of fired ceramic vessels is also a fundamental part of the human encounter with the material. More than just a metaphor, the breaking of ceramics embodies the irreversible workings of time, giving broken pottery a special set of meanings in relation to death. Enslaved Africans working on the southern plantations in the United States sometimes placed broken pottery on graves—an act that was frequently misinterpreted as a form of votive practice. "White observers persistently saw these as 'offerings' while black informants made statements about dividing off the dead from the living and about the rupture of time, preoccupations also marked by the placing of stopped clocks on graves."[2]

In a different vein, the Bakongo *dibondo* also speaks of the entanglement of ceramics with cognitive acts. The term *kubika ɛ bundu*, literally "the art of organizing" or "bringing together," refers to the act of creating an object in wood or clay, recognizing that "vessels could be understood as a source and medium of language."[3] That is, ceramic could be both the medium of expressing a worldview *and* the wellspring of that worldview, shaping human understanding of the environment, cosmos, and self through encounters with its material qualities. In medieval Arabic philosophy, clay (*ṭīn*) appears on occasion as both the prime matter of the universe and the substance of the imagination itself, receiving impressions from the internal and external senses while also retaining the capacity to be molded into new forms. Across time and space, ceramics have been shaped by humans, but humans have been shaped by ceramics too.

Those who make ceramics leave traces in the world that can outlive them by years, centuries, or even millennia. This chapter will close with a final pair of objects that bring two nineteenth-century ceramic artists, working far distant from each other, into sharp focus through the traces they have chosen to leave behind. The first, a glazed wall tile in Sultaanat-Abad palace in Tehran, gives a rare glimpse into the workshop of the tile painter [FIG. 15]. Is this a self-portrait of the painter? Or is this

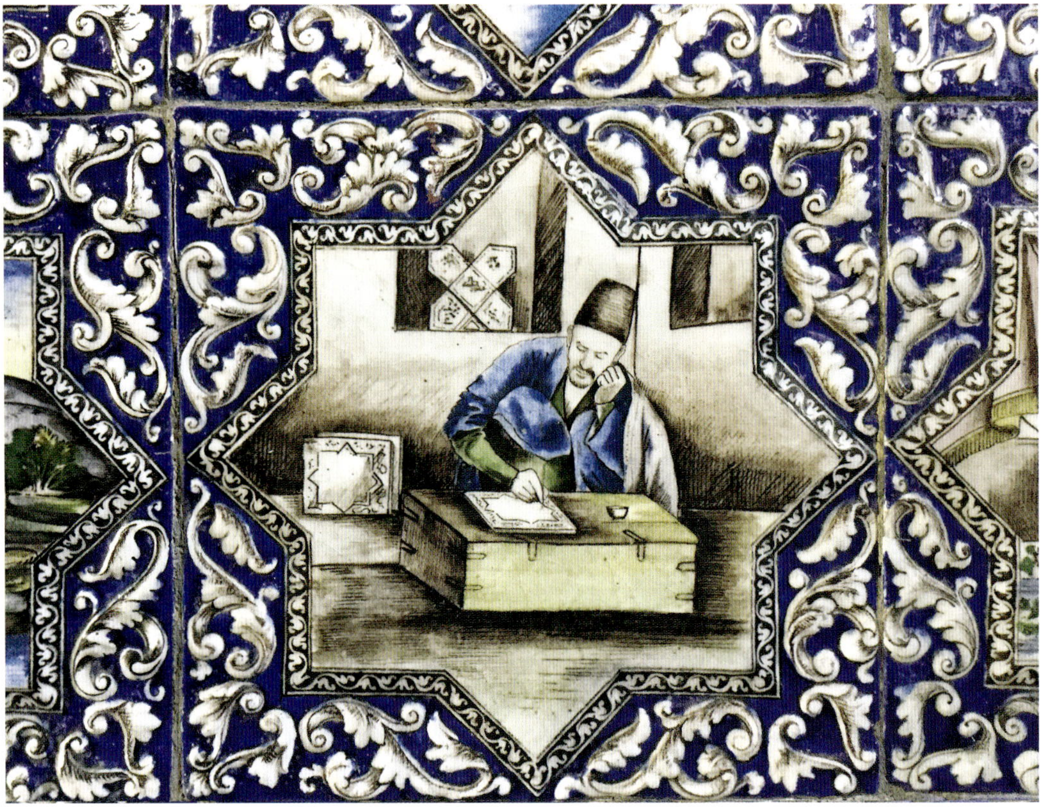

[FIG. 15]
A (self-?) portrait of the tile painter. Molded frit-ware (stonepaste) tile with polychrome paint and clear glaze. In situ at the Sultaanat-Abad palace, Tehran, Iran, 1886–87. Photograph courtesy of Kianoosh Motaghedi.

one tile painter's portrait of another, looking across the room in search of inspiration while working through a large order of luxury pictorial wall tiles, and lighting on his confrere as an interesting and novel subject? The careful observation of the painter's pose captures a moment of such precise and intimate informality that it must be documentary: wearing an astrakhan hat, he sits on the floor and leans his face on his left hand while doing fine brushwork with his right, holding the slim brush like a pencil for maximum control of fine lines and working with the paintpot placed carefully out of the way of his painting arm to avoid accidents. The square tiles with star-shaped fields on which he paints are, of course, analogous with the tile on which he is painted; two more blank ones are stacked up behind him, waiting to be filled with the battles, women, cats, and musicians that appear on the rest of the tiled wall in the Sultaanat-Abad palace. It is at once a self-conscious reflection on the act of making—a deliberate insertion of the maker into his product—and a startlingly spontaneous portrait of a moment in late nineteenth-century Iran. The robe or blanket draped over the painter's shoulder suggests it may be cold in the room. Is it the end of the day? The last painting of the order? Is the light fading outside?

The graphic image is one way to record human presence in ceramic. Another method, perhaps more intuitive to the medium, is the incised mark—including words inscribed into the unfired surface. The famous alkaline-glazed jars by Dave the Potter (also known as David Drake, ca. 1801–1870s), an enslaved man who worked at the stoneware factories in Edgefield, South Carolina, in the middle decades of the nineteenth century, bear witness to their maker not just through their monumental proportions and impressively well-turned forms but also in the short texts that he incised into their bodies along with his name and the date of manufacture [FIG. 16]. The earliest inscription attributed to this exceptional figure is the single word *concatination* on a two-handled, unsigned storage jar made in 1834. This unusual and satisfying word (usually spelled *concatenation*) is strikingly apposite to the multisensory medium of ceramic; it refers to things linked or occurring together to produce a particular outcome. It also carries the etymological weight of chains, being derived from the Latin *catena* (chain). The word seems almost eerily prescient as the surviving prelude to a unique set of short texts, often in rhyming couplets, embodied in a sequence of stoneware jars that make tangible an enslaved man who might otherwise have been largely lost to history. At a time when it was illegal to teach slaves in the southern United States how to read and write, Dave the Potter played with words and preserved them in the surface of the jars he turned—jars that are among the largest products of the potter's wheel in the nineteenth-century United States, with such powerful physical presence that contemporary potters were amazed by the strength and technical skill necessary to their creation.

The tactility of Dave's words, written with a sharp point in a cursive script into the surface of the stoneware body before firing, forms a physical poetry that acts in synchrony with their content. Like the painter of the tile in Sultaanat-Abad palace, Dave the Potter has inserted himself into his work to leave behind evidence of the potter as world maker—not just his name, but words that illuminate his experience of the world. His couplets refer to the future contents of the jars, locations, God, individuals including his owners, homilies and holidays, and the jars themselves. Most poignant is one dated May 17, 1857, that reflects on his own dislocation: "I wonder where is all my relations / Friendship to all—and every nation." In some of the other inscriptions, his tongue seems more in cheek. The example illustrated here, dated a few months later, refers with some irony to the economic conditions of his existence. It seems fitting to let Dave the Potter have the last word:

Lm Aug. 22 1857
Dave
I made this Jar for Cash–
though its called—lucre trash
Dave

* * *

Without presenting this as a global survey, I have brought together objects from across the world to make my case for the study of ceramics as an art historical venture. No one chapter could hope to touch on every ceramic tradition, and I hope that readers will forgive me if I have overlooked their favorites or skewed toward one region at the expense of another. The three different lines of inquiry I've proposed here—ceramics as markers of human presence, as subjects of manual and global movement, and as medium and source of cognition—have all been prompted by ceramic art that I have encountered and studied over the years. Every one of the pieces I have discussed in this chapter is an object that has jumped out at me from a display case or the pages of a book and given me a sense of wonder. But these are just three possible avenues toward a materially and culturally informed art history of humankind's most enduring medium of creativity. The other writers in this book reveal other ways that ceramic art can be approached and understood in the studio, laboratory, archaeological trench, and collecting cabinet.

Without my intending it, the watery matrix of the sea has turned out to be a leitmotif of this chapter. The importance of the oceans as conduits

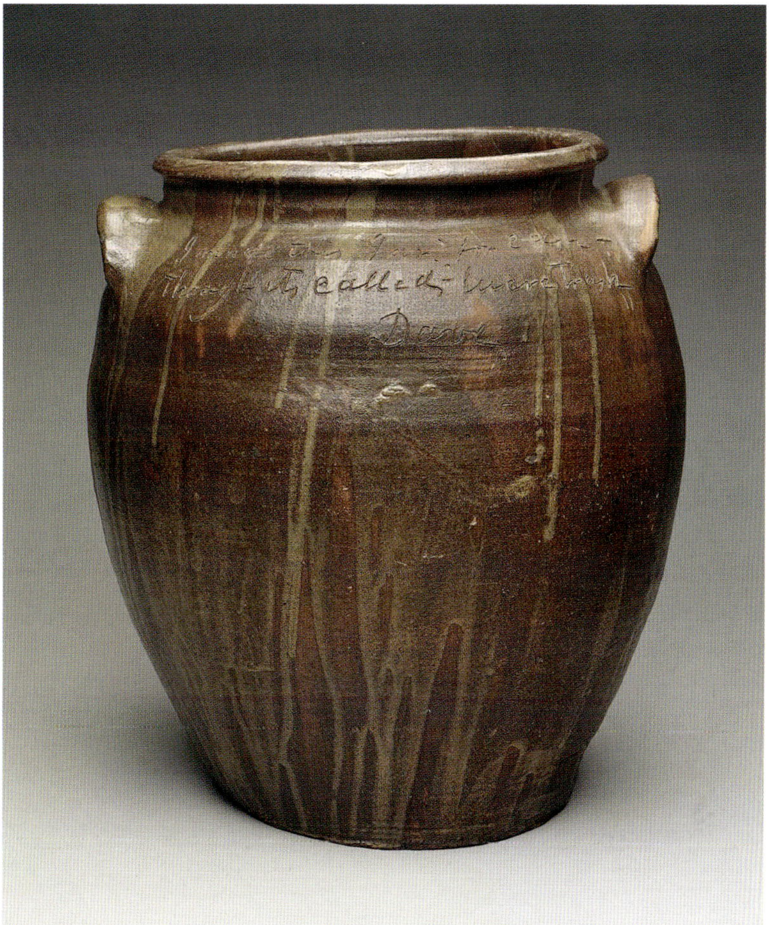

[FIG. 16]
Stoneware jar with alkaline glaze, made by Dave the Potter (ca. 1801–1870s) and inscribed "Lm Aug. 22 1857 / Dave / I made this Jar for Cash / though its called—lucre trash / Dave." Edgefield County, South Carolina, dated August 22, 1857. Height 48.3 cm. Boston Museum of Fine Art, 1997.10.

for ceramics (as well as the concurrent brutalities of slavery and empire) is an obvious historical fact, but writing this piece has made me realize that there is also a personal dimension to this. As a child living on the east coast of Scotland, I picked up hundreds of pieces of broken ceramic from the beach that we walked on daily. Much of it was blue-and-white ware that probably came from nineteenth-century factory discards dumped into the North Sea. The edges of each piece had been worn smooth by the movement of the sea, and the glazes were no longer shiny, but the designs remained. Foremost among them was the all-conquering willow pattern. Fragments from the middle parts of the design, with identifiable images of people, birds, and buildings, were rare; more common were pieces from the rims, with their chinoiserie bricolage of scales, cartouches, and geometric shapes. For a magpie-eyed child, these treasures felt like transmissions from other worlds, always incomplete and yet unending; every day the tide would take out the old and bring in the new from mysterious underwater currents that went around the world. No doubt the hours I spent looking for pieces of patterned ceramic among the stones, seaweed, and rubbish have had more impact on my adult career and preoccupations than anyone could have guessed at the time. Most abiding, though, is the impression left in my mind by those ceramic emissaries of the oceans that if you stood at the edge of the sea for long enough, eventually everything in the world would wash up at your feet.

Crazing, Shivering, Golden Cracks and Rivets: Preserving the Value of Flaws

Vicki Parry

For the life and afterlife of the ceramic object, conservation is one of many possible events that adds to its biography and continues past our interaction with it. The conservators who do this work document and preserve an object's complete history for those who come after us. We do this by identifying any previous restorations, which are made of materials not original to the object such as new handles or rims, and acknowledging the value they add to the life of the ceramic. It is vital to preserve this information and justly allow the object to represent its history. As conservators, we are not attempting to change the value or information contained in the object but rather to document and preserve it as needed. Sometimes this involves a discussion about slowing deterioration due to inherent conditions, or removing harmful or deteriorating components from previous restorations. This discussion may also include exploring the removal of historically significant yet culturally insensitive interventions while acknowledging their history and context. The following chapter describes the necessary dialogue and documentation that are vital to the conservator's practice.

Society and Ceramics: Intertwined Nature

Ceramics are all around us and have been part of human life, our daily lives, for millennia. We use them in our homes for cooking and serving food, and they provide beauty and practicality in the form of wall and floor tiles. Ceramic is defined chemically as an inorganic nonmetallic solid that is heated to create a strong but brittle material that is corrosion and heat resistant. This solid is formed from natural clay minerals and usually decorated with the same. Although there are additional types of ceramics used in high-tech fields that push the boundaries of that definition, they are beyond the scope of this chapter.[1] For the rest of this chapter, I will focus on traditional ceramic arts.

Traditional ceramics have been found in the earliest settlements of humans. The date changes with new excavations and reexaminations of existing materials, but it also depends on what type of ceramic object is being considered. At present, the earliest ceramic object is still the "Venus" of Dolní Věstonice dated to 28,000 BCE and excavated near Brno, Czech Republic, although many other early figurines, both human and animal, have been found too. The earliest functional pottery was discovered in Xianrendong Cave, Jiangxi Province, China, and dates to about 18,000 BCE. The earliest functional ceramic finds in Japan and Central Europe followed a few thousand years later. They began appearing in North and West Africa by the tenth century BCE, and the Americas by the eighth century BCE. Keep in mind that these are vast geographic areas with a range of cultures and histories, so each will have variations in the development of ceramic use. Archaeology is continuing to unearth finds that challenge these dates, so it is prudent to remain open to updates and corrections. As we continue to make discoveries and reexamine what has already been discovered, we will learn more about the earliest ceramics and their development, and ultimately more about this remarkable material that has become integral to our lives.

Ceramic as an art material at its basic level is chemically the same throughout the world regardless of what form it is made into or when and where that form is created. This means that traditional ceramics are all subject to the same ways of making, flaws in firing, and deterioration mechanisms. Beyond their creation, differences arise in how they are used, repaired, and valued. These differences evolve and depend on cultural values and histories that are also continuously changing. For as long as we have made and used ceramics, their repair and restoration have also been practiced. Early humans used locally available materials to extend the life of their ceramic bowls, ewers, and so on. As ceramics became more commoditized, so too did the need for repair. Niche professions such as china menders have been around for hundreds of years in Asia (mainly China) and Europe. These professions as well as allied or similar ones are the ancestors of the modern conservators who work at archaeological sites, historical societies, galleries, libraries, museums, and private labs.

In traditional academic programs based on conservation philosophies developed primarily in Europe and the Americas—but also taught in Africa and some regions of Asia—student conservators begin by being introduced to the chemistry of the materials they will study. For ceramics, this starts with the general information most ceramists will know: types of clay, forming and decoration methods, tools, and kiln/firing basics. As conservators continue in their academic studies and training, they gain more knowledge about materials. If they are specializing, then they may focus on ceramics from specific cultures or regions. Beyond the particularities of ceramics' manufacture, what varies and changes most across them is their life after production, which provides the challenging variations in physical condition and the value of that condition that conservators must document, understand, and ultimately preserve.

Ceramics and Conservation

Starting with their ancient production, ceramics were made of materials that were readily and locally available to the maker: clays and temper (leaves, shells, and sand). Over time, the acts of gathering, preparing, and manipulating the clay used for traditional ceramics developed into traditions that became instilled in local societies and beliefs. These included restrictions and social rules about who collected and worked the clay, who decorated it, and who fired it. There are multiple examples recorded in texts or paintings from many cultures that describe this social structure. This ingrained use of a material and its success within societies have allowed ceramics to remain a chemically consistent material throughout most of human history. Its success is primarily due to the medium's most useful characteristics. Its plasticity when wet, stability after being fired, and widespread accessibility from nearly anywhere water has carried and deposited it have allowed humans to recognize its value, and manipulate it to store food as well as move foodstuffs and other goods over longer distances.

These qualities of clay and the ceramic product have undeniably impacted its role in our societies. One commonality across cultures and time periods is that ceramics were made to last. Even ceramics created for funerary purposes were made to exist into that person's afterlife, such as the funerary terracotta figures, heads, and vessels of the Akan people in Ghana from the sixteenth to nineteenth century, ceramic figures from pre-Columbian shaft tomb cultures in Mexico, and painted *mingqi* from the Chinese Han dynasty (206 BCE–220 CE) and Tang dynasty (618–906 CE). These ceramics vary in age and culture of course, but all were formed to accompany the deceased into the afterlife. Often these wares do not receive restoration in their tomb lifetime, but their value is clear. What happens to their usefulness or life once excavated or collected?

A ceramic's intended use or original purpose does not necessarily change when excavated, or when it enters a museum collection. The biography of the ceramic acquires new meanings or layers as it changes context, building on what was already there. Remains of residues from ritual use or past restorations are important and add to the biography of the ceramic. Frequently what happens, or what we experience in looking at and studying ceramics, is that our current scholarship about a type of ceramic object and the culture it comes from will inevitably be the basis for how we experience them. These experiences will influence how we conserve these objects, and can be a troubling path that is often not fully recognized until there is a better and more complete understanding of a culture and its materials. It is a challenging issue we are dealing with now in the United States and generally worldwide. For example, restoring ceramics using metal rivets is a technique used for hundreds of years, and its use is indicative of the value of the ceramic object. The rivets are pieces of metal (think staples) designed to bridge a crack in a ceramic object using holes drilled on either side of that crack. Clearly this took skill, which took time to acquire, and it frequently required the use of relatively valuable metals such as copper. For decades in the early to mid-twentieth century, these metal rivets were removed. The empty drilled holes left behind were filled with new "modern" materials that were advertised as scientifically advanced, and therefore of a higher value and more aesthetically pleasing than the rivets they were replacing. This was the philosophy at that time. By the late twentieth century, the removal of rivets was routinely questioned as a technique and now is generally not done unless there is an urgent need to prevent damage from corroding rivets.

Today there is a reckoning in conservation between historical inequities that have had undeniable impacts on communities and their cultural property, and what feels like an earnest desire to learn about, understand, and appreciate the material culture of all groups of people and cultures equally. This reckoning is a topic of discussion that often comes up in conservation. It is essential to recognize it and acknowledge its vital place when discussing conservation outcomes and expectations. It is critical to talk and listen to all interested parties. These parties may be a person or group having a vested interest in the conservation of an object or collection; in a museum this may be one curator or a curatorial department. Equally, it may be one or a combination of donors, artists, or cultural groups. The Smithsonian's National Museum of the American Indian in Washington, DC, provides an amazing example of an institution where parties representing Indigenous groups have a strong voice. The acting director as well as many on the board of trustees are Indigenous peoples. They manage the museum's day-to-day operations and maintenance of a comprehensive collection that includes the largest group of Native American ceramics in the United States. Regardless of who or what groups comprise the interested party or parties, discussions about the expectations of a ceramic object's examination and conservation treatment are important, and their documentation is essential.

In conservation, like many professional fields, our ethics shift and evolve with changes in society. These shifts are often encountered during capital projects, such as a major renovation and reinstallation of a museum gallery, when large groups of objects or whole collections are reexamined, conserved, and possibly restored for the project's end goal. During this process, curators and conservators may encounter such situations; for instance, what was acceptable and ethical for restorations on ceramics in the 1970s is different from what is considered acceptable and ethical forty or fifty years later. Additionally, some older restorations, such as early twentieth-century restorations on twelfth- and thirteenth-century mina'i ceramics from Iran, now cross over into historical evidence. Further illustrations of this can be found in Asian ceramic collections throughout the world, such as at the Rijksmuseum in Amsterdam, where the head conservator of ceramics, Isabelle Garachon, has been researching the use of separately fired restorations. These situations create a challenge for conservators and are occurring more frequently as rightful historic value is given to past restorations. Understanding that "value" is complicated. What we end up needing to know is the nature of the materials that were used and what the earlier restorer's goal may have been. As we will see in the following sections, this materiality is complex.

As with any material, modern ceramics conservation starts with observation, which entails a careful and extensive visual examination of the object's condition. These observations inform the conservator and influence the development of an approach to conservation treatment, if needed, by providing information on the condition of the ceramic body, glaze, and other decorative components. This practice coupled with an understanding of ceramic as a material, and how ceramic objects are made and decorated, will inform the conservator. For example, crazing—a network of glaze cracks that is the visual manifestation of unstoppable physical forces continually pulling the glaze apart—when observed in a glaze may be intentional, as seen with crackled glazes from China's Southern Song dynasty (1127–1279 CE). Crackled glazes, intentionally formulated to craze (crack), are unmistakable, and have been in use for hundreds of years. Sometimes this intentional imperfection is deliberately enhanced with pigments or resins that are wiped over the glaze surface and settle into the crackled glaze. Still, although it is used as a decoration, crazing remains a valid condition issue that implies poor glaze fit, possibly leading to glaze loss. The process of making, glazing, and firing a ceramic object always involves the physical forces of expansion and contraction through the intense heating and then cooling of the firing process. During drying and firing, clays will contract (shrink) a given amount depending on their chemistry. Glazes do too. If one contracts more or less than the other, then this is where problems of "glaze fit" arise. Crazing is a sign that the glaze is too snug for the ceramic body. In other words, the glaze wants to contract more than the ceramic under it so it is under constant tension (pulling apart), which manifests as cracks or crazing. Shivering is essentially the opposite, where the glaze did not want to contract as much as the ceramic under it, and that can manifest as areas of flaking glaze, especially on rims. It is equally important to understand that crazing and shivering are processes that release energy over time. The release of that energy is unstoppable; therefore a crazing glaze will continue to crack and form new cracks in order to release energy. More cracks mean more potential damage for the ceramic object such as glaze loss. However, understanding ceramic as a material, how it behaves and how an object was created, is only part of the story. We must also recognize a history of conservation or specific restoration campaigns—defined periods when conservation treatment is performed, often for a specific reason or goal. This is not always straightforward, particularly when examining ceramics from a range of cultures and historical periods.

In the following sections, I look at five condition issues common to glazed ceramics that typically pass through the hands of a conservator. Actions are taken along each object's path from creation to its collection and beyond, resting for a brief time in the hands of a conservator whose decisions and actions add to that path or history. Because the bulk of my professional experience is with ceramics from cultures on the Asian continent, they will be the focus of my discussion and examples. Ceramics are ceramics no matter where and when they were created. The challenge to conservators is recognizing when certain conditions—like crazing and shivering (flaking)—are intentional and integral to the value of the ceramic. Likewise, with previous restorations that have a long and important history in their own right, such as *kintsugi* (discussed below) or metal rivets, the conservator's path forward may not be so clear. Historic restorations indeed hold value in technique and their history of development, but they also then impart a story to the ceramic on which they are used.

Biography of Intent: Crazing

Regardless of age, one of the most common flaws for glazed ceramics worldwide is crazing, which has also enjoyed a significant role as decoration. Interestingly, most of the common flaws that makers encounter have been used as a decorative technique; even shivering, which will be discussed in the following section on *ko-sometsuke*, is a characteristic flaw that was valued in a specific period of ceramic production in China.

Ceramics as a commodity did not become successful without having flaws that prompted the makers, users, and collectors to decide on discarding the ceramic object or keeping it. These flaws along with the desire to correct or replicate them are what steered makers in different

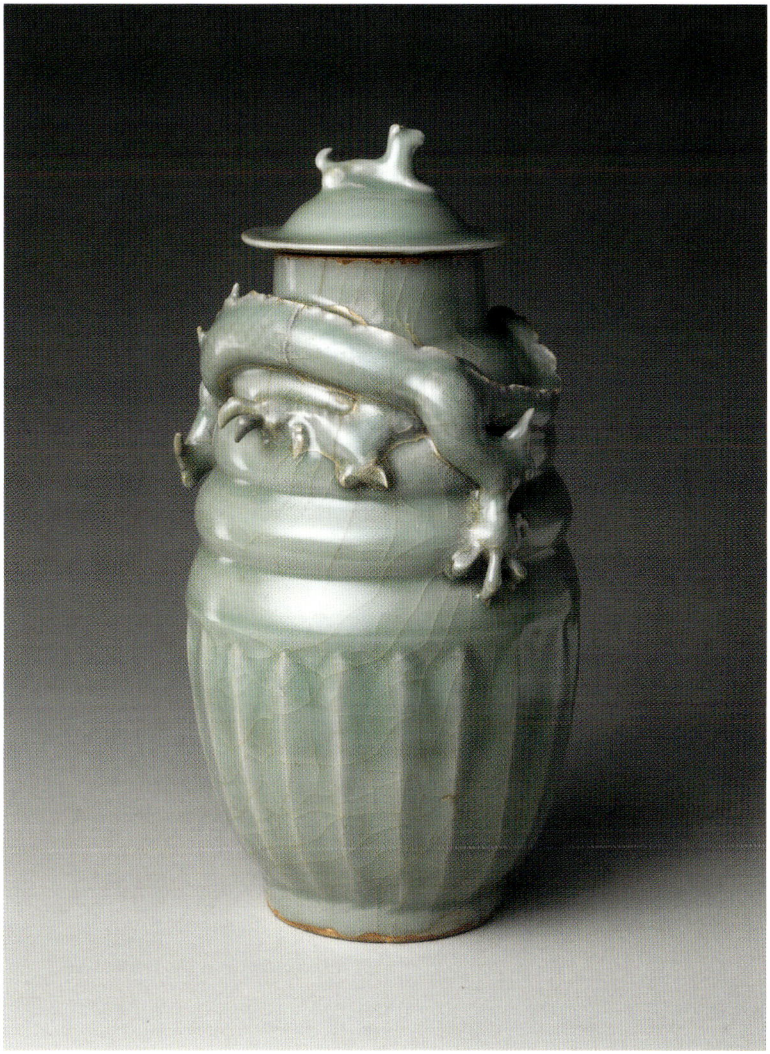

[FIG. 17]
Funerary jar with dragon. Longquan celadon, crazing; tomb vase. China, late Song / Southern Song dynasty, twelfth to thirteenth centuries CE. Height with cover 25.4 cm. Rogers Fund, 1918; Metropolitan Museum of Art open-access image, 18.139.1a, b.

directions to achieve those goals. As ceramics increasingly began to occupy the functional and artistic worlds, and were exported or traded across cultures and vast geographic areas, some "flaws" increasingly became markers of value. To be clear, each of these flaws has had known "fixes" that range from altering glaze and body recipes to changing firing conditions and time. Because they exist as something to be corrected, but have also been pursued (and still are) as valuable characteristics in some cultures, it is worth noting that these are still flaws that lead to the reduced long-term stability of most ceramics that exhibit them. This is the challenge for the conservator: balancing artistic intent with aesthetic appearance and slowing the physical instability that results from inherent forces already at play such as crazing, which continues to form cracks leading to potential to glaze loss and deeper cracks in the ceramic body (under the glaze) that will lead to the object's disintegration.

Longquan celadons from China's Song dynasty (960–1279 CE) were a departure from traditional refined Jingdezhen and Dehua white porcelain, and embraced the green celadon glazes and deeper iron-rich colors in the clay bodies. Although these celadon wares are remarkably like their perfect porcelain cousins in many ways, they were more prone to crazing due to differences in thermal expansion between the body and glaze [FIG. 17]. The main culprit was the glaze, which was higher in alkalis from potassium than sodium. This inherent tendency to craze became paired with the glaze's jade-like color and translucency, and these sought-after wares were produced until the early Ming dynasty (1368–1644 CE). Close rivals to the Chinese celadons are those from Southeast Asia, especially the kiln sites in Thailand at Si Satchanalai, starting in the Sukhothai kingdom (1248–1438 CE) primarily in the thirteenth and fourteenth centuries [FIG. 18]. Crazing is inherent for these ceramics, too, as the technical knowledge for creating celadons moved through cultural contact such as trade.

It is important to reiterate here that crazing, regardless of whether it is a flaw or desired trait, is a process of change and progresses over time, continually releasing energy through the formation of cracks. The more a glaze crazes, the more unstable it is, and this affects the overall stability of the whole ceramic object. In figures 17 and 18, note that there is a difference in the appearance of the crazing. Some cracks look more defined because they are ingrained with minute dust particles and oils or other organic materials that transfer to the surface through handling and being on display. Dust and dirt attract more dust and dirt. The lighter a crack appears, the more recent it may be because it has not had the same long-term exposure to dust and handling. These cracks are narrower as well, but they will expand over time as crazing progresses, allowing more particles of dust, dirt, and oils to deposit and build up in the cracks in

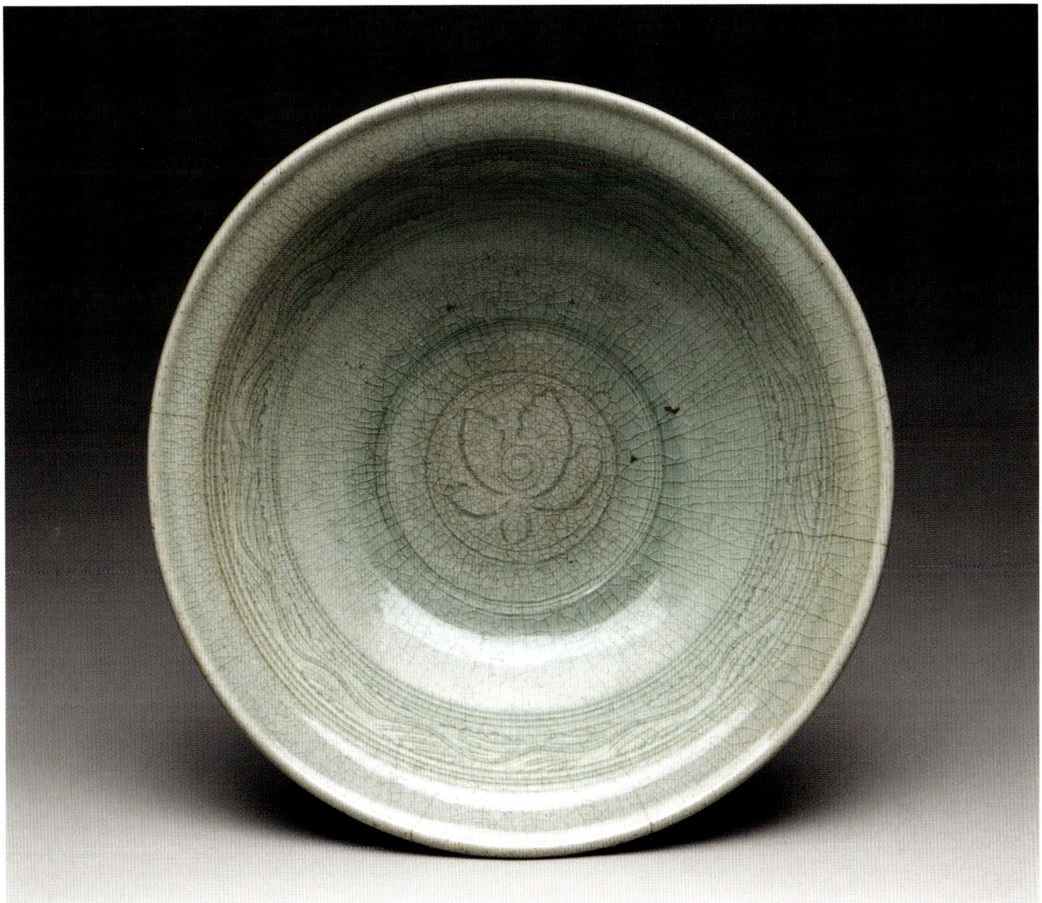

[FIG. 18]
Bowl with lotus. Stoneware with incised decoration and celadon glaze (Si Satchanalai ware). Thailand, fifteenth to sixteenth centuries CE. Height 11.4 cm, diameter 30.5 cm. Gift of Betty and John R. Menke, 1992; Metropolitan Museum of Art open-access image, 1992.72.37.

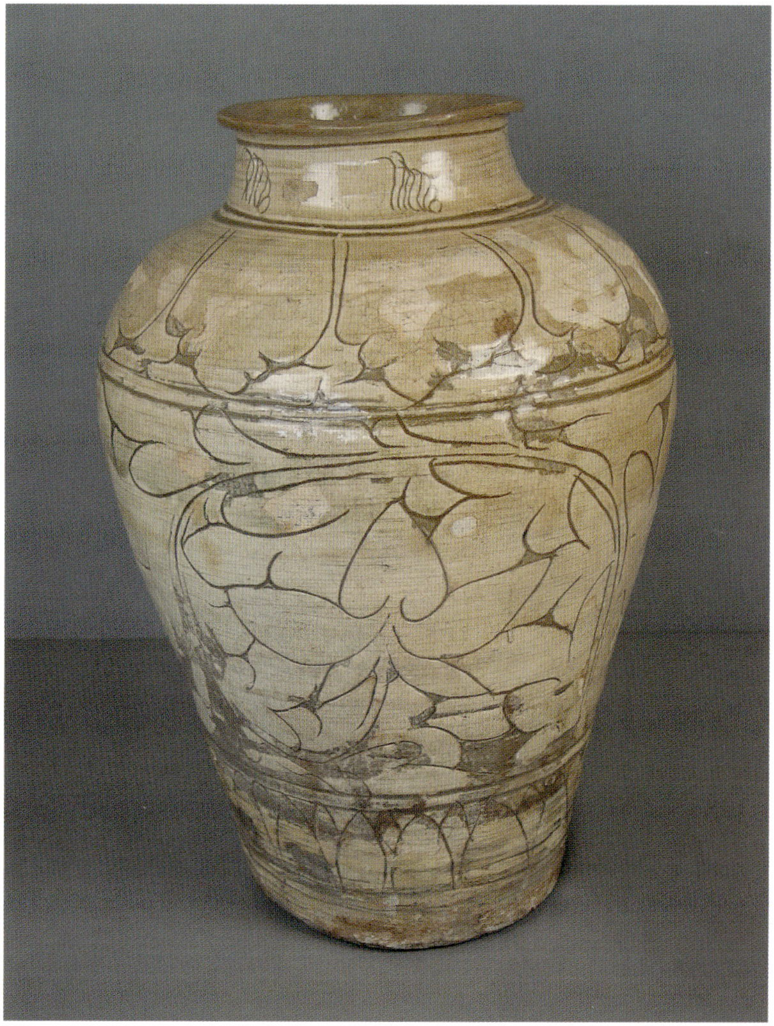

[FIG. 19]
Large jar decorated with peonies. Buncheong ware incised with sgraffito. Joseon dynasty (1392–1910 CE), late fifteenth century. Height 38.1 cm, diameter 27.6 cm. Rogers Fund, 1916. Before treatment image by Vicki Parry, 2012, Metropolitan Museum of Art open-access image, 16.122.1.

the glaze. In figure 17, note the slight vertical seam on the dragon. This is a previous restoration attempt to disguise a crack that was visually distracting because it was too wide. Although this is at the back of the vase, or perhaps because it is at the back, one suggestion may be to remove the restoration and perhaps some of the ingrained dirt/dust inside that crack, if possible. Leaving it unfilled may be better in that there would not be a material to discolor and possibly stain the ceramic. Its removal could also prevent further damage if this material was prone to expanding and contracting beyond what the ceramic could tolerate.

Crazing is clearly a stability issue for ceramics where the crazing glaze is falling off, leaving patches of jagged-edge losses that are more prone to damage. A conservator would aim for stabilizing the glaze/slip/body system, thereby reducing the likelihood of further damage from environmental conditions and handling. For example, figure 19 is a beautiful Korean *buncheong* ware jar from the Joseon dynasty (1392–1910 CE). These are typically wheel-thrown stonewares with a light-colored slip applied over the whole surface; the design is then created by carving away the slip to reveal the underlying body (usually darker). The glaze of these wares does craze and unfortunately often does not fuse with the body. Essentially, when this happens the glaze is floating on the slip—or to be more accurate, the glaze is a skin or shell that is easily broken and lost. Preventing glaze loss and preserving the jar's integrity along with its technical information were important goals for the previous conservation campaigns as well as a recent one. The same choice made across several decades in a traditional Western museum may not be surprising. Although the materials are different, the goal was the same. The downside of each is that there is visual change, but hopefully the newer material and resin will not discolor as it ages.

Introducing an adhesive resin under the glaze to adhere it to the underlying ceramic body and slip will add strength to an inherently weak bond and prevent imminent losses. The resin, however, will alter the way light interacts with the object's surface. Saturation of the slip will create dark areas or shadows along the loss edges. This creates a slight visual alteration of the ceramic that is undesirable. Similarly, the darker discolored appearance of the area consolidated in a previous campaign is not desirable. Both campaigns aimed to prevent glaze loss, but both altered the jar's appearance, even if it is slight.

Should the interested parties for each campaign have made a different choice? Open discussions between conservators and curators may lead to an agreement on the goal of long-term care for this buncheong jar as well as whole ceramic collections. With the understanding that the jar will become less stable as time passes, and the desire to slow and prevent loss, we can discover the best balance for the path forward.

Biography of Intent: *Ko-sometsuke*

With its many land and maritime routes, the trans-Eurasian trade networks of the so-called Silk Road influenced cultures for centuries through the movement of people, ideas, and goods across vast geographic areas. In the sixth century, Buddhism spread via Silk Road routes through China, Korea, and into Japan. By the eighth century in Japan, through its links to Buddhism, the appreciation and practice of drinking tea followed. Although the tea ceremony began as a Zen Buddhist practice, by the fourteenth century it had developed immense cultural importance.

Tea ceremony wares created in Japan increased in popularity and value as the significance of the ceremony increased. The demand was so great for these wares showing an appreciation of a humble aesthetic, *wabi sabi*, that Japanese potters could not keep up. As a result, patrons increasingly turned to China, where the mass production of wares to suit a specific aesthetic or fashion was already possible and successful.

During the Ming dynasty, the imperial kilns at Jingdezhen were kept busy with orders for the emperor and court. As the dynasty started to decline in the late sixteenth century, however, the imperial kilns experienced a reduction in financial support from the court and fewer orders, and with the chaos in the north affecting their production, the kilns closed in 1608.

Some imperial kilns remained closed until the early years of the Qing dynasty (1644–1912 CE), while others were destroyed. Potters for these kilns were still in need of work so they found patronage from Japan. With the trade bans lifted in 1621, an amazing period of trade emerged with their new patrons, spurred on by the popularity of the Japanese tea ceremony and the ceramic implements it required.

Ko-sometsuke, the ware created by the Jingdezhen potters for their new Japanese patrons, was distinct from any earlier and later wares. The use of finely levigated (sorted) clays to create the precise, thin, and even walled ceramics with the symmetry and refinement of skill that characterized the typical imperial work was set aside. Instead, these potters embraced their Japanese customer's desire for the *wabi sabi* aesthetic, featuring "natural" variations, signs of wear, and a visual history of use that tells a story. For these wares, the clays were poorly levigated, thrown quickly, and glazed with quick carefree hands. Because these exported wares were a clear and specific departure from the traditional Chinese aesthetic, it may not be a surprise that they were created solely for export and are rarely found in museum collections in China. Due to their manufacturing techniques, they have intentional flaws—firing cracks, glaze crawls, and shivering—intended to be viewed as damage, and embraced as signs of age, wear, and a useful life. It may be difficult to recognize these imperfections as an original condition that should be documented and preserved.

The most characteristic "flaws" of these *ko-sometsuke* ceramics are the glaze losses on rims and corners. Those that result from the natural flaking or shivering of the glaze from the body are sometimes easy to spot. Glaze loss on a rim resulting from shivering will be accompanied by a pocket or gap between the glaze and body to either side. These pockets are the perfect place for dust and resins to be drawn in, as if by capillary action. Over time, staining will become visible and travel deeper into the minute space between the intentionally poorly fitting glaze and poorly levigated body. As visually distracting as this appearance can be, it is also important to recognize that it results from an intentional manufacturing technique. The goal of that technique is to make the ceramic appear to have been used and aged.

In such a case, the interested parties should discuss the goals of conservation treatment as well as their expectations. Even if staining is the result of an intentional manufacturing technique, conservation attempts at reducing the appearance of it may not always give a visually consistent result or even be possible. For most stain reduction techniques commonly used in conservation, one challenge is getting the active chemical that reduces the stain to travel far enough into or under a glaze so that it contacts as well as surrounds the stain. This may not be possible if the dirt and oils sandwiched under the glaze have traveled too far under the glaze and away from the original pocket where it started. What can be done? What, if anything, should be done? Again, understanding a ceramic's history before it came to the conservator's hands is vital for understanding the complete picture of an object's biography. Past documentation and examination may elucidate the paths that the ceramic has taken and present a way forward. Deciding not to remove ingrained dirt and stains may be the ideal goal for a conservator as this staining is not usually impacting the overall stability of the ceramic. Still, additional options may be more realistic for others, such as an owner lending to a museum, or a museum curatorial department that may be concerned about the appearance of a stained white porcelain object in an exhibition. For these situations, options may include reducing the intensity of the staining through localized cleaning or moderate stain reduction. It will be essential to communicate with curators or owners that "cleaning" and stain reduction are not reversible actions, and therefore the expectations of using those actions must be fully explored. Likewise, educating and sharing information with museum patrons, who also have a vested interest, may be a worthwhile goal to include when discussing broader goals for an object or collection.

In traditional Western museums, including the Metropolitan Museum of Art, I have observed an acceptance of flaws originating from manufacturing processes or a maker's (artist's) intent. We are lucky in this twenty-first century because there is a greater cumulative understanding of the history of pieces like these unusual export ceramics created during a narrow period of a few decades in the seventeenth century. It is remarkable how much information we now have because of the ritual and cultural value placed on them by Japanese patrons wanting wares that honored the *wabi sabi* aesthetic and thus the tea ceremony.

Biography of Restoration: *Kintsugi*

The art of *kintsugi*, a traditional method of ceramics repair, is actually an urushi (Japanese lacquer) technique. Its use for the repair of ceramics is believed to have its origins in fifteenth-century Japan when the shogun Ashikaga Yoshimasa sent a damaged *chawan* (tea bowl) back to China for repair. It was returned with metal staples as the repair technique. The shogun was displeased with its appearance and motivated his artisans to improve on it. The *kintsugi* technique uses urushi to fill losses and adhere fragments of a broken object together. The surface of the urushi is dusted with gold powder and burnished to create a smooth, lustrous surface that seems to celebrate the losses. It developed around the tea ceremony, and was influenced by the aesthetics and philosophical meaning valued by the ceremonial practice. By the seventeenth century, it was well established in Japan, and has been found on ceramics and other objects outside Japan since then.

The presence of *kintsugi* on ceramics originating outside Japan is not uncommon in major ceramic collections, however the painful history between Korea and Japan up through the early twentieth century makes its presence on Korean ceramics deserving of closer attention. A more delicate issue would be discussing the possible removal of these repairs at the request of a concerned patron, cultural group, or other interested party that may see the repairs as a mark of oppression as well as a painful history that is outshining the beauty and value of an important Korean ceramic.

The use of Korean ceramics in tea ceremony practices in Japan began in the mid-sixteenth century and continued into the eighteenth century, when the tastes of the tea ceremony again turned to ceramics originating in Japan. Japan's invasions of Korea from 1592 to 1598, sometimes referred to as the "pottery wars," were instrumental in bringing Korean artists and craftspeople to Japan, and ultimately influencing the trajectory of ceramics as well as other arts. Although there is contradicting evidence regarding the nature of the transfer of Korean potters to Japan during this period, there does appear to be agreement concerning the inhumane treatment of the Korean potters in Japan. The history between Korea and Japan should be considered when discussing overlaps in collections, and this certainly applies to *kintsugi* on Korean ceramics. Through photographic and written documentation, the conservator can guarantee that the location and condition of the *kintsugi* will be documented. Identifying the date of a ceramic, its restoration date, the intentions of the collector or restorer, and the goals and concerns of a collection curator or current owner should all be conducted ahead of any conservation action.

Conservators do not advocate for the wholesale removal of *kintsugi* or any historical restoration technique. Nevertheless, sensitivity to a ceramic object's community or culture is prudent. The removal or reduction of past restorations is not unheard of, but again, societal norms and expectations evolve and change. Conservators are in a unique position to encourage relevant conversations, preserve information, and speak on behalf of the ceramic, while being sensitive to cultural hurt and concern.

Unfortunately, removing *kintsugi* is not straightforward. The lacquer (urushi) will have stained the ceramic, and over time, the cross-linked resin will become more irreversible and unfortunately darker in appearance. Also, the traditional process of polishing a *kintsugi* fill to prepare it for the gold finish often damaged the adjacent glaze surface. This damage is usually subtle at first glance, but it generally means a loss of surface gloss (leading to a matte appearance), and provides a surface that is easily ingrained with dust, dirt, and oils from handling. These conditions along with the likelihood that the ceramic will always appear stained due to the urushi (or other resin used) should be made aware to all concerned so they understand that the visual clue of that history will always be there, visible although reduced.

Does it matter when the repairs were done? Are they more "important" if they are older? If they are historical, should they automatically be allowed to remain untouched? What if they were applied by a recent previous owner in the 1960s? Does it make them less significant or impactful to the history of the ceramic? In the case of an object like the bowl in figure 20, what if the owner was a Japanese citizen or someone of Japanese heritage? What if the owner was a Korean citizen or someone of Korean heritage? Of course, these questions open a broad range of possibilities and perspectives to consider that will ultimately have multiple possible answers. Still, it is essential for all parties, including conservators, to understand that the answers will vary for each object, and the acceptability of those answers in society will also change over time. All parties must be prepared for this, and understand that conversations regarding the value of past restorations will continue well past a current examination or conservation campaign. A small bowl from Korea's Goryeo dynasty (918–1392 CE), possibly made in the twelfth century, serves as a good example of this complexity [FIG. 20]. It was sold to the Metropolitan Museum of Art by an established collector and dealer, Yamanaka and Company, in 1922. At present, only the last century of the eight-hundred-year-plus journey from Korea to New York City is known. Although it was made in Korea several centuries before the Japanese invasions at the end of the sixteenth century, the presence of *kintsugi* serves as a visual reminder that it likely spent significant time in a Japanese collection. The bowl's inherent connection to tea also tells us that it was likely collected, ending up in Japan, for that reason.

Although the presence of *kintsugi* rarely creates a stability concern for a ceramic, a curator felt that partial removal would promote the bowl's delicate appearance while slowing some of the visual changes that would be inevitable. Continued darkening and eventual staining from the urushi as well as the ingrained dirt and oils along the *kintsugi* fill edges were a concern. If no action was taken, then these areas of staining could further alter the appearance of the bowl, making it more difficult to see and interpret the design, and possibly implying to some observers that its care was not of importance.

In figure 20, the image on the bottom is "after treatment" and shows the tea bowl as it appears today. The dark appearance of ingrained surfaces was reduced. The thin gold veins that traveled into the bowl were removed and the urushi staining was reduced while keeping the *kintsugi* restorations of the rim in place. There is no doubt the bowl was valued in the Japanese collection for having survived so many centuries, the meaningful restoration of a damaged rim celebrating its history and continuing life.

Biography of Restoration: Fired Restorations and Metal Rivets

Fired restorations and metal rivets are commonly encountered by conservators when examining ceramics that have been restored in the past few centuries. Yet one should be aware that rivets (metal or organic) may be the older of the two techniques. Frequently they are also found together, either because they were used in one campaign, such as when rivets are used to secure fragments/restorations to the ceramic, or they may be from different restoration campaigns separated by many years. The latter is the case for a Chinese Qing dynasty famille verte vase discussed below. The evidence for the concurrent techniques is not easily seen at first, but thinking and reasoning through the processes as well as understanding some of the materiality may be the key. First, I will address fired restorations.

Basically, there are two types of fired restorations. The first is the use of restoration fragments made from separately fired ceramics. These fragments may be from other (possibly similar) ceramics that happen to be available to the restorer, or may be custom-made, fired, and affixed

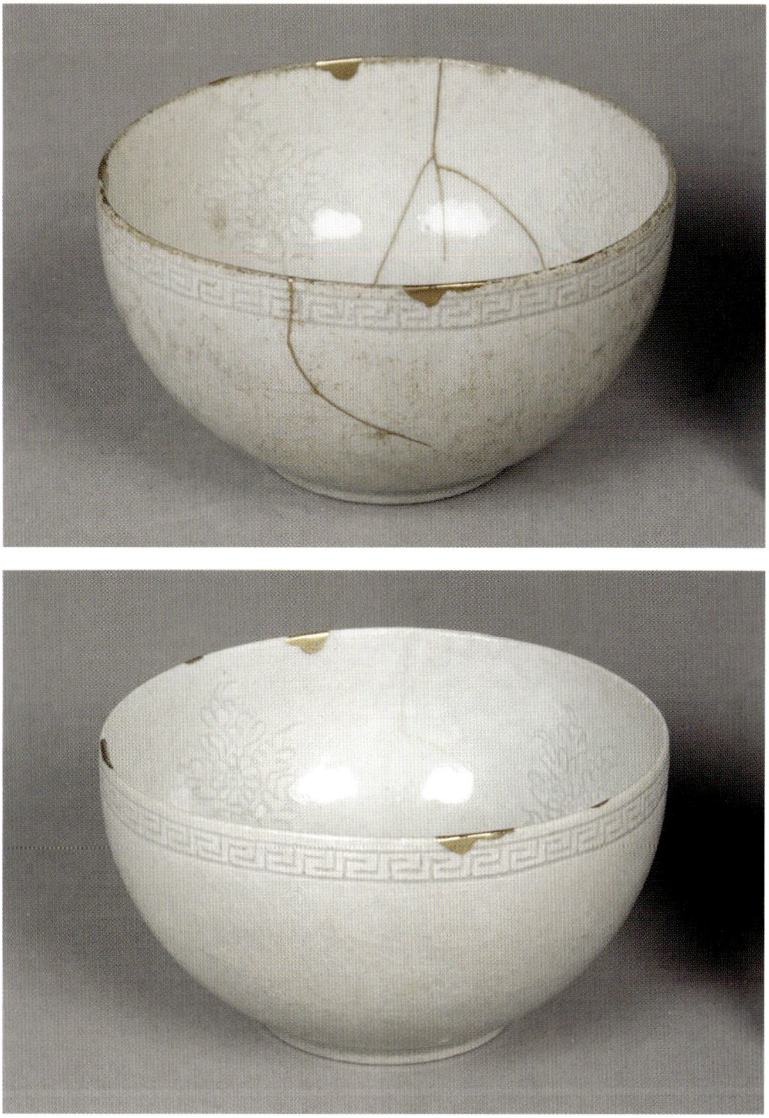

[FIG. 20]
Small bowl decorated with chrysanthemum. Porcelain with incised decoration. Korea, Goryeo dynasty (918–1392 CE), twelfth century. Height 4.4 cm, diameter 8.4 cm. Rogers Fund, 1922. Before and after treatment images by Vicki Parry, 2015, Metropolitan Museum of Art open-access image, 22.141.35.

with adhesive to the ceramic in need of restoration. The history of this technique is an extremely interesting and complex topic that is beyond the scope of this chapter, although this topic has had recent publications from Garachon (Rijksmuseum) and others listed in the further reading section. The second type of fired restoration involves fusing the restoration to the original ceramic using extreme heat—usually a small kiln. The materials used to create these restorations were low-melting pastes and/or a high-lead enamel. This in situ fired restoration appears to have a much shorter history, showing up in manuals, advertisements, and other documents in the eighteenth and nineteenth centuries in Europe. From the explanations of these sources, it seems clear that this technique grew from a need to satisfy wealthy owners or collectors who prized a restored appearance more than restored use. It must have been an expensive and somewhat unpredictable technique—probably going wrong many times. After all, any ceramist will confirm that reliable, repeatable outcomes from glazing and firing are difficult to achieve, and take much time and expense to figure out. Still, the technique could produce a somewhat seamless repair with no metalwork or glue that essentially looked as good as the original.

The significant challenge for conservators confronted with in situ fired restorations is that they are not reversible. Common solvents used in modern ethical conservation practices, such as acetone, ethanol, methyl ethyl ketone, mineral spirits, and water will not dissolve a fired, glassy restoration. The mechanical removal of such restorations is not usually discussed as an option because it would involve using mechanical means that may put the adjacent surfaces, or perhaps the whole object, at risk of damage. In an example of the issues raised by in situ fired restorations, the restored area on the lid of a tiered box from the Edo period (1603–1867 CE) ([FIG. 21] and [FIG. 22], left image) was not aesthetically consistent with the rest of the box—the color was different, and the design in the original glaze had been lost. It was, however, providing structural completion of the lid, and its shape and thickness were accurate. It may have been the original corner, but instead of organic-based adhesives or other joining methods, the restorer used heat along with a low-melt bonding agent and low-melt glaze or enamel. The glaze texture around the join is rough compared to the rest of the lid, suggesting localized heating. The corner was first noticed while I examined the box for an exhibition because there were some concerns for the stability of the glaze at the corners due to stresses from stacking the box components. The corner restoration was stable, although the appearance, once pointed out, was visually distracting, and the best solution was to use acrylic paints to better integrate the appearance with the adjacent original glaze surface. The outcome was acceptable and is reversible, should informed future

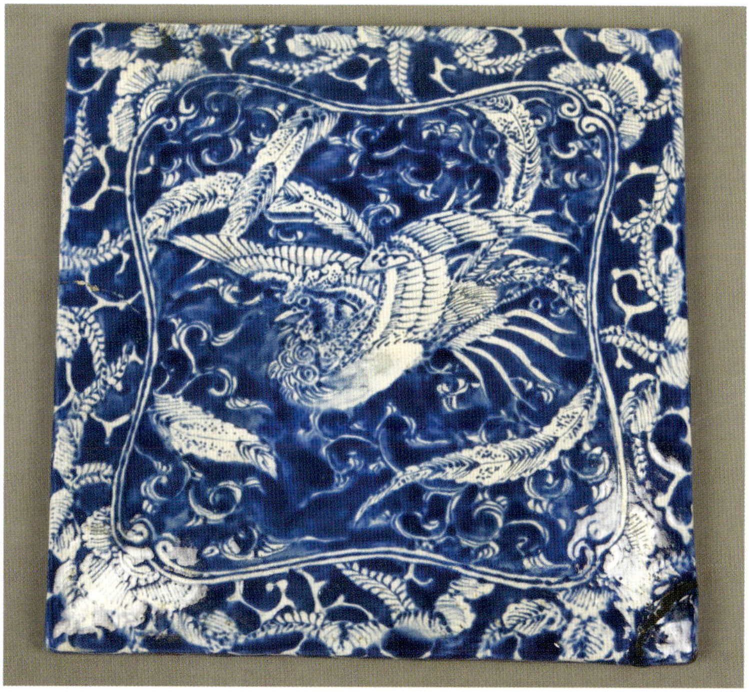

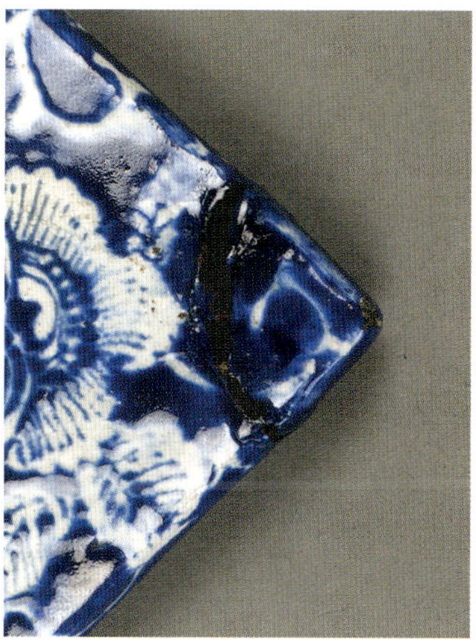

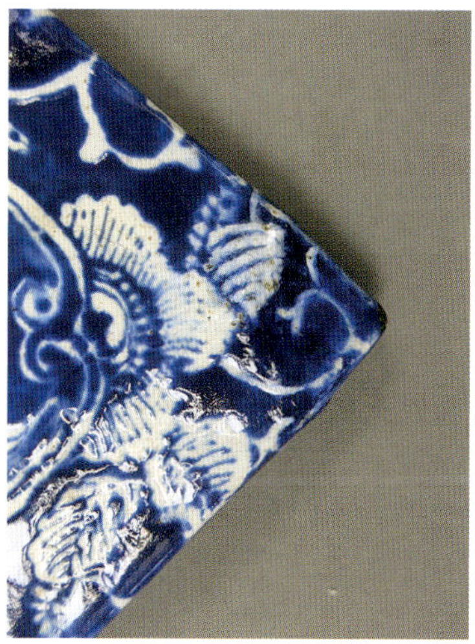

[FIG. 21]
Tiered box with Westerners and landscapes. Faience (tin-glazed ware) decorated in the delft style (Kyoto ware). Japan, Edo period (1615–1868 CE), second half of the eighteenth and early nineteenth centuries. Gift of Mrs. V. Everit Macy, 1923. Before treatment image by Vicki Parry, 2015, Metropolitan Museum of Art open-access image, 23.225.255a–e.

[FIG. 22]
Tiered box with Westerners and landscapes (details of fig. 21, before and after treatment).

decisions mean that the in situ fired restoration is to be fully displayed ([FIG. 22], right image). We are lucky that this restoration was quite localized, with minimal damage and change to the surrounding ceramic. This isn't always the case.

Finally, rivets. The practice of repairing ceramics—a brittle material—using a riveting technique that involves creating holes in the object in order to repair it seems counterintuitive. It is, however, a technique with a truly long and successful history. It is difficult to pinpoint the earliest use of materials to "stitch" a ceramic back together to restore its usefulness, but there is evidence for it as early as 7000 BCE. First, holes were drilled into the ceramic, along the break edges, and then a material (sinew, cord, etc.) was threaded through and used to sew the ceramic fragments together. Often plaster or similar self-hardening paste was used to seal the crack or break further. These repairs have been noted in finds from the Middle East. There is also evidence that bronze was used fairly soon into its era for repairing ceramics, as was iron. Lead has been used throughout history too.

In Asia, the use of metal staples, rivets, and wire appears to have become a sought-after repair technique by the early seventeenth century. The ubiquity of ceramics, especially porcelain, beyond Asia and into Europe and the Americas, and the evolution of china menders as a niche profession, tells us that porcelain/ceramics were of value, and deserving of the time and cost of their visual repair as well as the restoration of their function. Rivets were preferred because owners and menders understood that resins/adhesives had a short life span, especially if the ceramic needed to be returned to a useful life—cooking, food service, food storage, and so on. Metals such as iron and copper alloys, if used on the exterior of ceramics, may last longer than adhesives alone. Since the 1980s, there have been efforts in the museum and conservation professions to preserve "historical" restorations, yet the defining date or date range for "historical" has not been formally defined and so is discussed on a case-by-case basis.

Several references can be found for the term *china burner* in documents from the seventeenth to nineteenth centuries that speak of the unsightliness of the metal rivets; it is during this period that other materials were also being promoted to restore ceramics—plaster, organic resins, and lead pigment/paint. So for several centuries, there existed a complicated range of techniques being employed for ceramic restoration. Wealthy families and collectors during this period may have driven the use of certain techniques more than others. In demonstration of their financial means, they may have wanted to repair expensive china pieces so they could continue to use them as a visual confirmation of their wealth. Collectors, likewise, would want to purchase wares that were visually appealing, without flaws. We can make this assumption based on the popularity of the restoration methods that arose claiming to create perfect repairs, as good as new.

For example, a Qing dynasty porcelain vase from the Met (accession number 14.40.418) bears at least three different restoration techniques—all used to restore the surface's visual appearance. Putting aside that we do not have the complete history of this vase, we can certainly start from when it was last examined, which was in 2017, and work backward. The body of the vase appears to be in one complete and original piece, however the neck has had several repairs. Rivets (or staples) were used across several of the breaks on the inside of the neck, which is fairly common, and these had been removed. What is interesting is that rivets were used on the outside of the neck too, possibly interfering with the glazed design. These were also removed, but some of the holes were filled with fired glaze. These filled holes are next to unfilled holes in a pattern that suggests possible reriveting, but apparently just on the outside of the neck. Why? Were the metal rivets affecting the aesthetics of the vase and driving down its value? If so, why was the technique used again?

In an earlier restoration campaign, the previously removed rivets on the interior of the neck were filled with shellac and other unidentified materials. Finally, they were painted with latex paint, which was used in the mid- to late twentieth century and exhibits a color-shift problem common for some modern paints as they age. The shellac used in the rivet holes and along the joins is a natural resin that has been used for centuries. It becomes darker and less soluble over time, leaving dark red-brown discolorations. Even porcelain, as vitrified as it is, is not immune. This is a similar issue to the challenge of reducing urushi stains on the Goryeo tea bowl. Since this is the case, should conservators stop trying to remove or reduce the appearance of shellac? Depending on the interested parties involved and current social desires, there may be a range of options. There is the challenge of conserving the metal rivets as well. If they are extant and corroding, they may be conserved in situ, but it has also been proposed that if they could be gently removed, they could be conserved separately and then returned to the ceramic when they are stable. This may not always be possible, of course, and that is one reason why discussions between all interested parties are vital.

Afterlife of the Ceramic: Conservation's Role

What role does conservation play in the afterlife of a ceramic object? Conservation treatment, examination, and documentation serve as a confluence for the path of a ceramic object's journey through time, documenting the condition of the ceramic by analyzing resins, x-raying to identify the use of pins and rivets, and identifying restored cracks and other losses. Ceramics and conservation may intersect at various times in the ceramic object's afterlife, when events make it essential to consider condition, stability, and all that the object has endured, documenting and archiving those traces of the past for further and future conversations. Ultimately, conservators, as one group of many caretakers of collections, want a ceramic object's conservation history to be discussed and shared with all who have a vested interest. In this way, a modern conservator serves as the librarian or archivist for that information as well as the detective and inspector. The conservator is part of the continuum of a ceramic object's afterlife. It is our goal—honestly—to document all that we see (and don't see) and preserve that as well as the ceramic itself so that it can continue on its way. Maybe it goes back to a secure storage cabinet. Perhaps it will be put on permanent display or loaned to a museum on the other side of the world. Wherever it goes, its life will continue.

Pots with Structure and Purpose: A Chance Encounter, a Potter by Chance

Magdalene Odundo

> In Japan you had intellectual potters consciously working to achieve an aesthetic, a naturalness of unsophistication, but they were going through an arduous intellectual process to get there. . . . I saw this in the African pots through a completely different pathway, where potters with an unsophisticated consciousness were subscribing to the same aesthetics as the Japanese tea ceremony. One is very intuitive and spontaneous and a response to basic needs versus an intellectual and arduous approach.
>
> —Douglas Dawson, "A Potter's View on African Ceramics"

> [Shattering Perspectives] is a way to sort of counter this idea that there exists a monolithic singular entity of Africa, bringing people's attention to the fact that it's made up of many countries full of many different, diverse, specific, unique cultures.
>
> —Dr. David Riep, Colorado State University

The curators of Shattering Perspectives, an exhibition put together by students and staff of Colorado State University, were seeking to illustrate through the museum collection the misconception generally held that Africa is a single country. Africa is a continent with diverse societies, people, cultures, languages, and ethnicities.

> Instead of a presentation organized by region, as is customary in ethnographic museums, this exhibition offers a design-historical examination of the vessels and figures, starting from the objects themselves. This approach enables a new, fresh look at ceramic production in Africa, examining form, function, decor, and materiality.
>
> —Press release for African Ceramics: A Different Perspective

In 2019, the Design Museum (Die Neue Sammlung) in Munich mounted a spectacular exhibition, African Ceramics: A Different Perspective, curated by Barbara Thompson, a historian of African art, from the collection of the Duke of Bavaria. This exhibition marked the first time a collection of African ceramics had been displayed in the context of global design, shown alongside ceramics from around the world as pieces of design rather than as specifically African objects. His Royal Highness Franz, duke of Bavaria, donated his collection of over six hundred works of African ceramics to the Design Museum. The collection was previously well-known within professional circles, but is now available for the public to see.

Ceramics from Africa are as diverse as the countries that make up the continent—countries constructed of boundaries invented under colonialism. Most of the best ceramics are considered antiquities, speaking to traditions some thousands of years old, yet some can be traced to the last hundred years. What unifies many of these ceramics is that the best examples of forms, sculptures, vessels, and pots, made to the best design and with the highest skill, are generally seen in Western museums and private collections. These collections include secular vernacular pots and utensils as well as ritual and ceremonial ceramics that are often sacred to the people who made and owned them. Many of these African ceramics were collected during the colonial period, although a substantial number date from the postcolonial period and are recent acquisitions.

Unlike ceramics from other cultures, many works from Africa up until recently were frequently classified as part of anthropology, ethnography, natural history, and primitive art collections. Most likely the labels would give the country of origin under colonial boundaries, and at best the village or community might be included. Most were regarded as artifacts and attributed to anonymous and unknown makers, as in the Different Perspective exhibition. Many, if not most, Western museums have been forced to reevaluate the labels and designations of work from the continent due to contemporary politics and world movements, such as Black Lives Matter and the present global coronavirus pandemic. The intellectual property movement has exerted pressure on Western countries and museums to repatriate artifacts. Academic institutions have also been forced to decolonize cultural studies, with students from African countries placing more emphasis on the subject in their research. Ceramics have been one of the beneficiaries of this shift in perspective.

The vessel form, essential to people all over the world, is central to my own work. It echoes the human body, the vessel that contains our own humanity. In this way, my pots are anthropomorphic; I often refer

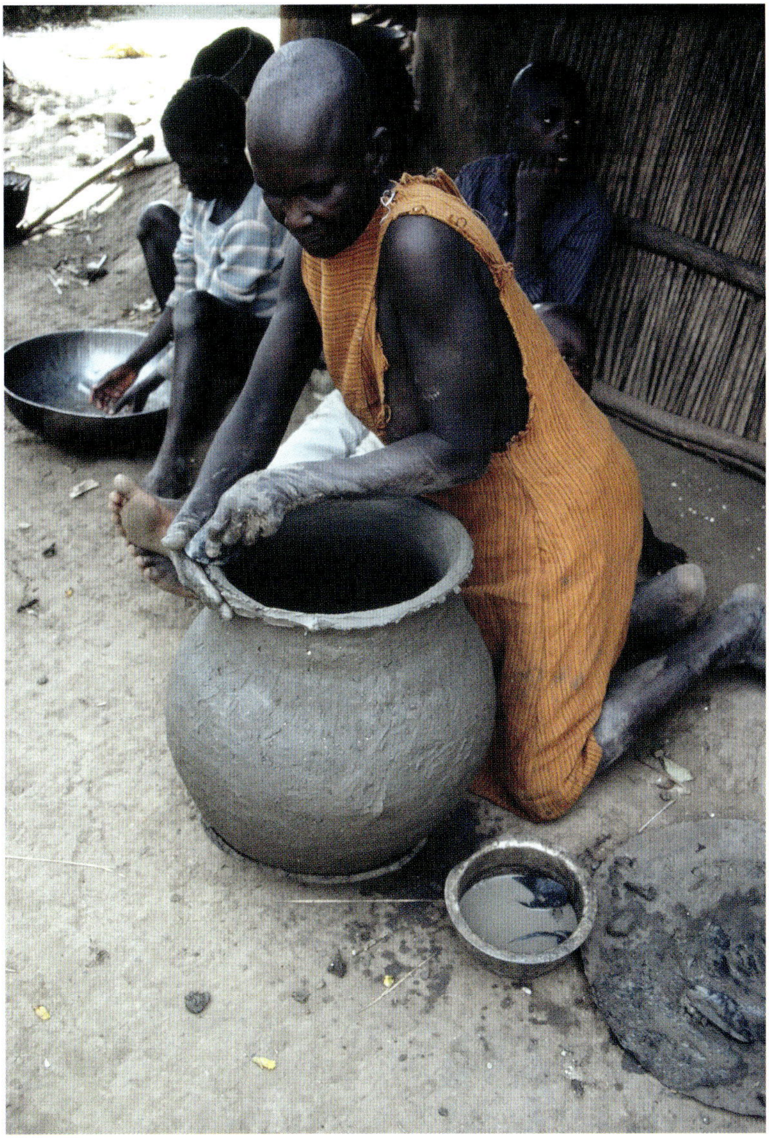

[FIG. 23]
Potter from Bunyala, western Kenya, building a pot, ca. 1974.

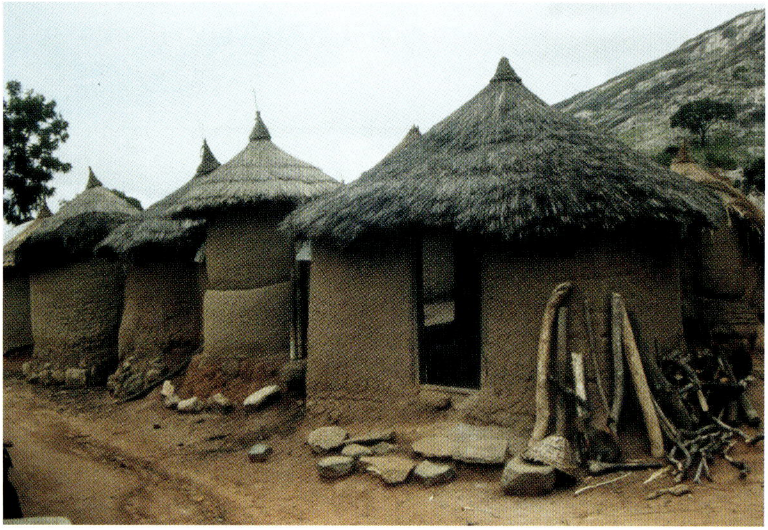

[FIG. 24]
Village granaries in Bunyala, western Kenya, ca. 1974.

to my pieces as people or children. In my own work, my vocabulary is deliberately minimal. I do not want my pots to require lengthy explanation. I want people to be able to understand them visually and feel empathetic. Viewers are welcome to imbue my work with whatever they want, but the words come second. The work, the vessel, must come first. My interest in pots as vessels is driven by my desire to construct, build, and make objects with meaning beyond utilitarian function. Drawing ideas of containment from pottery objects is for me an acknowledgment that the potency of a container to sustain life is as strong as the potency of a container that mediates beyond its function as a vessel.

I have always considered the art of making pots as a form of constructing and building objects with clay [FIG. 23]. Pots are constructed in a similar way to dwellings, and like them, pots shelter and protect, and are made to be inhabited. They contain a potent, resonant, symbolic space, reminiscent of the womb. Like dwellings, pots are constructed with a solid outer wall, which provides a structure that can hold matter, spirit, and ideas, giving us a sense of space that allows us, as human beings, to relate to everything beyond ourselves [FIG. 24]. But pots made from clay specifically have the capacity to allow for some transference between the interior and exterior. This is similar to our skin, which protects our flesh, but through its pores also helps to breathe life into us. Historically, many low-fired pots were central to ceremonies, rituals, and rites of passage. In many traditional societies, there is a belief that spirits are contained within these vessels, and that rituals connected to the pot both please the ancestors and appease the living, allowing the souls of both the living and dead to be at rest. It is the sense that vessels are objects that are structured to contain and have a strong, defined exterior presence, occupying space in that same way that a person does, that resonates with my notion of what it is to be human. Vessels imbue one with a sense of space, both inside and outside.

The connection between vessels and buildings resonates particularly strongly in some ceramics, including a group of rare Kenyan pots, about which little has been written. Made by the Endo-Marakwet people in the Marakwet area of the Rift Valley of Kenya, there are few examples of these pots in any public or private collections, other than that of the National Museums of Kenya in Nairobi [FIG. 25]. These enormous, sculptural vessels are encased in hide, which has stretched over time. This makes the pots less porous, reducing the transference between the interior and exterior, but also changes their appearance, making them look as if they are covered in glaze. The largest were used for storing beer or water during ceremonies such as weddings, or rites of passage such as family burials, while gourd-shaped pots were used for gathering honey or for milk. For me, the form of these pots echoes those of built forms, such as granaries and remind me of the architecture of the vernacular dwellings in which my family and community lived, plastered with clay slip mixed with cow dung and later decorated at the base with lime splash. Over time, vernacular shelters changed. Dwellings that had been constructed to protect whole communities were broken down to accommodate nuclear families and became more and more insular and individual, just as the design of ceramics has been adapted to accommodate the needs

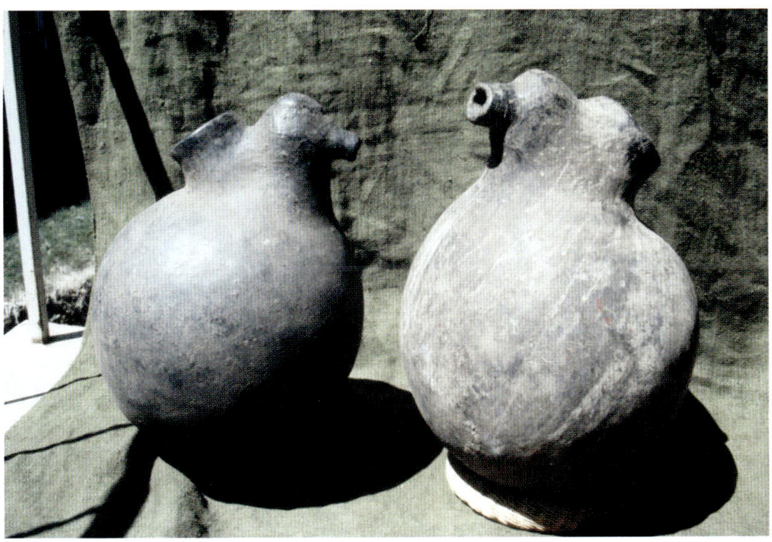

[FIG. 25]
Beer pots, Endo-Marakwet culture, collection date 1978. National Museums of Kenya, Nairobi.

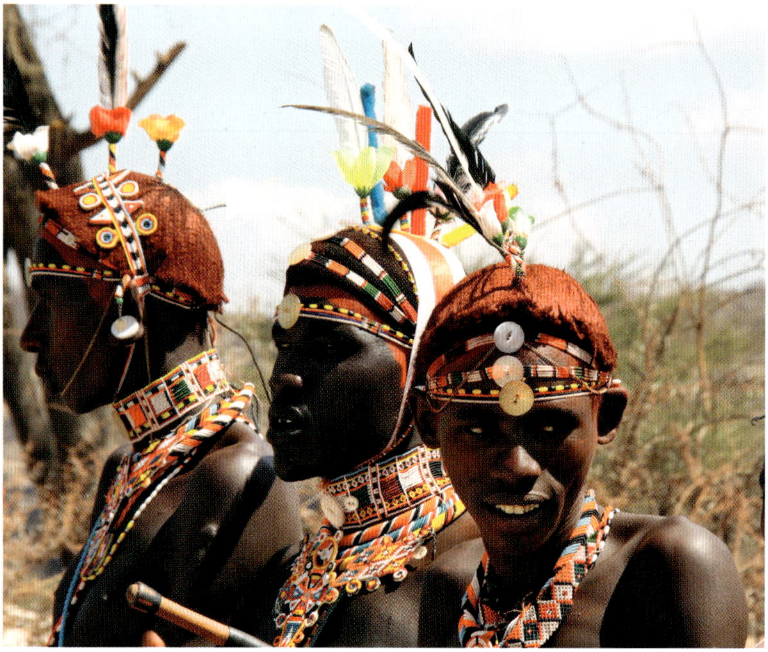

[FIG. 26]
Maasai warriors with traditional head-dress and ocher. Alamy, image ID CW3DEB.

of contemporary utility. But it struck me that these pots, granaries, and dwellings were made by a people that loved to work with clay.

Clay is expansive and versatile, and used in many different forms. In Kenya, Ethiopia, Uganda, and Sudan, clay has long been part of a wearable material in the form of headdress and coiffure. Clay was used to adorn, both as body decoration for everyday wear and part of performances during rituals and ceremonies, and as decoration for the individual too, as is still evident among the Karamojong, Turkana, and Maasai in Tanzania and Kenya. Among the Mursi and Omo of Ethiopia as well as the Nuer and Dinka of South Sudan, ocher clay slips and pastes are often used in body decoration. But the use of clay for coiffure and body decoration by the Maasai at initiation is a live practice [FIG. 26]. At puberty, one's hair is shaved off, gathered, and then preserved in a red ocher clay as a wig, which is held together in a plaster of clay, adorned with ostrich feathers and lined with human hair. It becomes a wearable piece that, when appropriate, is removed to reveal the shape of the wearer's head. Clay is important in forming the cap as well as holding together the feathers, beads, and human hair. When the headdress requires refreshing, it is done by removing the whole solidified mass of hair from the head and reworking it using fresh, vivid ocher red clay. In order to make this hairstyle, the back part of the hair is plaited into a thick bun and glued with clay at the nape. This removable headdress molded in clay forms part of the warrior age group ceremonies undertaken by young men, marking the end of their childhood and emergence as adults. Therefore, here too, clay plays a crucial role in rites of passage and life progression. Like vessels, which contain so much both literally and conceptually, the clay headdress holds, or contains, this particular stage of life as well as cradling the human, physical form.

Looking at objects and materials and making connections between forms has always been key to my practice. Because of this, museum collections have always been important to me, and my interest in looking at different kinds of ceramics and vessels dates from early on in my training. Museums are key to helping us perceive pots as containers that are essential for us. When we view ceramics, we think of the development of skill, the magic of the design, and embodied form and shape, all enabling the eye and brain to relate to those objects along with the people who made them. In 1971, I moved from Kenya to the U.K. to take up a place at Cambridge School of Art, where I intended to study commercial art. Instead, the combination of a brilliant pottery teacher and the exciting and varied ceramics on display in museums in the city changed my trajectory. I have worked in clay ever since.

In Cambridge, I studied the ceramics on display at the Fitzwilliam Museum and the Museum of Archaeology and Anthropology. For the first time, I understood the versatility of clay, and saw how cultures from around the globe have explored a universal language of shape and pattern. These pots demonstrated the connection and universality of our human experience. Working recently with a curator at the Fitzwilliam Museum, I chose a number of objects that reminded me of my time in Cambridge and that have stayed with me throughout the last fifty years, for an exhibition titled Magdalene Odundo in Cambridge (October 5, 2021–July 24, 2022). The ceramics I selected tell us something about the people who made them and the communities in which they lived. These ceramics provided makers with an opportunity to express themselves, describe their cultural norms, and preserve their society. Now these objects help us make connections between pots, places, and people.

At Cambridge School of Art, the foundation course was comprehensive and offered a wide range of art practice. In my second year, I tried to focus on commercial art and advertising. That did not work for me, and as I became disengaged, I got more interested in pottery, printmaking, and jewelry. Zoë Ellison, the wonderful pottery teacher there, encouraged me to think more seriously about fine or applied arts. With her advice, I put together a portfolio and applied to West Surrey College of Art and Design, Farnham, now the University for the Creative Arts. It is thus largely because of Ellison that I became a potter. She urged me to explore the museums and galleries in Cambridge and beyond, and look at historic and contemporary art and objects as examples of what and how to make. She introduced me to contemporary studio potters, jewelers, printmakers, and sculptors, like Robert Welch, based in Suffolk. She brought to her classes works by her contemporaries, which she collected and later gave to the Fitzwilliam Museum. Ellison also introduced me to Ian Auld and Gillian Lowndes, both studio potters. Auld had traveled widely, to India, Turkey, and Iran, and in 1970, he, Lowndes, and their son spent a year traveling around Nigeria, extensively collecting Nigerian art. On their return, they started selling what was at the time called "tribal" art in their shop in Camden Passage, North London. This was one of the few places that you could see African art in London at that time and it was my first experience with handling Nigerian pottery, textiles, metalwork, and wooden sculptures.

Also as a student in Cambridge, I often went to the Museum of Archaeology and Anthropology to study the enormous range of objects on display. It was the first time I had seen objects from so many parts of the world in one place, allowing me to make connections between them. For example, I noticed how the Ichi patterns on the Nigerian vessel [FIG. 27] echoed the lines made on a Ugandan milk pot [FIG. 28], and that the double vessel form appears in many different cultures. I was struck by how similar the decoration on the pots from Vanuatu was to that on pots from Nigeria. I saw how cultures from around the globe had always used similar patterns, proving the connection and universality of our human experience. Although I hadn't thought about pots when I was growing up in Kenya, seeing Kenyan ceramics in the museum made me appreciate the variety and range of pottery designs and forms bought from the markets for different uses, especially for carrying water, storing grain, and giving as wedding gifts. This was before aluminium cooking pots (*sufurias*) and cheap, ghastly colored plastic containers became the "norm" in Africa.

Thus by the end of the academic year of 1973, after this rich exposure to beautiful historical objects that filled me with joy and wonder, and with the encouragement of my tutor, Ellison, I put a modest portfolio together and showed it to Henry Hammond, then head of the department of three-dimensional art and design at West Surrey College of Art and Design He invited me to an interview at the college, and a week later, I sat around a table with people asking me about visionaries in ceramics that I had never heard of. Three weeks later, I got my acceptance letter, packed my bags, and went home to Kenya for the summer vacation having decided to abandon a promising career in commercial art, advertising, and designing neon signs to study a subject I had scant knowledge in. In my Farnham acceptance package were pamphlets about the town, including a map with traditional ceramic sites, preregistration study assignments, and books

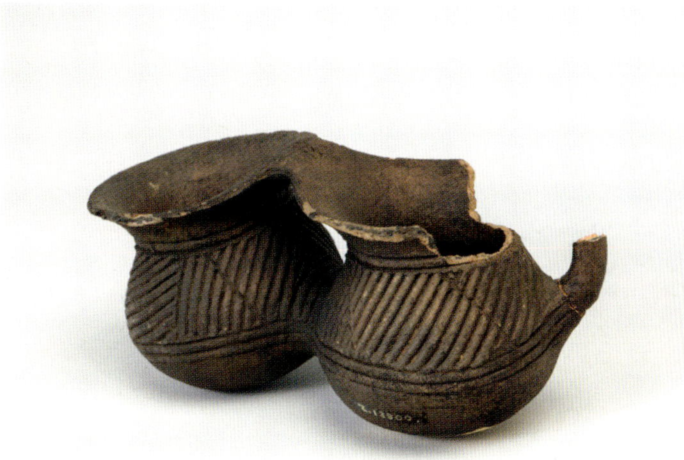

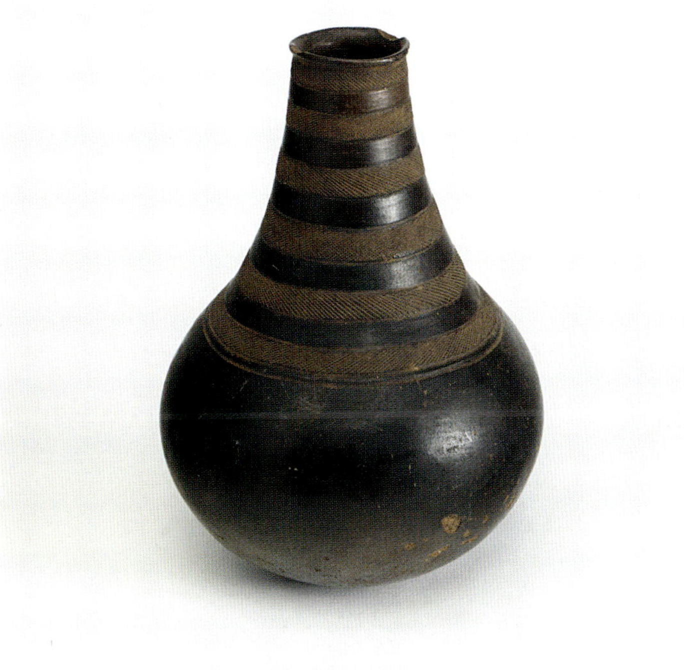

[FIG. 27]
Double vessel, unknown maker of the Igbo people, made in Nibo, Nigeria, from local clay. Museum of Archaeology and Anthropology, University of Cambridge, Z 13800.

[FIG. 28]
Milk pot with incised lines, unknown maker of the Ganda people, made in Uganda from burnished earthenware. Museum of Archaeology and Anthropology, University of Cambridge, ROS 1920.127.

to read. The books were *A Potter's Book* by Bernard Leach, *Pioneer Pottery* by Michael Cardew, and *The Story of Art* by Ernst Gombrich. We were also asked to visit and conduct some research on local potteries over the summer, and keep a sketchbook of museum studies of interesting pots.

In Nairobi, there were a couple of pottery projects, one of them the college's Eastleigh Community Project, which happened to be run by a former student of Colin Pearson, whom I met when I returned to England with presents from the Kenyan pottery project. I visited an industrial sanitary ceramics company that treated Kenyans so badly that it felt like living in the colonial era. The visit highlighted the true ills of the colonial mentality and the enslavement of Africa, and as such, made me not want to work in that industry. Yet the visits to the National Museums of Kenya, Nairobi, and Fort Jesus, Mombasa, gave me the prep work I needed for my two essays of the first term of my undergraduate studies. As I struggled to learn how to throw a cylinder on a wheel, I began to look back at the images of ceramics I had photographed at the National Museums of Kenya and wondered if I would ever master enough skills to emulate such strong structured pots—those pots that echoed the architecture of my childhood. The challenge was real and frightening.

During a study trip to Cornwall in 1974, I met the well-known potter Michael Cardew. He spoke with passion of his time in both Ghana and Nigeria, and talked fondly of the potters with whom he had worked. He spoke of learning from his experience, especially how he had gained the sense of generosity of spirit from those around him. He felt that he had adapted the techniques he used to make his own work through being with potters at Abuja Pottery. I had the opportunity to see what Cardew had meant and what he was so excited about on my arrival at Abuja Pottery in Nigeria in 1974. There, I was overwhelmed by the variety of forms, vessel shapes, sculptures, and adobe clay architecture that were artistic works to be admired. In fact, Nigerian art and crafts were intact in all aspects—utilitarian, decorative, and ceremonial—unlike those of East Africa. The colonial histories of Kenya and East Africa were different. The Europeans had settled in East Africa and practically colonized the arts, or in a brutal manner, rendered them "pagan" and forbade their practices, stifling local artistic traditions.

At the Abuja Pottery Training Center (now Ladi Kwali Pottery Center in Suleja), I learned Gbari (Gwari) hand-building techniques from Ladi Kwali, Lami Toto, and Asibi Aidoo, and throwing from Kainde Ushafa, George Gharba, and Peter Boko [FIG. 29]. The pots were made from a lump of clay placed on an upturned mortar used for pounding yam and other food, or as was the case at Abuja, on a sagger or wood stud of approximately sixteen inches high. From the lump of clay, one gouged out a section and then pulled it to form a cylinder by placing the pulled clay on the inner

[FIG. 29]
Ladi Kwali at Abuja Pottery, Nigeria, 1974.

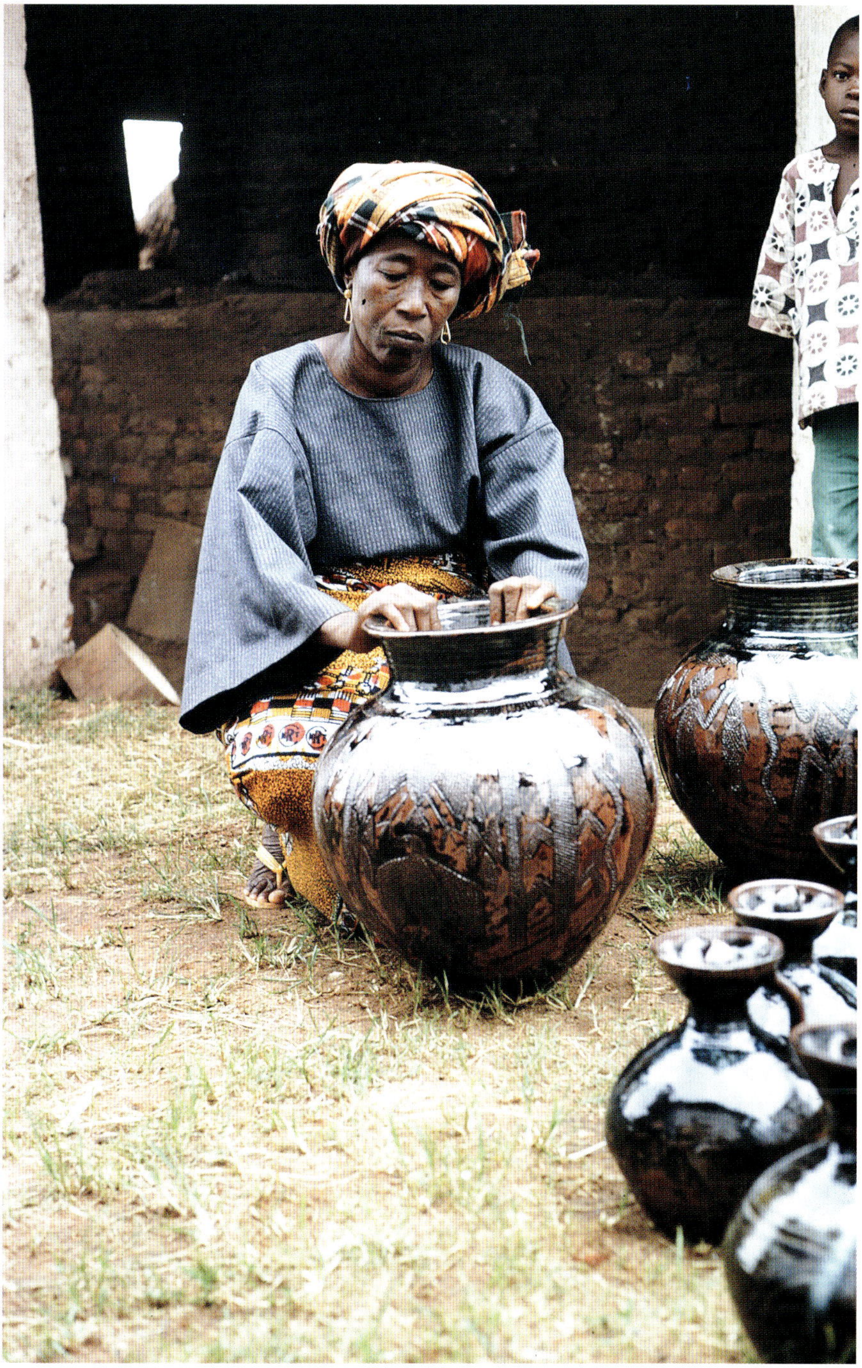

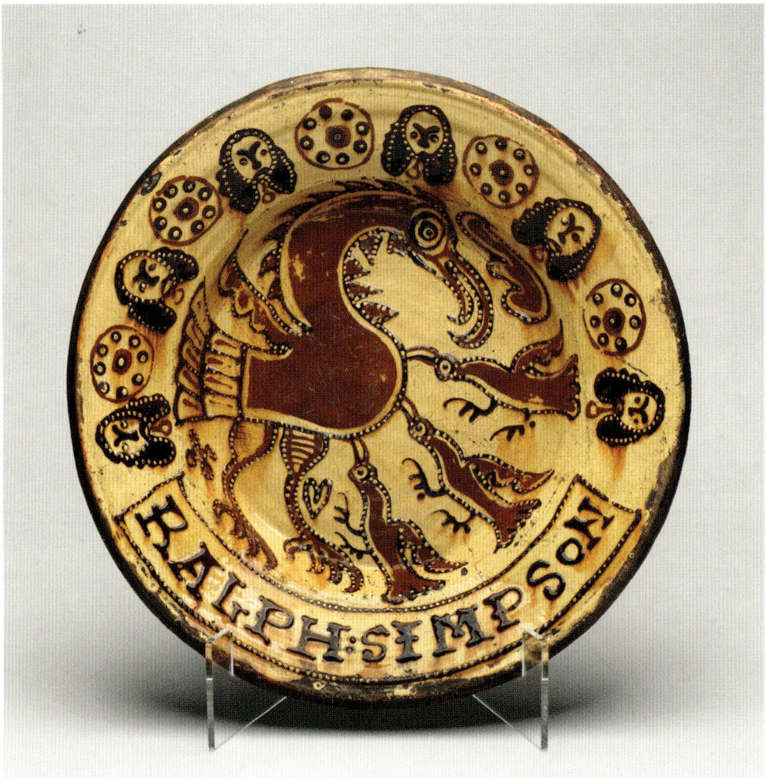

[FIG. 30]
Ralph Simpson (1651–1724 CE), "pelican in her piety," ca. 1670–80, glazed earthenware. Fitzwilliam Museum, Cambridge, C.215–1928.

edge to build the wall upward, while walking around the pot backward in a circular motion. Short, fat coils were then used to build up height; only then did they pick up a shaped gourd rib that was used to smooth and shape, creating a symmetrically balanced wall inside and outside. When the body and shoulder of the pot was complete, the latter was moulded inward to allow for the neck to be built and then the rim carefully turned outward. The pots would then be left to stiffen to leather hard before they were decorated.

I studied and observed every movement, gesture, mark, and nuance made as I watched the women hand-build large pots and throw on kick wheels designed by Cardew. I tried to make work like they did. Both Ladi Kwali and Lami Toto were excellent at decoration, but Ladi Kwali's ability to animate her pots and tell stories through her precise incised decorations was incredible as well as mesmerizing. I mimicked every stance and practiced the rhythm in dance they performed around the pot, but at the beginning I lacked the finesse of Ladi Kwali. Most artists who are starting out study the work of others and then practice their skills by making similar work to that of their teachers. This is a process that helps one to gain experience, acquire information, and assimilate knowledge as a maker practically, visually, and mentally. When describing this process, I have often used the analogy of a child learning to walk, step by step, until they can do what the adult is doing, which is to walk without falling. Only then with instilled confidence do they begin to try out their own stance and deviate from this mimicry!

When I returned to Farnham for my second year, it was the wheel throwing that had taken hold of me and I began to explore further the English slipware tradition. At the time, I wanted to create ceramics that I thought were more cheerful and bright than the green and brown of Abuja, but glazing has never sat comfortably with my own work. I thought back to my experiences as a student, visiting the Fitzwilliam Museum in Cambridge, where I had been struck by the work of Thomas Toft and Ralph Simpson, who made slipware in Staffordshire in the 1600s. This pottery later became, and remains to this day, my favorite of the English pottery traditions. These chargers tell us about the society in which they were made and also display the incredible skill and dexterity of the makers. Their painting with colored clay slips has a great sense of animated enjoyment and liveliness. Some pieces portray ideas, such as the charger showing the "pelican in her piety" [FIG. 30], while others depict events or people of the time. English slipware embodies the capacity of pots to tell us something about the people who made them and the culture in which they lived, their animals, traditions and customs, rituals, and beliefs. Ceramics allowed these ancient and contemporary makers to express themselves, to describe their cultural norms, and preserve their society.

There is a lot of storytelling in ceramics, and it is a tradition that we see on pots from all over the world, throughout the ages. Similarly, visiting the Museum of Archaeology and Anthropology in Cambridge enabled my first encounter with ceramics from South America, including the amazing examples made by the Nazca people who lived in southern Peru, between 100 BCE and 800 CE (see the chapter "Animating the World"). At the time, I knew nothing about Peruvian culture and was intrigued. These were the first ceramics I had seen that truly combined strong forms with artistic surface decoration. The later Inca pieces surprised me too. Years later, on a visit to Santa Fe, New Mexico, I watched the Pueblo potters burnishing the pots, as I had done in Kenya, Nigeria, and Ghana. It was fascinating to watch the same technique repeated in different cultures. The seductive, smooth burnished surfaces of the Inca ceramics I handled in the Museum of Archaeology and Anthropology have remained a constant influence on my decision years later to use burnishing and polishing as finishes for my own ceramics, and perhaps have also influenced my passion for mezzotint and etching in printmaking.

For me, visual literacy, looking and noticing, is the most important thing. Developing a vocabulary in visual literacy has been a crucial element in the evolution of my own work and helped improve my communication skills when I was teaching. While studying for my foundation course, researching, observing, and recording ideas, designs, and forms through objects became a habit, and visiting museums enabled me to examine objects from many cultures within a manageable space. Visual literacy is an aspect of our education that is underused and underrated. Before going to Cambridge, I had only had access to the National Museums of Kenya, Nairobi, and Fort Jesus in Mombasa. To experience the many museums in Cambridge gave me an opportunity to reflect on the varied objects on display, their provenance, and the implications of the transportation of all the pottery and art from Africa, Oceania, and South America. And the experience set me on a journey into the exploration of material culture, art, and objects, especially in museums. Museums hold the key to helping us develop this visual literacy, and my own work continually draws on museum artworks I have seen and handled [FIG. 31].

I further developed my visual literacy skills working as a museum educator at the Commonwealth Institute in London (1976–79)—a role that involved handling Institute artifacts as tools for demonstration, communication, and teaching. It is therefore not surprising that I became bored with my MA thesis project, which instead involved endless clay analysis and experiments. I returned to studying ceramics in museum collections for inspiration. The Victoria and Albert Museum, with its many ceramics galleries, was just next door. Artist Eduardo Paolozzi, my tutor at the Royal College of Art, was a frequent visitor to the British Museum and the now-closed Museum of Mankind, and he introduced me to curators at those institutions, providing me with endless access to the library and collections in storage. My focus turned to world ceramics, cultural studies, material culture, politics of identity, colonialism, displacement, loss, and material appropriation. My time at the Royal College of Art was difficult, but it allowed me a period of self-appraisal and self-reflection. I began putting together the visual materials, ceramics, and objects I had collected from visits in Kenya, Nigeria, Ghana, London's Portobello Market, and elsewhere. Every material I studied, examined, or collected became an *aide-mémoire* for making. My trips to experience kiln firings at Cardew's Wenford Bridge Pottery in Cornwall were tied in with memories of making at Abuja in Nigeria. All of these reminded me of early historical pots from Egypt and the delicate Kerma pottery from Sudan/Egypt. The need to bring these elements into my work became a quest that continues even today. Making became synonymous with my search for an identity.

My working process typically begins with sketching. I make quite a few full-scale drawings as I think about relationships of volume, silhouette,

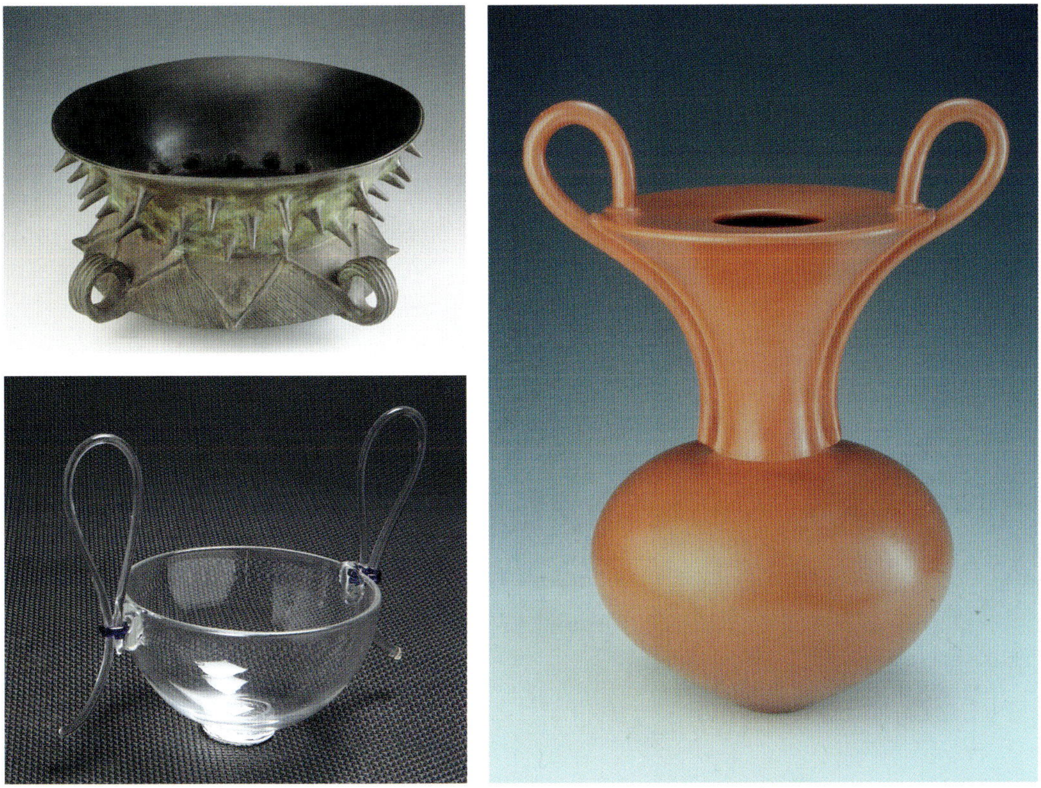

[FIG. 31]
Vessels made by Magdalene Odundo. *Clockwise from top left*, bronze vessel, terracotta vessel, and glass vessel.

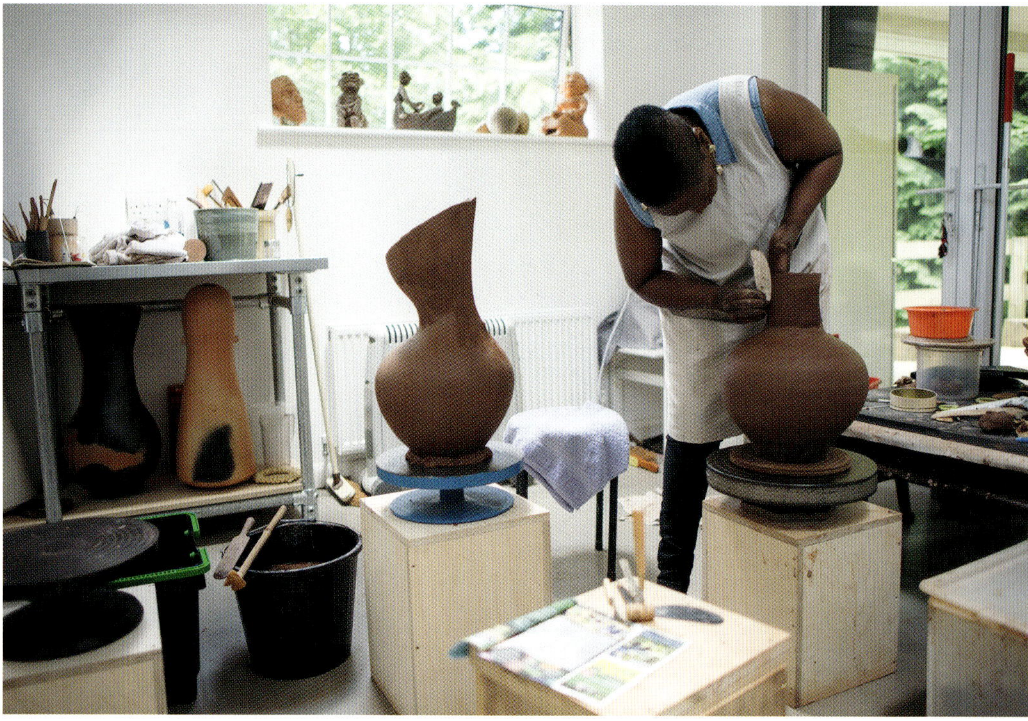

[FIG. 32]
Author at work in her studio, ca. 1995.

and line. After I have worked out a direction on key relationships in the form, I begin to work the clay. I start at the base of the vessel, opening up a ball of clay to have walls and an interior [FIG. 32]. As the clay gets firmer, I build up the walls using large coils that I compress and shape as I go. The form emerges slowly, and as it does I respond to both its nuances and my original sketch. I continue to thin the walls, refining the form and adding any loops or bumps to the surface. When the form holds its presence, seeming both complete and alive, I add a layer of fine clay called terra sigillata to the surface and then burnish it with various burnishing tools, including polished stones and metal spoons. This usually takes several days. I typically work on three to four pieces at a time, with the group taking several months to complete. After the forms are fully dry, I fire them in a gas kiln. To achieve the carbonization that echoes the historical work that inspires me, I add a combustible material to the kiln. Some of the work is fired multiple times to achieve the right balance of color across the surface. The combination of surface character and color variation should reveal further aspects about the form. By working slowly, I am able to focus on the subtleties of each piece. I generally know right away when a work is successful, although I am still surprised how works look different over time.

It is true that to master any skill and knowledge is an ongoing learning process. I have been making vessels in clay professionally for many years now, and every time I have exhibited a group of my vessels, I always see many aspects of the work that I feel require improvement, both in production and their aesthetic. Each time, I realize that there is so much that needs to be said and that the stories that I wished to tell have not been told in this last group of work. Therefore with each new body of work, my process is reflective and critical. I find this time difficult, painful, and mentally exhausting. They are times of conceptual turmoil, with long periods of anguish, doubt, and fear. I have the will to make, but I am in limbo or a dark period, unable to make work. Often, teaching and participating in interactions with students helped me to retrain my brain, eyes, and hands. I would be required to come up with creative solutions to solve problems and have some knowledge of the needs of individual ideas and concepts of students, which necessitated reading and research. I have also been fortunate throughout the last forty years to have worked on diverse projects that diverged from my studio practice but related to my thinking process. Moreover, I have a strong belief in the benefits of a deep spiritual and physical connection to my identity. This sense of belonging is entwined with my cultural background, upbringing, and education. Schooling has played an important part in my education. I did not become the ceramist I am today intuitively, though it is true that my engagement with art runs through my family too.

I see my vessels as part of my quest to create an understanding of the significance of making by using humble materials such as clays. Through making vessels with clay, I am able to trace the marks of toil and history of that making; in the end, the finished vessel can become something that embodies our desire to make objects that speak to who we are as human beings. I also hope that the vessels are imbued with a deep spirituality. Pots as vessels of containment were important in many African cultural activities. They provided links to extended families and were central to many ceremonies and rites of passage. I have always thought of my ceramic vessels as forms that are constructed and built using clay, similar to a dwelling or constructed enclosed container designed by an architect, but built or put together by an experienced builder or bricklayer. I think of them conceptually as structured to contain matter, enclosed within the inner space, but from the outside they have the presence to occupy a notional space. These structured objects might transport us beyond ourselves, thus enabling us to carry out our purpose as human beings within spaces that are real or imagined, and walk with our shadows, occupying negative or void spaces, leading us to find a balance that sustains our daily perceptions of who we are. I think that like architectural objects, these vessels can comfort and intercede to protect, heal, and sustain. Throughout human history, we have invented norms and traditions around vessels, structures, and objects, thereby transporting us through ceremonies and rituals. Pots are used to contain medicines to heal and perfumes to please the senses. They can provide nourishment for our mind, body, and soul. Vessels are objects that satisfy the real "us" as well as connect us to the other "us"—that which inhabits the unknown and is out of reach. Vessels are important in transporting our minds beyond our bodily reality. The vessels contain and uncontain the spaces we inhabit.

Vessels are therefore crucial for the rites we perform daily and those that help us connect to unknown ancestral worlds. Clay as a material has been used to form, build, and construct throughout the ages and across most cultural traditions. We have built structures in clay to withstand time and natural elements (water, fire, and air), through necessity but also for spiritual attainment and sheer pleasure. Where clay is used to make structures used as human dwellings, it provides protection, seclusion, and even isolation. Pots are inanimate narrators of immaterial and material culture. Their forms and decoration, including symbols, hieroglyphs, and pictorial depictions, supply us with knowledge of social structures and societal norms. Along with grain, water, and medicine, pots can hold everything that embodies human well-being—belief, spirits, ailments, exorcism, and healing—and can act as the go-between, mediating between the living and the ancestors. They hold both that which is known and unknown, and contain and uncontain much potency. Pots not only offer us insights into the lives of the people who used them but also a means of connecting us with the makers and their art. Vessels are the most important and fundamental objects on this planet and can be found in every society as well as museum on earth. Looking again at the Endo-Marakwet pots described at the beginning of this chapter reinforces my belief that vessels have a magical capacity and can amaze and astonish. Looking at them, I begin to internalize and process their visceral nature and understand the way that one's eye is drawn to them. One's attention is caught by the rim and shoulders, sparking a desire to look within, to an interior that is more often than not hidden.

Case Studies in Ceramic Art

Animating the World: The Ceramics of Ancient Peru

Ulla Holmquist Pachas

> The ancient inhabitants of Peru were great potters and the archaeologist has at his disposal this great source of information to do a detailed study of all of Peru's prehistoric cultures. In a remarkable way, ceramics reflect the cultural state of the people who produced them. Furthermore, sculptural and pictorial ceramics, especially those that depict a scene, are an open book, whose many, vividly interesting pages are rich with information for the scholar.
>
> —Rafael Larco Hoyle, *Épocas peruanas*, 1963

Ceramics have the character described in the epigraph above by Larco Hoyle, archaeologist and founder of the Museo Larco, as a result of combining earth, water, fire, and air. The hands of artists from the past and present have shaped different objects by mixing claylike earth with the right proportions of water and other plastic and nonplastic materials. The makers of clay pots and sculptures ensure that the air surrounding them sets the new forms without overdrying them, and drastically transform their products using a carefully controlled fire. It is thus that wet, shapeless clay has been able to transcend time and space, eternalized in ceramic forms that still tell us stories today.

Ceramic objects reveal the art and know-how of different peoples from around the world. For example, the ceramics of ancient peoples reveal the potters' degree of access to sources of diverse clays, the techniques they developed over time to make different objects, the types of firing that enabled them to achieve different looks and levels of hardness, their preferred pigments for coloring their creations, and whether these were applied before or after firing, among many other things. We can also catch a glimpse of their daily activities by studying the pots they used in their domestic lives; likewise, we can learn about their ceremonial life through the ceramic objects that were part of their ritual paraphernalia.

In some parts of the world, like the central Andes, pottery became a highly developed expressive art form. It was not just a means of making pots, vessels, and containers for carrying and storing foodstuffs but also a way to model the world and communicate a vision of the universe. Therefore when we visit Peruvian museums whose collections include archaeological objects from ancient Peru, like the Museo Larco, we might be surprised by the large quantity of ceramic pots. It is almost like entering a library whose shelves are laden not with books but rather with these ceramic objects, which Peruvians call huacos. It is likely that the word *huaco* is related to the Quechua word *huaca*, meaning sacred being or place. These ceramic objects are considered to be sacred because they were used in ceremonies and funerals, and were associated with water. Such an impressive abundance poses some basic questions: Why are there so many of them? Why were they made? What kinds of objects are these?

Ceramics in the Andes

Ceramics were first produced in the central Andes around thirty-eight hundred years ago. Ceramic technology probably came to this region via the northern Andes (present-day Ecuador and Colombia), where it had developed two thousand years earlier. The first evidence of early ceramics in the central Andes comes from Cajamarca (in Peru's northern sierra), Ancon (on Peru's central coast), and Kotosh (eastern Peru).

Prior to the development of ceramics, dried gourds (*Lagenaria vulgaris*) were used to store and transport water. With the introduction of pottery to the Andes, pots and containers started to be made in clay, especially terracotta, but the use of gourds was not abandoned. The gourds used in early eras were decorated with incisions and in some cases they were pyroengraved with a heated implement. The oldest ceramics from the central Andes were decorated by means of incisions too. Over time, experimentation resulted in new firing and decorative techniques, such as negative painting, an effect achieved by covering parts of the pieces with clay during firing so as to achieve a combination of dark, smoky surfaces and lighter ones, since the covered surface was not burned in the same way. Then surfaces of the pieces began to be decorated with pigments mixed with resins after firing and later with pigmented slips before being fired. The modeling of different forms was also complemented with the use of molds and casts that made it possible to make objects that, although not exactly identical, were similar to each other.

The ceramic techniques of the central Andes were relatively simple. Potter's wheels were absent, but the archaeological record does include potter's plates—slightly concave plates that could be rotated manually to shape objects. Trowels were used to build the walls of the pots, as was the rolling technique, both of which are still in use among artisanal producers in the different communities who make ceramics in Peru today. Molds have been used since early times, but as time went on, they became more frequent, such that some societies could mass-produce objects to meet the demand for prestige objects generated by a growing polity (such as the Chimu Empire of the northern coast, 1100–1450 CE).

Etching was used to create designs and scenes on the surfaces of objects, and texture was added by means of objects with serrated edges or pointed tips. In some cases, as in the Paracas culture, pieces were painted with resinous pigments after being fired, but in most styles corresponding to the different archaeological cultures, slip was applied to the surfaces prior to firing. This made it possible to create a smooth, even finish, and more important, to experiment and achieve levels of virtuosity by using different colored slips that yielded painted containers with well-made designs, figures, and polychrome scenes. In addition to these finishes, the pieces were carefully polished to remove imperfections from the surface while making sure not to smudge the edges and silhouettes of the designs. As mentioned above, the pottery techniques were not especially sophisticated; nevertheless, thanks to their aesthetic and expressive sense as well as highly developed notions of scale and design, the ceramic tradition of ancient Peru stands out prominently among the pottery achievements of the world for its originality and communicative quality.

Ceramics were adopted in the central Andes around 1800 BCE—that is, approximately twenty-two hundred years after their northern neighbors. These were highly complex societies that had already developed an intense ceremonial life, as indicated by the existence of extensive and monumental preceramic centers for coming together, exchanging goods and knowledge, and engaging in ritual community celebrations. As we have seen, ceramic technology enabled the inhabitants of the Andes not only to make containers and utensils for culinary use but also to create hollow sculptures, figurines, and musical objects, like drums and wind instruments. Some objects, known as *pacchas*, functioned more to channel liquids than to contain them.

For approximately thirty-three hundred years, ceramics were the primary artistic and expressive medium of ancient Peru. Clay was the material used to model the world as well as communicate ideas and beliefs. Potters combined earth, water, air, and fire, turning a shapeless plastic material into objects that fulfilled a variety of functions and represented a wide variety of things and beings.

Figure 33 shows a ceramic drum that represents a shaman. The body of the drum is completely decorated, except for the lower cream-colored band, where the head of the drum was attached. The form of the drum seems to correspond to that of a funeral bundle. The face is covered by a funerary mask. A pair of snakes emerges from its nostrils and encircles its eyes. The figure's cheeks feature two motifs in the shape of stars, which might represent a cross-section of a seven-pointed San Pedro cactus, one of the plants consumed by shamans in ancient Peru to commune with other worlds. The figure wears a diadem with a feline head on its front. At the back of the figure's head, there is a serpent's body shaped like the stem of the same cactus. From where the head of the diadem meets the cactus stem, six more snakes come down from the figure's head. A yellow serpent is discernible across the crown of the head, from left to right. The figure's neck is adorned with what seems to be a necklace made of pendants in the shape of feathers or reeds. Three tonguelike features come out of the figure's mouth. The thickest of these is a maroon color and resembles a cactus stem; it coils around the scepter in the figure's right hand. This snake with the body of a cactus has a feline head, which like the feline diadem, has a septum piercing. A second, slender white snake also emerges from the figure's mouth. The third one corresponds to a gray rope or cord that ends at an offering of a head wearing a gray diadem. This rope is attached to a cassava-man held in the main figure's left hand. The figure's chest features the face of a Pampas cat (*Leopardus colocolo*), an animal that is frequently represented in Nazca art, from whose mouth there are two prolongations in the shape of snakes that encircle the body of the drum and terminate in feline heads. In the lower part of the main figure there is a yellow band with a stylized representation of an offering of heads outlined in black.

Taken as a whole, this drum presents us with a set of elements that convey a message about the shamanic experience, one of the central themes of the Nazca religion. Shamans consumed psychotropic substances to facilitate contact between the inner world (*Uku Pacha* in Quechua) and the outer one (*Hanan Pacha*). The figure on this drum has the strength and agility of a big cat; like a bird, it can fly to the world above; and like a snake, it can cross over into the subterranean depths. The shaman drum thus expresses the ancient shamans' power to connect the different worlds.

Drums and pipe flutes were essential to Nazca ritual activity, and because of its function, this drum also manifests the role of the ancestors buried in the funerary bundles, regarded as the continuously regenerated origin of life. Plant life is born from this subterranean world where the ancestors are buried. The snakes on the figure's body could also symbolize sources of water, which were primarily underground in the case of Nazca society. The Nazca ingeniously channeled aquifers into reservoirs with which to irrigate the land. They were thereby able to create fields for agriculture and survive in the challenging desert landscape of Peru's southern coast.

The ancient inhabitants of Nazca used these drums to beat a rhythm that sounded like a heartbeat, in accompaniment to their processions

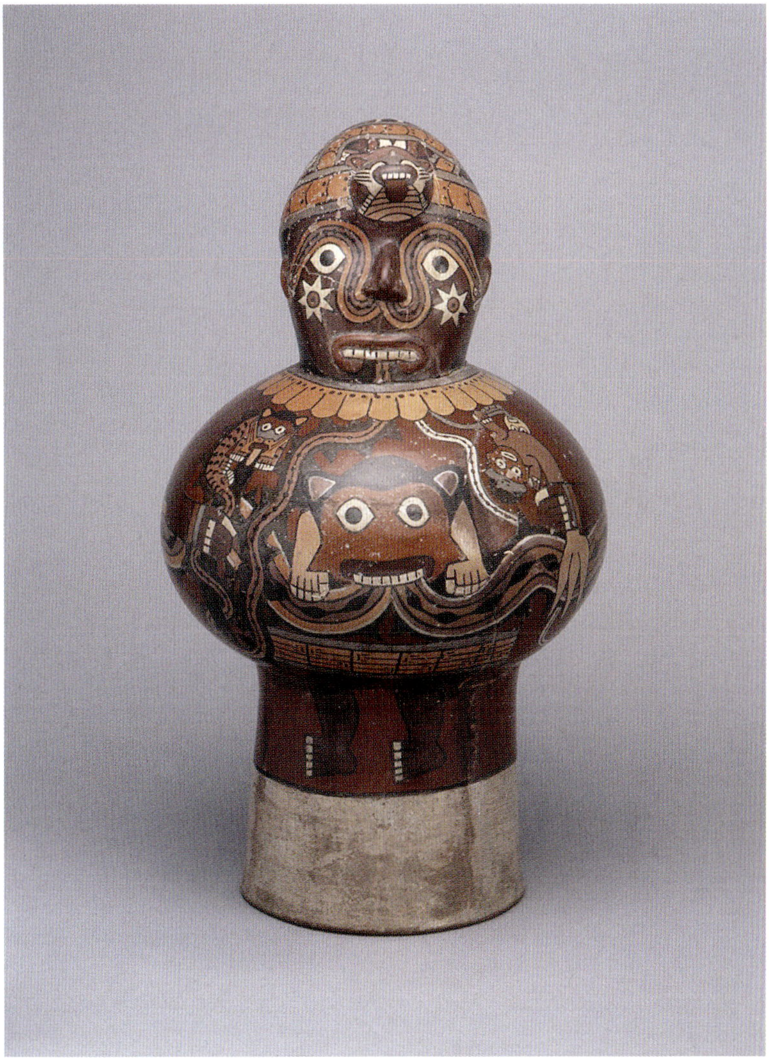

[FIG. 33]
Shaman drum. Nazca ceramic. Southern coast of Peru, 100–600 CE). Width 27, height 44.5, depth 27 cm. Museo Larco, Lima, Peru, ML013683.

and ceremonies. The fine ceramic drums joined the deceased on their journeys to the underworld, as if they were returning to their mother's womb, where they would continue hearing the rhythmic beating of that inner world. Many of the different original Andean societies also created ceramic objects known as *pacchas*, ritual objects that functioned as "channels" for liquids. They were probably used to make offerings of chicha, or corn beer, to the earth.

This pair of *pacchas* adds the meanings of the component objects that make them up: the *urpu* or aryballos, a container for chicha; and the *chaquitaclla*, or Andean foot plow, an agricultural tool used to turn the soil [FIG. 34]. Liquid was poured through the mouth on top of each *urpu* or pitcher, running through it and exiting via another orifice or spout on the bottom of the elongated tip of the object, corresponding to the *chaquitaclla*. This agricultural tool is made from wood with some metal parts and leather straps, but in this case everything is represented in clay. At other museums of the world where similar pieces have been found, the residues inside them have been analyzed. These analyses have revealed residues of soil and sand within the pieces as well as markers of corn beer, indicating that these objects were driven into the ground, chicha was poured into them through the *urpu*, and this chicha went into the earth. In other words, these objects were used in pairs in agricultural rituals. They made it possible for a society organized into halves, in the Andean style of communicating the complementarity of opposing pairs or *yanantin* (whether in terms of one half being the upper part of the community and another half being the lower part, or one group of men and another of women), to pour libations to the earth, *Pachamama*, and thereby encourage a good agricultural cycle.

Vicus pottery, which developed in the northern part of the central Andes, is largely characterized by negative painting on its surface—a technique that consisted of achieving a color contrast in the designs by covering certain sections in clay during firing, hence preventing them from darkening or becoming "smoky" like the rest of the surface. Even more striking than this widely distributed feature of Vicus ceramics is the quantity of ceremonial objects that produce sounds, like the vessel flute shown here [FIG. 35]. It consists of two bodies, one being sculpted, where the flute mechanism is found, and the other a container or bottle connected to the first via a tube and handle. Holding the object by the handle, one would pour water into the bottle and move it around. The water moves through the tube and pushes against the air in the sculpted body, creating a whistling sound. These bottles or clay bodies were activated with water, and "spoke" or "sang" in different tones and volumes.

This piece is composed of a rear bottle attached to a vessel consisting of the molded body of a naked man adorned in body paint. The figure

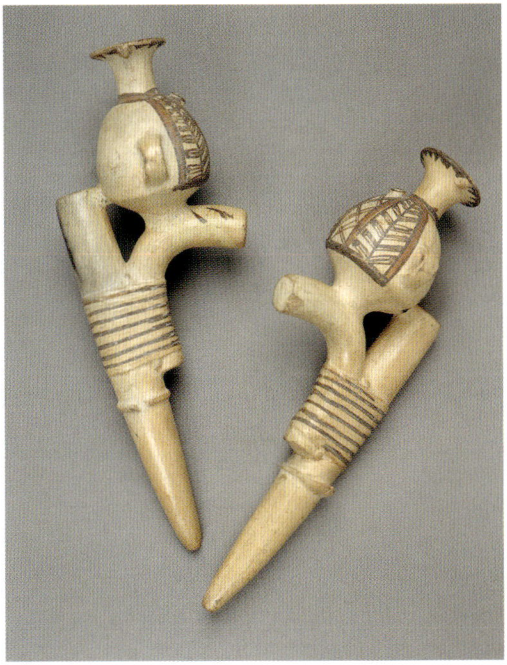

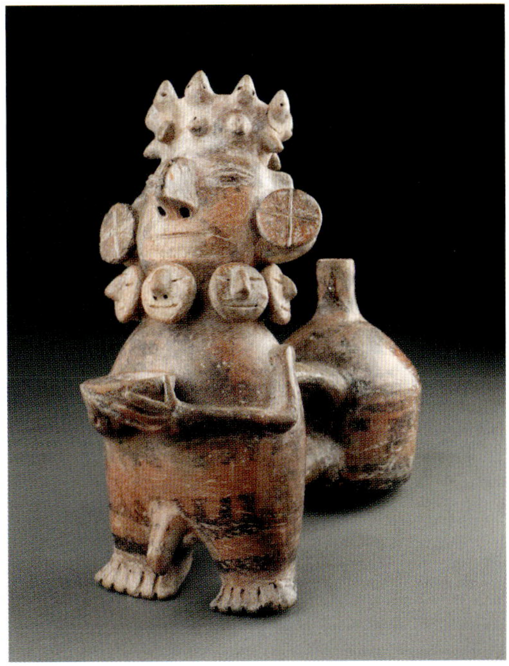

[FIG. 34]
Pacchas in the shape of *chaquitacllas*. Inca ceramic. Southern sierra of Peru, 1350–1532 CE. Width 11.5, height 35.3, depth 14.8 cm. Museo Larco, Lima, Peru, ML018892–021102.

[FIG. 35]
Ancestor. Vicus ceramic whistling vessel. Northern coast, 500 BCE–200 CE. Width 12.7, height 23.2, depth 27.8 cm. Museo Larco, Lima, Peru, ML031834.

wears a crown made up of small birds pointing upward. Its nose has been represented as a bird's beak. The figure also wears large earrings, a symbol of his high rank, and a collar consisting of beads that represent human heads. This figure wears garments that would have been made in metal and feature offerings of birds and heads. The intent of showing the male sex organ might have been to communicate that this ancestor is still sexually active and thus can impregnate the subterranean world. He is an ancestor who is able to fertilize the earth and also holds a bowl, indicating his connection to water. He probably represents an ancestralized community leader, already inhabiting the underworld, and as such he is represented in the nude, but adorned with ornaments that emphasize his link with the forces above.

Huacos as Channels for the Animating Forces of the World

Traditional Andean forms of expression stressed the physical and visual qualities of objects. In this sense, art objects constituted highly symbolic systems of visual communication. Notable among the different kinds of art objects created by ancient Peruvians are ceramic objects that cannot be categorized as "crockery" but do have forms similar to pitchers, bottles, basins, bowls, and cups. Here we can recognize an intent to enclose empty space, thereby creating forms or structures that embody the coexistence of opposites in a single physical entity. Form and empty space coexist in each piece: there is an invisible inside of the "vessel" giving shape to that which becomes apparent from outside, which in turn constitutes a pictorial space expressing categories, concepts, relationships, mythical narratives, and ritual actions. In the Andes, ceramics were the privileged means of representing the world and creating "microcosms." In other words, "the vessel is a miniature of the cosmos where a number of worldly agencies are presented and articulated (opposed to each other)."[1]

As I mentioned above, the vast majority of huacos are containers or vessels. Some of these were used to contain water, chicha, and even the sacrificial blood offered in some rituals. Their value and importance are linked to their ability to contain liquids or fluids, literally or symbolically. Some of these vessels were never even used in this world but were instead made as offerings to accompany the dead in the underworld, or animate or activate vital forces in that subterranean space where the ancestors reside.

The objects that we now learn about through display cases at our museums and different collections originated mostly from the burials of rulers, priests, and priestesses, most of whom were elite individuals in the societies of ancient Peru. Some of the other objects in these tombs had been used in various ceremonies before being buried with the dead. These objects were made centuries ago to facilitate the interactions mentioned above, establishing channels between the living and dead, between humans and other intermediary beings, and between humans and the forces of nature. They also served to communicate their users' identities in each activity in which they were used, and in many cases to mark hierarchies and express the power relations that existed in each society. The messages of these objects were activated within the specific context of their use and according to the agents through whom these objects came into play.

It is important to underscore, however, that within the cosmovision of the original societies of the central Andes, objects are regarded as animated beings, active agents in a world in which they interact with other beings. All objects are expressions of the creative power of their makers, sharing a common animate essence.

Some themes and forms recur more than others in ancient Andean funerary and ceremonial ceramics: on the one hand, there is the theme of the representation of the "head," and on the other, there is the form of a bottle with a neck or handle in the shape of a stirrup, characteristic of the northern tradition, or a bottle with two mouths and a handle bridging them, typical of the southern tradition.

Heads as Powerful Containers

The body had an important function in the processes of consolidating and configuring power in the Andes. The extraction or accumulation of heads, whether physically or figuratively, was a way of symbolically appropriating the powers of the other. As the part of the body that concentrates the senses through which we perceive the world, the human head was frequently and recurrently represented in pre-Columbian ceramics. Mochica ceramics modeled heads of male figures with a high degree of detail and physiognomic exactness, as a result of which these objects have been called huaco retrato. The individuals portrayed were members of the ruling elite, priests, warriors, and notable artisans, some of whom were represented at different moments of their lives. The faces of deities were also depicted. Many of these portrait pots show traces of having been used before they were buried in tombs.

Among the Nazca, obtaining human heads was central to the ritual of war. Nazca burials have included trophy heads that may have been symbolically sown like seeds in agricultural land. The fact that these trophy heads have been represented with plants sprouting from their mouths reinforces the symbolic relationship between war, the human head, and agricultural regeneration.

One of the most ancient funerary bottles in the collection at the Museo Larco is a Cupisnique bottle featuring a striking representation of a head [FIG. 36]. This is a sculpted ceramic bottle from Peru's northern coast, made approximately three thousand years ago and fired in a kiln with a reducing environment, yielding a dark lead color. It shows the characteristic form of Cupisnique funerary vessels: it has a connective bridge- or arch-type handle and single spout—a form known as a "stirrup spout vessel." The bottle's chamber is in the shape of a head, but it actually seems to consist of two heads, or two half heads, one within or "beneath" the other. The right side is a face with a mix of human and animal features. One can discern a circular eye, and above it an eyebrow like a serpent that extends to the ear in the shape of a deer's head. There are two nasal openings, and above these, the waxy or fleshy membrane that some birds have over their beaks. A serpent's head emerges from the thick-lipped mouth. The face on the left presents itself as a synthetic elaboration that follows a geometric pattern in which we see the eye, nose, and mouth of a feline with crisscrossing incisors, similar to the stone sculptures from the formative era that represent ancestral figures or divine beings.

From early on, ancient Peruvians represented the sacred animals that symbolized the different worlds: birds were symbols of the world above, or *Hanan Pacha*; snakes were symbols of the underworld, *Uku Pacha*; and large cats were symbols of our world, *Kay Pacha*, the space where the world above and the underworld met. The political and religious leaders of ancient Peru expressed their earthly power by taking on the power of the cat, but they also needed the powers of the other animals in order to mediate between the earthly plane, celestial world above, and underworld below. These "transformations" were achieved by consuming the juice of either the San Pedro cactus (*Echinopsis pachanoi*) or ayahuasca plant (*Banisteriopsis caapi*), which had hallucinogenic effects and produced visions. This would explain the representation of possible portraits of shamans who gradually took on the facial features of the jaguar in Cupisnique art.

The Northern and Southern Traditions: Two Bodies of Hydraulic Knowledge Modeled in Clay

The stirrup spout vessels that have characterized the ritual and funerary ceramics of northern Peru for over three thousand years are really hollow sculptures connecting inside and outside through the formal component of the handle. If a liquid is poured into the mouth, it will flow inward through both channels, reinforcing the symbolic sense of connection. Nevertheless, to pour out the liquid in the bottle, two different fluids have to circulate: air has to enter one channel, while liquid flows out of the other. Given that stirrup spout vessels are associated with funerary rituals, they are understood to be highly symbolic objects referring to the connection between the outer and inner worlds that occurs precisely in the death trance. They can be regarded as small hydraulic systems that

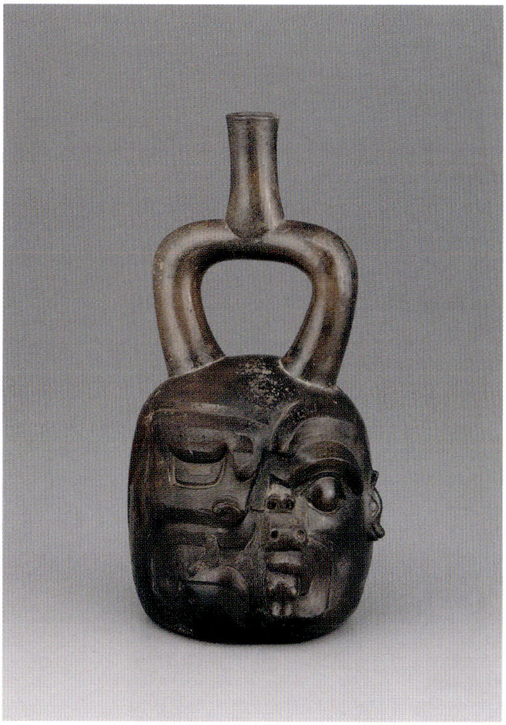

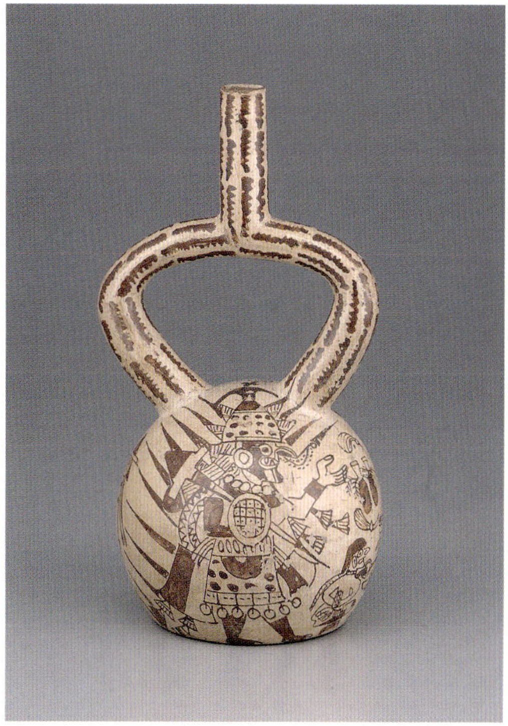

[FIG. 36]
Head in shamanic transformation. Cupisnique ceramic. Northern coast, 1200–1 BCE. Width 13.4, height 24.3, depth 12.8 cm. Museo Larco, Lima, Peru, ML040218.

[FIG. 37]
Sacrifice and presentation of the goblet. Mochica ceramic. Northern coast, 100–800 CE. Width 14.8, height 24.6, depth 13.4 cm. Museo Larco, Lima, Peru, ML010850.

symbolically refer to the vital, continuous water cycle that sustains life as well. These sacred bottles re-created the circuit of water that the inhabitants of northern Peru experienced: from the snowy peaks of the sierra, the meltwater drains down both sides of the mountain. With river water, agriculturalists could irrigate their fields, directing the moving water through canals, or *pacchas*, until it ultimately reached the sea, the great container.

Spherically shaped stirrup spout vessels made it possible to develop cosmological narratives in greater detail. The connective handle divided the vessel into two sides, organizing the narratives depicted thereon in accordance with notions of opposition and complementarity. The handle generated a sense of *tinkuy*, or the generative encounter of opposed forces in the hollow sculpture, as we can see in some of the most iconographically developed bottles like the Mochica one.

Just as the northern style of container with connective handles (commonly known as a stirrup spout vessel) was a ubiquitous, highly symbolic object for three thousand years or more, in the south the form known as a "double spout and bridge vessel" reveals the relationship with water that characterized the arid southern coast. The water contained in the inner world, or the great lagoon, runs through puquios or springs that dot the coastal landscape, never fully flowing out, but remaining underground, flowing through subterranean channels and rivers. The iconography on the sides of these containers is always associated with the ancestors, flows, canals, and beings that are ultimately linked to the vital potency of water. This type of bottle recalls the underground flow of water rising toward the world above [FIG. 37]. Just as some Mochica pieces capture the great calendrical scenes in all of their extent and detail, others depict just a few actions or main characters linked to specific rituals or mythological episodes. This ceramic bottle features a mythological scene in which one of the most important Mochica deities presents a goblet to another. One side of the piece features a representation of the diurnal solar Radiant God, dressed as a warrior in a conical helmet with a crescent-shaped ornament or *tumi*. Rays shoot forth from his body; he wears face paint, and has incisors in his mouth, circular ears, a septum piercing shaped like a half-moon with flaps, a necklace with circular beads, bracelets, a shirt and skirt with circular pendants, and hip protectors in two colors. He wields a club and circular shield.

The other side represents the God of the Milky Way, lord of the starry night sky and wet underworld, holding a cup and a plate that seems to be made from a gourd, which might indicate that it had served to cover the cup. He wears a crown in the shape of an octopus, a posterior plume of feathers, and a cape on his back that culminates in a serpent's head. His mouth reveals feline fangs; he has a half-moon-shaped nose piercing with flaps, and wears rectangular earrings with snakehead pendants, a chest plate, bracelets, a shirt and cape with rectangular plaques, a skirt with symbols linked with volutes, a snake for a belt, and body paint.

Beneath the arched handle is a feline man wearing a shirt with a tiered design and skirt with cruciform symbols, sacrificing a naked man whose hands are tied behind his back and whose neck is in a noose—a captive warrior from the ritual combat. Above them are a pair of birds along with a pair of ulluchu fruits (identified with the genus *Guarea*). On the opposite side we find the litter on which the sacrificial blood would have traveled to the world of the gods, surrounded by animated clubs.

Ceramics as an Open Book

The examples of ancient Peruvian ceramic pieces featured in this chapter allow us to get a sense of these objects' meanings and imagine them in action, since they do not constitute pots meant for consuming food or drink. Instead, they must be understood as objects that model the world and the forces that exist within it, capturing the relationships among the beings that inhabit it, in the inner as well as outer world. These objects do more than tell stories; they act. They make things possible, enable them to be what they must be, and foster contacts, flows, encounters, and regeneration.

In ancient Peru, the experience of the world was not written sequentially in words on paper but rather was sculpted, skillfully and masterfully, in three dimensions. Ceramic vessels were the privileged artistic means for modeling the world and expressing a vision of the universe. Our huacos were real and symbolic containers for liquids, but more important, they were containers for messages, meant primarily for the underworld. Together, they constituted a system of communication. Therefore Larco Hoyle, founder of the Museo Larco, regarded ceramic vessels as an open book in which to learn about ancient Peru. And today we continue to do so, from the most diverse disciplinary perspectives and with a greater quantity of methodological tools, laboring to read the legacy of ancestral knowledge contained therein and recognizing the significance of each step taken in the process of creating them: the choice of materials, their preparation, the interaction with their creators' bodies, the gestures of the potters' hands, the techniques for achieving forms and representations, and, ultimately, the uses and meanings that each of these works had in the past.

Cycladic Bird Jug

Carl Knappett

The ceramic arts of the Aegean Bronze Age—from mainland Greece, the Cyclades, and Crete especially—are justly famous. They appear in museums across the world. Heraklion Museum on Crete provides a remarkable material history of Bronze Age pottery and is visited by many thousands each summer.

And yet art history does not quite know what to make of these objects. We can begin to understand the challenge they pose through comparison with the much later Classical vases of Greece with which the art historian is more familiar. The latter not only have complex figurative iconography but often also text integrated with the image. Such text aids interpretation of the iconography, as do the texts beyond the vases that describe a historical and mythical world in some depth. Their Bronze Age counterparts, however, are rarely adorned with figurative scenes, thus resisting the kinds of iconographic analysis performed by art historians. In those cases where we do see figuration, there is no accompanying text—either on the vase itself or in the wider cultural universe it inhabits. That is to say, Bronze Age cultures are prehistoric, lacking deciphered texts—at least ones that have anything at all to say about art. Are we to treat these ceramic arts—if they even qualify as art by these standards—as a kind of primitive precursor to the later Classical achievement? That sometimes seems to be what happens. Or are we to work on these vases as anthropological evidence, signs of an ancient society that can tell us about past lifeways and social practices? In which case, the whole "art" question recedes from view.

In a way, then, the very selection of an *individual* object for particular attention is a choice that aligns us with a particular tradition. Art history may be at ease with the selection of individual objects, but (prehistoric) archaeology is generally not. To select an individual piece in this manner is almost to agree that an individual artist made choices that were designed to elevate an object above others—and so by extension it is then also acceptable for us to put it on a pedestal and single it out. We have little sense in prehistory that the individuality of an artist was ever recognized in this way—notwithstanding their evident skill and creativity. The closest we get to identifying singularity is in attributing products to regional workshops. Ceramic objects were generally not conceived of as singular pieces but instead as parts of sets—both in terms of their production and use. Potters typically made the same designs repeatedly, and ceramic vessels were intended to be used as parts of extensive assemblages, whether in a household or palace. From the archaeologist's perspective, there is also the fear that fetishizing individual objects and putting them above others is an outlook that implicitly encourages the kind of appreciation that feeds the desires of collectors, and ultimately the illicit antiquities trade.

Hence I have chosen an object that is not really one object but rather a set. I do so to keep in mind the inherent limitations of this procedure. We are forced in the process to recognize the "assemblage" qualities of the object and how these, as much as any intrinsic properties, are what render it remarkable. The selection I have made is deliberate in the prominence of its figurative decoration too, thereby offering an opportunity to confront the challenge of iconographic analysis in a prehistoric setting. The set chosen here has a remarkable story to tell, exemplifying the many different dimensions that come into play when we seek satisfactory interpretations of ancient material culture and ceramics specifically.

Cycladic Bird Jugs on Crete

The vase type selected here is known to Aegean Bronze Age archaeologists as a Cycladic bird jug. Here you can see examples that were all found at Knossos, but are now housed in scattered locations [FIG. 38]: Heraklion Museum on Crete [FIG. 38A]; Oxford's Ashmolean Museum [FIG. 38B]; London's British Museum [FIG. 38C], and the Metropolitan Museum of Art in New York City [FIG. 38D]. The one from the Ashmolean has been restored, and the British Museum example is a large upper-body fragment, also restored in plaster. Most (if not definitively all) of these were found in the Temple Repositories of the "Palace of Minos" at Knossos by Sir Arthur Evans during his excavations there in the early 1900s. These vases date to some thirty-six hundred years ago, or the end of the Middle Bronze Age. "Cycladic bird jug," however, is a condensed, specialized description that does not help the general reader much; neither does saying it comes from the Temple Repositories. So let us step back and talk about what stands before us in more straightforward terms.

First, we can simply remark that this is a ceramic *container*. And it seems that it must have been a container for liquids because it has a spout

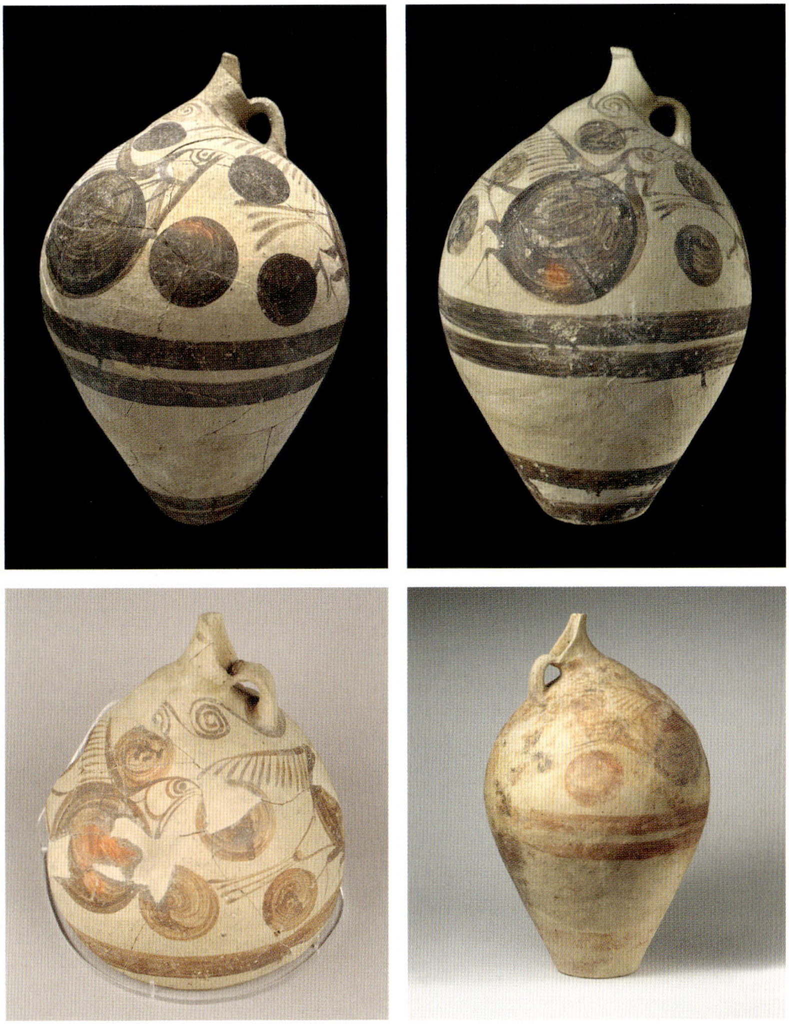

[FIG. 38]
Cycladic bird jugs found at Knossos: (a) Heraklion Museum, HM2595; (b) Ashmolean, AN1896–1908. AE.807; (c) British Museum, 1906,1112.95.a–b, 1700–1600 BCE. Height 36.8 cm; and (d) Metropolitan Museum of Art, 11.186.13 ca. 1700–1600 BCE. Height as restored 54.4 cm.

and an opposed vertical handle—a combination designed for pouring. Moreover, the mouth is quite closed and narrow, and so it would have been difficult to view the contents, refill the vessel, and even clean it. Might these features suggest it was only ever filled with its liquid contents once? The voluminous, globular shape suggests that some capacity was required; if the act of pouring in and of itself was primary, one could imagine a more slender shape, with a more prominent spout perhaps. No, this actually has more the shape of contemporary amphorae designed for transport. On this point, we must also recognize its size. It is just over half a meter tall, or to recognize the slight variability within the set, the Heraklion example is 56 centimeters tall, the one in the Metropolitan Museum is 54.4 centimeters (as restored), while the Ashmolean piece has a restored height of 53.5 centimeters. So this is not a typical jug of the period. Actually, if this were even close to full of liquid, it would not have been possible to lift with a single handle like this (and it might well have broken if one had tried). To actually pour from this vase, the person (or persons) holding it would most likely have had to place a second hand on the lower body of the vase for support. When one thinks about the size of the vessel in this way, the handle does not exactly invite contact eagerly. Is its design more about achieving an aesthetic unity than some functional affordance? Similarly, the spout does not reach out with great purpose either. The overall aesthetic effect is one of a vase that seems more set to contain than to release—perhaps indicating that it was designed to be emptied just once and not for frequent pouring.

With our thoughts turned to grasping, holding, pouring, and liquids, we might ponder the vessel's contents. As with most organic commodities from these distant periods, no visible traces remain. Still, sometimes residues of organic contents can be extracted from the porous walls of ceramic vessels; when subjected to certain kinds of analysis, such as gas chromatography–mass spectrometry, the compounds in these residues can be isolated and identified. The technique has been successful in finding animal fats and beeswax, and claims have been made for the identification of wine as well. This method has not been applied to the vessels in question or other vessels of this kind, so we cannot in this case deduce directly from such analyses what the contents may have been. Nevertheless, a vase found alongside these had an inscription incised into it in Linear A. Though this ancient script remains undeciphered, certain signs can be recognized, and one of the signs in the inscription is the logogram for wine. Thus it seems that wine may have been contained in broadly similar vessels found adjacent—so why not our vessels too, given that their shape strongly suggests liquid contents? What other liquid contents might we imagine?

Bird Jugs in the Cyclades

If we then assume that such vessels contained wine, we might also think about provenance and even terroir. Where did this set of vases come from? They all have a distinctive clay fabric that is white with a greenish tinge. On this basis alone they look unlike most vessels local to their Knossian findspot. When the fabric of other vessels of similar appearance has been studied in more detail, using ceramic petrography, small volcanic inclusions can be found in the fabric of a kind that cannot possibly be local. Yet there is an obvious place to look: the volcanic islands of Melos and Thera in the Cyclades some 120 kilometers to the north of Knossos. These islands have their own rich archaeological sequences, in which this kind of ceramic fabric is common. It is known as "Cycladic White." This fabric occurs on both islands, and it is currently tricky to tell their Cycladic White fabrics apart. We must then say that the clay suggests this vase could be from either Thera or Melos. We might also mention the forming technique used for the vases, namely that they were handmade with coils. The technique is significant because on Crete in this period, potters had long been making smaller vessels with the help of the wheel and were now increasingly making large vessels of this kind on the wheel as well. In the Cyclades, however, potters were much more attached to coiling techniques, and the wheel was barely used at all at this moment. It seems we have a set of vases made by potters on a Cycladic island, but that have found their way to the island of Crete around 120 kilometers to the south.

It bears mentioning again here the vase with a Linear A inscription briefly described above. This was actually just one vase among a set of four. These vases were in a quite different fabric, not greenish-white at all but red-brown (sometimes varying to gray due to firing), with angular white inclusions and abundant silver mica. This kind of fabric is not at home on Crete and can be linked to the Cyclades, quite probably the island of Naxos (which has a different geology than the volcanic islands of Melos and Thera). So here too we have a set of vessels coming to Knossos from a distant island to the north—perhaps in a shipment of wine with its own local characteristics.

These large jars likely imported as a set of four from Naxos are rather plain, and do not signal their provenance and contents in any conspicuous way other than through the Linear A inscription. That only one of them was thus incised may be explained if they are viewed as a set, with the one inscription labeling the entire "batch." Some of the Cycladic bird jugs also have incised signs, though less elaborate; they consist of a single sign at the handle, a triangle in a few instances, and a double axe in one case. Could these have functioned similarly to signal a batch or were these marks made by the potter for some other purpose? Either way, the

Cycladic bird jugs are stylistically far more distinctive than the Naxian wares. Melian and Theran potters had a specific way of decorating such vases that was quite different not only from what is seen on Naxos but also from wares produced locally on Crete. Whereas Cretan potters rarely decorated their vases with figurative motifs in this period, Melian and Theran potters worked within a tradition that put great stock in such depictions. We see various floral motifs, such as pomegranates, and even human figures. But it is birds that they paint most frequently. Here we see not just one bird shown in flight but instead three that seem to follow each other around the vessel's upper body. They have a distinctive "fat belly" rendered as a disk, with other similar, though smaller disks placed between the birds. The frieze is framed above by a running spiral pattern at the neck and two thick horizontal bands just below the maximum diameter; below these bands the lower body is empty, until two further bands that mark where the body meets the base. The paint is a dark brown to black, applied in a washy or streaky manner, and it is interesting that only this color is utilized; in an earlier phase, Cycladic potters painted such motifs in bichrome, using dark brown/black together with red, with the latter particularly for the bird's fat belly. The quality of the line depicting the birds' features shows free, confident strokes, but at the same time, the regular bands that frame the frieze are somewhat uneven in places. Painterly skill is also apparent in the use made of the vase's globularity in positioning the birds. There is a further design sensibility, moreover, in that the iconography finds a match with the vessel's morphology—such that the neck is tilted back and has a "swollen throat" to mimic a bird's neck. There is almost a playfulness here in the double meaning of "bird jug," with the shape mirroring the decor: fat-bellied birds flying around the vessel, which is itself a fat-bellied bird.

What elude us, however, are the associations these birds may have had. Indeed, can we even identify what kind of birds they are? While quite stylized, they might be red-legged partridges. Why would these containers, possibly full of wine, have been decorated with three partridges in flight? Does their arrangement around the vase represent the flocking behavior of partridges? Or can we speculate on a possible connection between partridges and vineyards? Some studies indicate that vineyards can be a good source of cover for partridges—perhaps especially useful in an environment (such as Melos and Thera) that may have had limited tree cover. Birds depicted in other media—such as the famous wall paintings from Thera made just a generation or two later that include a sequence of ducks in flight—may have had religious connotations. There is no particular reason to impute a cultic meaning to these fat-bellied birds that may be partridges, but there could well be other layers of symbolism that elude us entirely.

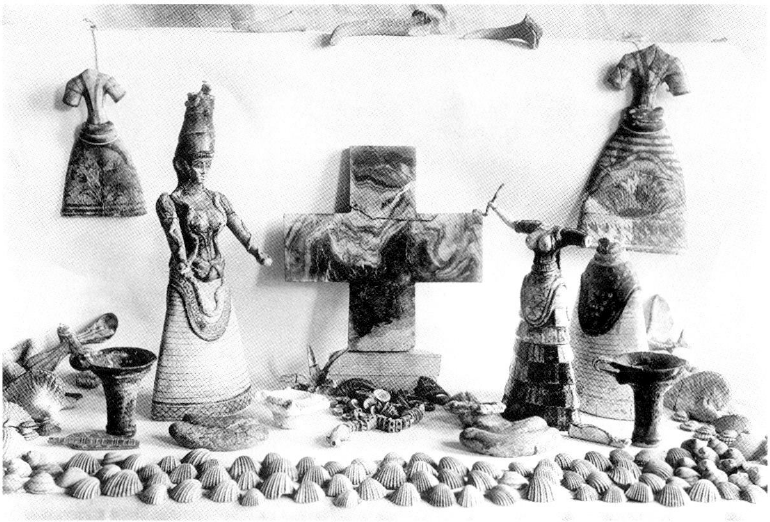

[FIG. 39]
Finds from the Temple Repositories at Knossos.

On their journey south from the Cycladic islands to the "mini-continent" of Crete, the appearance of these vessels may have been quite recognizably associated with their contents. They surely were just a small part of a larger cargo, some or all of which may have been off-loaded at the port of Poros on the north coast of Crete before being transported the few kilometers inland to the palace of Knossos, without question the largest and most powerful community of its time in the Aegean world. On such a journey, this set of Cycladic bird jugs may have been accompanied by other sets, as this was not the only such set found at Knossos. When one takes into account the other vases found alongside it, such as the set that includes the one incised with the wine logogram, perhaps they were all wine imports from the Cyclades; after all, wine from the volcanic soils of Santorini (Thera) is prized today, and the nineteenth-century traveler Theodore Bent described the extent and quality of wine production on the island in the 1880s.

The Finds in the Temple Repositories

To say that the vessels found their way to Knossos only begins to tell the story of their context. As briefly mentioned above, they were discovered in what are known as the Temple Repositories. These are stone-lined cists sunk into the floor of a shrine in the very heart of the Knossos palace. These cists were likely used to store cult paraphernalia that would be brought out and used in ceremonies. That said, they were not discovered with an orderly arrangement of objects but instead had clearly been filled in to create a kind of sealed deposit. It may have been that there was an earthquake that rocked the palace, destroying some of the shrine and its cult equipment, and that it was subsequently decided to close the cists in an act of "structured deposition," with objects deliberately placed in an act of final deposition. There are astonishing finds that were buried here, including the famous "snake goddesses" made of faience, thousands of seashells, gold, bronze, and ivory artifacts, and stone offering tables, to name but a few [FIG. 39]. In addition, there were forty-four ceramic vessels, many of which we see in a photograph from 1903 when the cists were being unearthed [FIG. 40]. A Cycladic bird jug—the one now in Heraklion Museum—can be seen in the left foreground. When we see, then, the context in which this set was found, alongside so many other vessels that could easily have been wine containers, we can imagine how wine offerings might have been an integral part of the cult activities associated with this shrine (and indeed such offerings are mentioned in the later Linear B texts). Moreover, it would not be an exaggeration to view this shrine as one of the most significant in the whole of the Aegean world at this time, given its position at the heart of its largest and probably most long-lived town. Given its significance, could it be that the Cycladic bird jugs and their liquid contents were specifically manufactured and shipped with this uniquely hallowed destination very much in mind?

Timing and Dating

If one begins to imagine this set of Cycladic bird jugs as a deliberate, targeted shipment for a palatial shrine, then the question of timing also arises. Wine kept in such containers would presumably have had a limited shelf life. Would it then have been shipped soon after being made—in the spring perhaps? One can imagine the needs for such imports being seasonal—connected with certain religious festivals perhaps—as well as taking into account the period of wine production and ease of travel with varying seasonal winds. While in the Cyclades these vessels were very much part of the local tradition and would likely have been made year-round, it is possible that their export as wine containers was seasonal.

For the archaeologist, however, vessels have a different kind of existence in time; we think more in terms of "dating" than "timing." It is vessels of this kind with a distinctive style that can be used diagnostically—based on the assumption that such styles change with some regularity and so can be linked to specific periods. Styles did not exactly see rapid overhaul; we could be talking about a generation or two. But this is the level of resolution we are faced with in prehistory, so being able to narrow stylistic development down to windows of twenty-five to fifty years' length is satisfactory. We are rarely able to work at the scale of decades.

In order to achieve some accuracy in dating, we have to look at the context in which these vessels were produced within the Cyclades. And

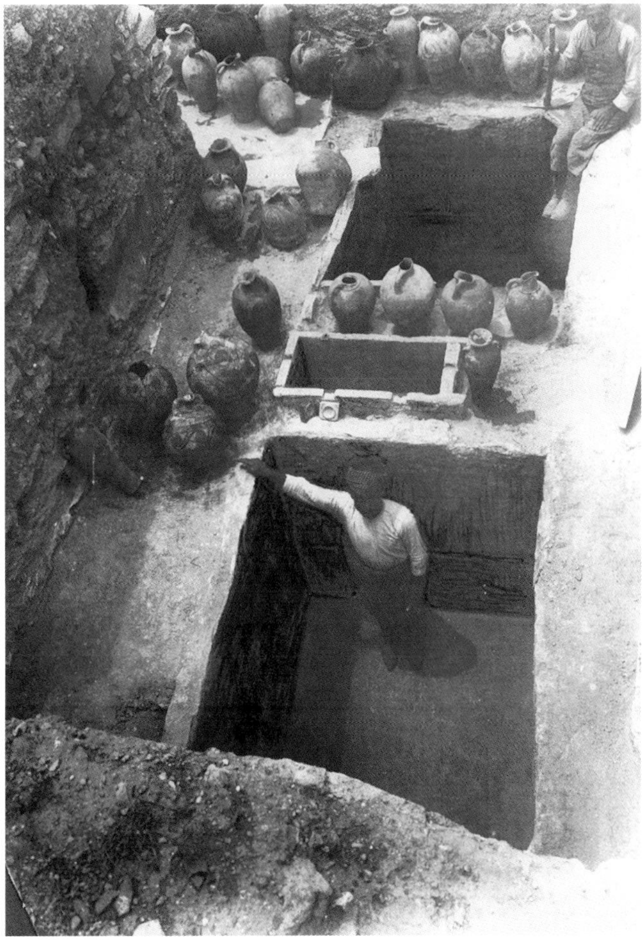

[FIG. 40]
Ceramic vases arranged around their findspot, the Temple Repositories at Knossos.

here we are provided with a remarkable freeze-frame: the destruction of the town of Akrotiri by the Theran eruption. The extensive archaeological remains from this site allow us to say that it occurred during a phase we call Late Minoan IA. There has been a huge amount of debate around the corresponding absolute chronology, but the first half of the sixteenth century BCE (or ca. 1550 BCE) seems likely. What is important here is that while the Late Minoan IA levels at Akrotiri do contain the same type of jug in terms of shape, they do not have the same kind of decoration as the bird jugs found at Knossos. Earlier levels at the site are also preserved, and these have jugs (of a different shape) with depictions of birds that are similar in their form, though typically bichrome (using both black and red paint) and hence distinct. These earlier levels are from the Middle Bronze Age, equivalent to the Middle Minoan IIIA phase on Crete (or ca. 1700 BCE). It could be that our bird jugs then fall stylistically between these two points—which would be the Middle Minoan IIIB phase. Yet this phase happens to be poorly represented at Akrotiri. So it turns out to be quite hard to pin down the period when the bird jugs were produced.

As for their context of deposition, the various other vessels found alongside the Cycladic bird jugs in the Temple Repositories point to a date in Middle Minoan IIIA or IIIB. There are ewers with retorted spirals in white on dark that were common on Crete at this time, particularly in the Mesara region, to the south of Knossos. We have to exercise caution, though, because pottery vessels, especially larger ones that might be quite durable, can be curated for generations. So a vase could be discovered in a deposit that was formed much later, even centuries after the vase was made. This argument is sometimes evoked for the Temple Repositories because of their many other finds, including faience figures and other figurative pieces, which some scholars feel are stylistically more advanced than Middle Minoan III. This nevertheless risks circular reasoning, as it is generally the more abundant pottery finds that form the dating backbone; it is risky to take or leave the dating evidence they provide according to whether their indications suit one's own ends or not. In any case, the time with which these vases are associated—let's say the Middle Minoan IIIB period, or the late seventeenth century BCE—is significant: it was a time when Knossos was acquiring ever more power across not only the island of Crete but the wider southern Aegean too. The discovery of these Cycladic imports at this very moment, then, is a sign of these wider geopolitical developments.

A Dispersed Cultural Heritage

Many of the finds from the Temple Repositories are displayed handsomely together in Heraklion Museum, providing a powerful sense of this varied cult assemblage. The finds were moved from their findspot at Knossos for display here, quite naturally—and this minimal separation (just six kilometers apart) is mitigated by the fact that many visitors to Knossos will also go to Heraklion Museum. The site and the museum form a natural pair. Still, though now curated by the Greek Ministry of Culture and Sports, these finds were uncovered in excavations conducted by Evans for the Cretan Exploration Fund at a time when duplicate finds were permitted to be taken out of the country. With the Cycladic bird jugs being so similar, as we have seen, they made excellent candidates for export under such rules—and so now individual examples can be viewed in the Ashmolean Museum in Oxford, British Museum of London, and Metropolitan Museum of Art in New York City, as noted earlier [FIGS. 38A–D]. The last of these had been in the Ashmolean too, but found its way to New York as part of a move that saw sixty-five Aegean artifacts traded from Oxford in exchange for a group of Cypriot antiquities from the Met's Cesnola collection. Ironically, the very standardization of the bird jugs—and their existence as a set—encouraged their separation. The colonial context for archaeology in the early twentieth century created a dispersed cultural heritage whereby each piece is now displayed as a singleton in four separate museums in three different countries. There are more pieces, such as the upper body of one bird jug in the Ashmolean and others held in the storerooms of Heraklion Museum—perhaps three more vases. Their fragmentary nature means they are not on display, and according to the study in the late 1990s by Marina Panagiotaki, it is not even certain that they are all from the Temple Repositories.[1] So there is a further dispersal of the assemblage due to an attitude to excavation in the early twentieth century that did not place great importance on keeping finds together. Panagiotaki's study was the first time the assemblage had been published as whole.

Final Remarks

Here is a vase type that has the features of a jug but the size and shape of a transport amphora. It may have only been filled once with a liquid commodity—let us say wine—and transported as a set by ship from a producer on Thera or Melos. After being off-loaded, most likely at the port of Poros, these bird jugs were brought up the Knossos valley right into the heart of the palace. Was the special quality of these vases' contents apparent to all from their bird design? There are hardly any others known from Crete, so this may have been a special shipment. In any case, their discovery in the Temple Repositories suggests their contents were consumed as part of some palatial religious ceremony. One could well imagine the wine containers themselves would subsequently be discarded. Yet it seems they were purposefully kept and curated, to be deposited in these deep stone-lined cists, among a deposit of forty-four vessels in total, local and imported, and alongside other remarkable finds of faience goddesses, thousands of seashells, and so on. This cult assemblage represents a kind of termination rite, as these materials were buried and even fragmented so as not to be recovered. But not long before their deposition, they must have been party to powerful religious rites performed in the palace. Why was Cycladic wine, if we can assume as much, offered in such ceremonies? Was it consumed by worshippers or dedicated to the deities (it is suggested that Minoan religion was polytheistic)?

Even though Knossos remained a major center, these vases lay untouched for millennia until Evans uncovered, restored, and published them, with a subsequent journey to the various museums where they are now displayed. They intrigue and enchant countless visitors with their theriomorphic shape and matching bird imagery, even though their meaning, symbolic associations, and the identity of the potters who made them remain elusive. While we might engage with one of these Cycladic bird jugs on its own terms as an individual ceramic creation, it is the nature of the set to which each belongs that is key to their understanding and interpretation.

Acknowledgments

My sincere thanks go to Irene Nikolakopoulou for her advice on all matters Cycladic, and Andrew Shapland for helpful input, particularly on the connection between partridges and vineyards. I am deeply grateful to Sequoia Miller for the invitation to contribute to this volume.

A Porcelain Set of Four Continents Fit for the King

Yao-Fen You

The allegory of the four continents was firmly established as a theme in European decorative arts by the eighteenth century. The division of the known world into four parts gained traction in early modern Europe, following overseas encounters with the Americas. Such gendered and frequently racialized personifications of Africa, America, Asia, and Europe—occasionally taking the form of tender putti, but more often that of nubile females of varying skin tones and in varying states of undress—served to perpetuate, reenact, and uphold the superiority of Europe. An outstanding example among Cooper Hewitt, Smithsonian Design Museum's collection of porcelain personifications is an exceptionally large ensemble modeled in soft-paste porcelain in which Europe, Asia, Africa, and America are represented as elegant female figures with an expanded range of attributes [FIG. 41].

Each of the four figural groups in this ensemble measures around sixteen inches high and eleven inches in diameter, and is vividly decorated in vibrant polychrome enamel colors. The continents stand gracefully on a rocky base of moss- and vegetation-covered stones, attended by their respective animal attributes, whose bodies have been elongated to wrap around their mistresses. Alongside each is a personification of a major river, taking the form of mostly nude and reclining bearded old men bearing urns overflowing with water. This pairing of the four continents with the four rivers, though found in paintings such as Peter Paul Rubens's *Four Continents*, is extremely rare in porcelain configurations. The compositional complexity and proportions of Cooper Hewitt's set are extremely impressive given that the figures are modeled in soft-paste porcelain, which does not permit the degree of detail or crispness that may be achieved in "true" or hard-paste porcelain since it is fired at a lower temperature and has a stronger tendency to slump in the kiln. Nevertheless, the modelers took advantage of its "doughy" quality to make the animals appear more affectionate. The malleability of soft-paste

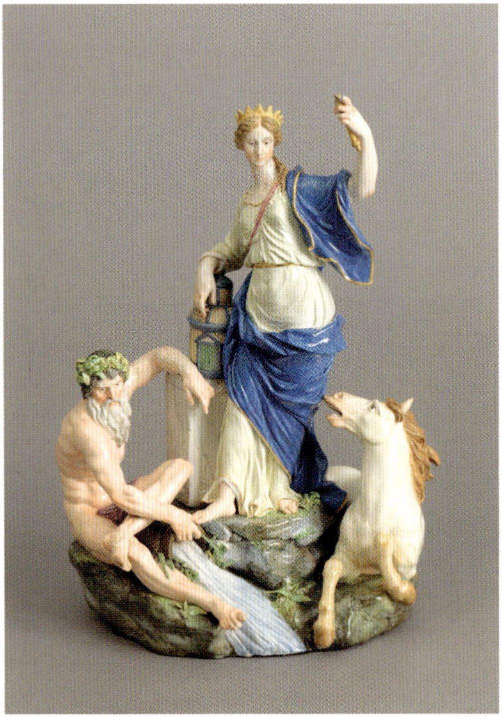

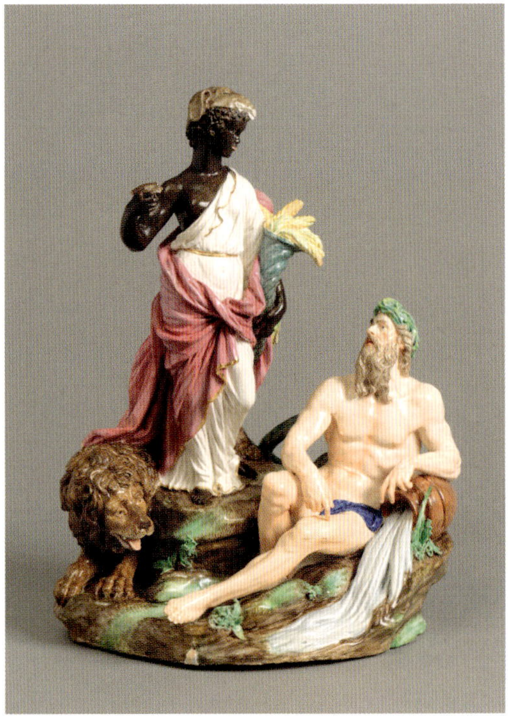

[FIG. 41]
Allegory of the four continents with the four river gods, Capodimonte Porcelain Manufactory (Italy), 1757–59. Soft-paste porcelain, vitreous enamel, gold. *Left to right*: 40.6 × 27.3 × 26.7 cm (Europe, 1960-1-51-b); 39.1 × 29.2 × 24.8 cm (Africa, 1960-1-51-c); 38.7 × 26.7 × 25.1 cm (Asia, 1960-1-51-a); 41 × 27.9 × 27.9 cm (America, 1960-1-51-d). Gift of the Estate of James Hazen Hyde, Cooper Hewitt, Smithsonian Design Museum.

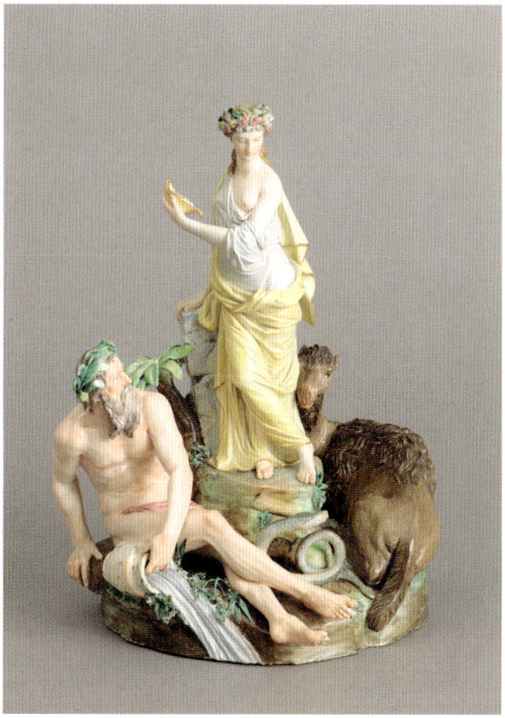

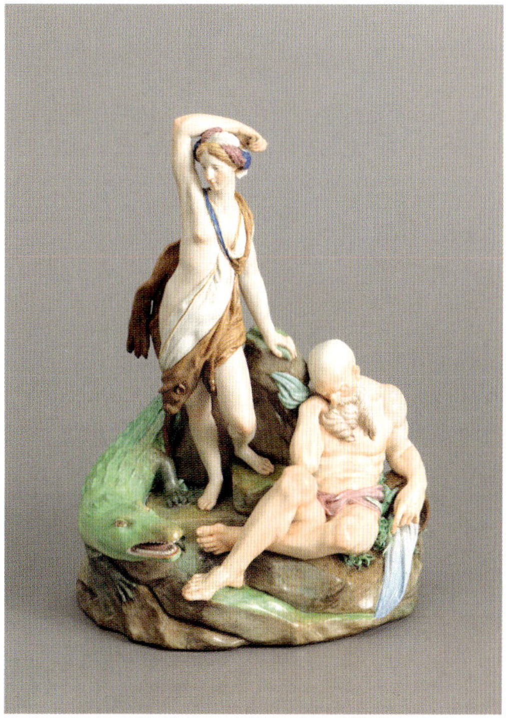

porcelain is ideal for conveying, for example, the lumpiness of a camel and its soft neck folds. The creative application of paint, including the differentiated flesh tones and faux marbling as well as the clever use of extruded porcelain filaments to mimic tufts of grass, compensates for the lack of crisp detail.

Although the allegory of the four continents had a long and rich history in the graphic arts, it only appeared in the medium of porcelain in the eighteenth century—at the peak of the theme's popularity—after being introduced by the Meissen Porcelain Manufactory in the mid-1740s. Between August 1745 and June 1747, Meissen modelers Johann Friedrich Eberlein (1695–1749) and Peter Reinicke (1711–68) collaborated on a large-scale series of the continents for Empress Elizabeth of Russia (1709–62), showing them as richly attired female personifications seated on animal attributes. This series formed part of a larger order of custom-made figures and tableware. Allegories of the four seasons and five senses [FIG. 13] were also included in the great "Russian order" of 1745. In the eighteenth century, such porcelain figures served principally as elements in an elaborate and fanciful garden centerpiece (*surtout de table*) on the banquet table during the dessert course. A four continents set was also included in the large gift of Saxon porcelain dispatched to the French foreign minister in 1747, the same year that Empress Elizabeth took possession of her order in Russia. The following year, Meissen introduced a smaller version of the four continents, reduced both in scale and attributes; modeled by Friedrich Elias Meyer (1725–85), this ensemble of figures sans animal attributes proved extremely popular. Count Heinrich von Brühl (1700–63) owned at least five sets of the four continents. A Meissen price list from 1765 notes no fewer than six different groups in varying sizes, some of them of putti. Meissen's models were widely copied, imitated, and adopted by other European porcelain manufactories, both within and outside Germany, into the late eighteenth and early nineteenth century. As historian Benjamin Schmidt has recently claimed, the story of their appearance in ceramics is very much intertwined with that of eighteenth-century European porcelain and "marks the moment of Europe's 'discovery' of porcelain."[1]

The Cooper Hewitt four continents porcelain group once formed part of a vast collection of decorative and fine arts objects surveying the evolution of this theme assembled by wealthy US collector and amateur art historian James Hazen Hyde (1876–1959). Hyde's collection of almost a thousand works of art was amassed when he was based in Paris between the two world wars. It is now divided among the Brooklyn Museum, Cooper Hewitt, the Metropolitan Museum of Art, and the New-York Historical Society. Unmarked and lacking a firm attribution, the Cooper Hewitt set has been associated with the royal factories of porcelain at both

Naples and Madrid that were active in the second half of the eighteenth century. Further analysis of this group, with an eye toward shedding light on their provenance and function, forms the subject of my case study. I will demonstrate that it was most likely produced in Naples at the Capodimonte porcelain factory for Carlo di Borbone (1716–88) during his reign as the king of the Two Sicilies from 1734 to 1759.

My argument for this attribution is based on three lines of analysis. First, the material composition of the porcelain body in the Cooper Hewitt four continents has been shown to be consistent with the prepared clay used at Capodimonte. The Capodimonte manufactory struggled with a high amount of waste—around thirty percent—in the initial years of production. Further, the paste used at Capodimonte possessed poor thermal shock resistance, forcing the factory to orient its production toward less functional wares like large figural groups and potpourri stands. Second, the specificity of the iconography of the Cooper Hewitt set accords strongly with the decorative program of key rooms at the royal palace initiated by Carlo di Borbone at the time of his marriage to Maria Amalia, princess of Saxony and Poland (1724–60), in 1738. Finally, the classicizing style and poses of the figures derive from major visual sources closely identified with the Bourbon king. These include the *Herculaneum Dancers*, which were unearthed outside Naples under the king's supervision and thoroughly identified with Naples. The illustrious sculptures in the rich collection of antique statuary housed in the Palazzo Farnese in Rome that Carlo inherited from his mother, Elisabetta Farnese of Parma, also served as visual models. Therefore the points of reference to Carlo within the four continents, in the choice of material, subject matter, and styling of the figures, all suggest they were commissioned by him between 1757 and 1759, while their size indicates they would probably have functioned as sculptural pieces for display in one of the more public-facing rooms in the royal palace rather than acting as occasional table decoration.

Attribution through Material and Production History

In earlier scholarship, the attribution of the Cooper Hewitt set has oscillated between the manufactories at Capodimonte in Naples and Buen Retiro in Madrid. The set was sold by London dealer J. Nachesohm to Hyde in 1927 as a work of the Real Fabrica de Buen Retiro (1760–1808), but subsequently ascribed to Capodimonte after it entered Hyde's collection. Active in Naples between 1743 and 1759, the Capodimonte porcelain factory was in fact the precursor to Buen Retiro. Established at the Royal Wood in Capodimonte by Carlo in 1743, the Capodimonte factory worked exclusively in soft-paste porcelain. The enterprise was active only sixteen years before it was dismantled and transferred to the palace of Buen Retiro when Carlo ascended to the Spanish throne in 1759 as Charles III. Forty-one employees and several thousand pounds of clay (and molds) sailed with him on October 7, 1759. Because the new factory continued to use the same prepared paste and the Capodimonte mark of a fleur-de-lis for its products—the flower being a reference to the Bourbon dynasty—the early wares and figures made at Real Fabrica de Buen Retiro in its first period of production (1760–83) are often difficult to distinguish from objects made at Capodimonte in the later years.

What, then, defined production at Capodimonte? The sculptural groups produced at Capodimonte, particularly by the chief modeler Giuseppe Gricci (1700–70), are frequently notable for figures with small heads, short torsos, and heavy limbs—none of which applies to the figures under discussion. Moreover, at Capodimonte, enamel and gilded decoration is often used sparingly to show off the beauty of the modeling and luminosity of the white porcelain body. Painted decoration usually consists of dainty floral patterns, gold accents to pick up on details of costume and dress, and occasionally stripes. The decorative scheme of Cooper Hewitt's set is quite different, exuberantly embracing color. Most of the surfaces are painted, and we observe neither the restraint of color nor the delicate patterns typically associated with Capodimonte pieces. The set retained the Naples attribution at the time of its accession to the museum's collection in 1960, but it was reattributed to the Madrid factory the following year. It was also redated to the nineteenth century. This is understandable in view of the classicizing manner and proportion of the figures as well as the use of flamboyant enamel decoration so often associated with Buen Retiro porcelain.

While the set is not characteristic of Capodimonte with respect to the presentation of the figures and the decorative scheme, however, recent technical examination by Dr. Thomas Lam at the Smithsonian Institution's Museum Conservation Institute confirms that the body paste dates to the eighteenth century. Preliminary semiquantitative analysis of the body and glaze by means of scanning electron microscopy-energy dispersive X-ray spectroscopy indicates that the porcelain body, with its high quantity of silica as well as small amounts of alumina and calcium oxide, is consistent with the reported literature for Capodimonte porcelains. The lead silicate composition of the glazes aligns with the manufactory's known reliance on lead-rich glazes, too.[2]

While this characterization of the paste as siliceous strongly suggests the possibility of a Capodimonte attribution for these works, the data is not entirely conclusive because of the shared history between the Capodimonte and Buen Retiro factories. A further complication is the absence of archival records for both factories. When Carlo departed for Spain in 1759, he ordered the destruction of the kilns and machinery he could not take with him as well as the documentary archives—supposedly to prevent his young son Ferdinand from running a porcelain factory in Naples. Subsequently, the molds and any other process materials brought from Naples to Madrid were destroyed in 1812, along with plans, drawings, and records related to Buen Retiro, when the factory was used by the British as an artillery base during the Spanish War of Independence (1808–14).

Iconography: Francesco Solimena's *Allegory of the Four Parts of the World*

Absent further paste and glaze analysis (as well as primary sources) that might shed light on the figures of the four continents, it is possible to locate them in the cultural milieu of Naples based on their distinctive iconography. They could have been grouped in any way, but I will describe them as laid out here [FIG. 41], from left to right: Europe, Africa, Asia, and America. Draped in a blue mantle, Europe thrusts her left arm triumphantly upward, her fingers curled around the handle of a now-broken scepter—a defining attribute. Her right arm rests on a miniature church; a gold crown perched on her head—also typical—is tilted ever so slightly down. At her feet, a unicorn stretches its head toward its mistress, looking up at her with a gaping mouth. The figure opposite, with a white beard and full head of gray hair crowned with a wreath of reeds, is presumably the Danube (though he could be the Tiber). With his torso tilted forward and one leg crossed over the other, he rests one arm on the plinth and steadies the mouth of the overturned urn in the other. Africa is a dark-skinned figure in a magenta mantle and elephant headdress. Her left arm is wrapped around a cornucopia, while the right carefully balances a scorpion (whose limbs have since broken off)—both typical emblems. A crouching lion at her feet wraps his body protectively around her, while the muscular Nile, languidly reclining in the natural rocky landscape, very much like a river himself, gazes up at her. Asia stands with one leg crossed over the other, dressed in a yellow mantle and crowned with a wreath of blended flora. She is identified by the incense holder she clutches in her left hand as well as the kneeling camel cuddled up beside her. A snake and miniature palm tree further confirm her "exotic" identity. Looking up at her is the river Ganges, whose torso is turned away as he steadies his urn. America is a scantily clad figure who raises her right arm over her head and rests her arm on the rock behind her. The fingers of her right hand are curved around the handle of what was once a bow—typically America's most striking attribute. She can also be identified by the ring of feathers crowning her head, animal hide draped around her nearly naked body, and fierce crocodile guarding her. Her bald but bearded male counterpart, either the Río de la Plata or Amazon, lies in slumber, blissfully unaware of the reptile's gaping maw.

As noted earlier, the coupling of the four continents with the four rivers is rarely found in porcelain, and this atypical pairing establishes a specific connection with the reign of Carlo di Borbone as sovereign of the newly independent kingdom in the Italian Peninsula. For his wedding in 1738 to fourteen-year-old Princess Maria Amalia of Saxony-Poland (1724–60), the twenty-two-year-old Carlo commissioned a cycle of paintings from the celebrated Neapolitan painter Francesco Solimena (1657–1747) to decorate the royal bedchambers. A highlight of the new interior program was the *Allegory of the Four Parts of the World* painted for the ceiling of the room adjacent to the king's alcove [FIG. 42]. This painting is critical to understanding the iconography of Cooper Hewitt's porcelain set.

Solimena's vertical composition—measuring approximately six by four feet in its present state—notably adapts a classic apotheosis scene (also popular in Europe in the eighteenth century) to the representation of the four continents, with their order of importance signaled by their scale and location in the painting as well as the extent to which they are sexualized. A fully clothed, queenly Europe reigns supreme in a throne in the upper right, one arm resting on a model of a round church as she looks down to hold the gaze of the viewer. Asia, also fully clothed but with a lower neckline, sits on a rock directly below her, holding an incense burner in her outstretched hand. She occupies the foreground. Next in size is Africa, who stands nude with one arm akimbo and the other hugging a large sheaf of grain; she is on the left side of the canvas, but in the middle ground. Barely perceptible is America, who is not only the smallest of the female figures but somewhat grayed out in the background too.

The upward spiral procession of female figures and tender cherubs from back to front, culminating in the inevitable triumph of Europe, conforms to traditional patterns for representing the four continents. But the painting deviates in one crucial regard: it includes a reclining male river god in the bottom-left corner between Africa and Asia. Like the sculpted river gods in the Cooper Hewitt set, he is shown as a muscular older man, supporting himself on an overturned urn overflowing with water. Like his porcelain counterparts, he is bearded and crowned with a garland of reeds. Although the river god is an uninterested bystander—instead of gazing upward toward Europe he looks away—he is, in fact, a charged symbol for Carlo's rocky relationship with the Holy See early in his reign.

The troubles with the Holy See started in 1735, when Pope Clement XII refused Carlo's *Chinèa*—an annual tribute in the form of a white horse laden with treasure paid by the kings of Naples as vassals to the pope since the eleventh century. Clement instead accepted the token of submission to papal authority sent from Austrian emperor Charles VI, even though Carlo had defeated the Austrians at the Siege of Capua. The desire

[FIG. 42]
Francesco Solimena (Italian, 1657–1747), *Allegory of the Four Parts of the World*, 1738. Oil on canvas. 184 × 127 cm. Gift of Dr. and Mrs. Henry R. Hope, Eskenazi Museum of Art, Indiana University, 74.83.

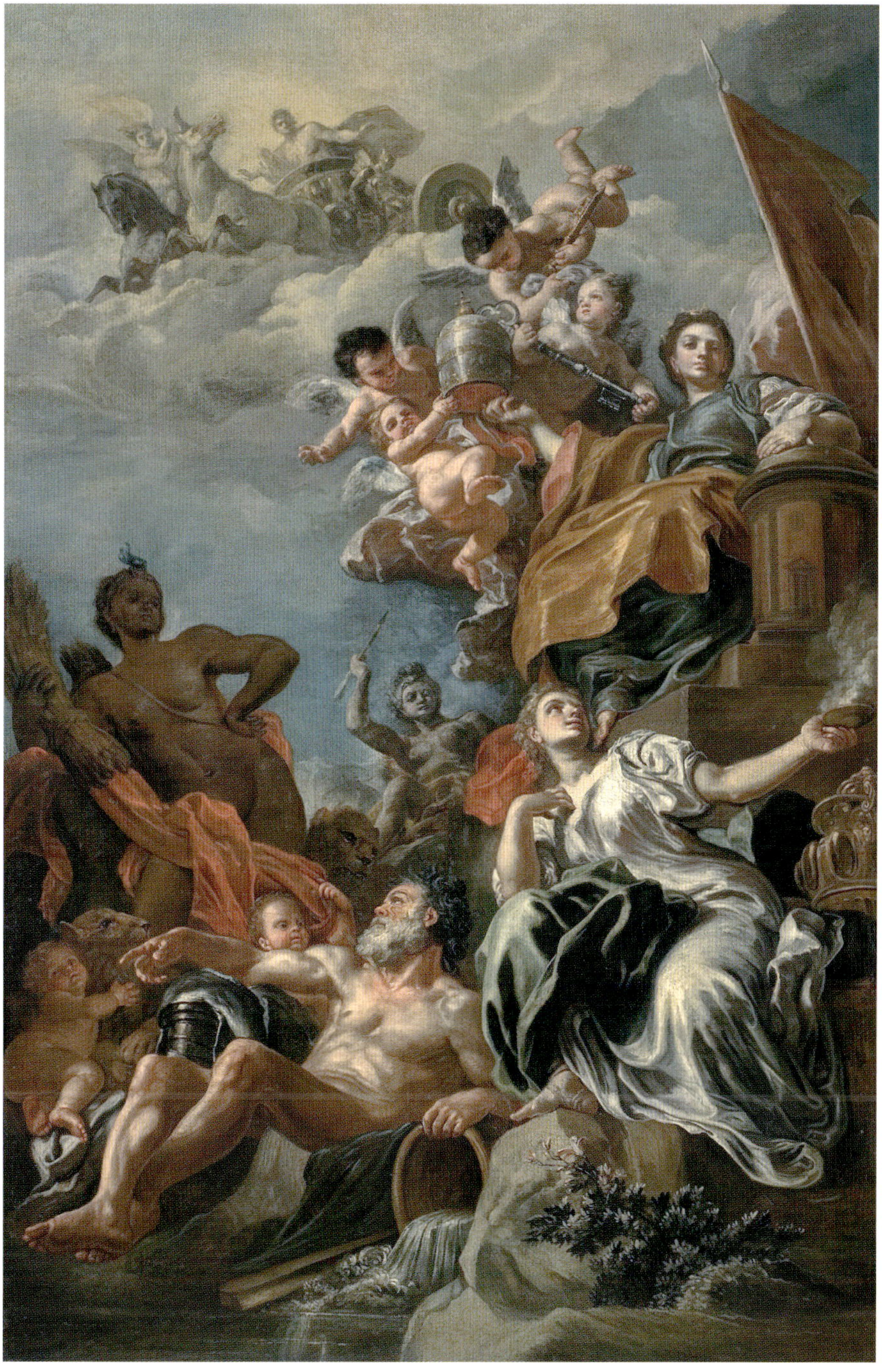

for recognition by the Holy See motivated the Bourbon ruler's choice of Maria Amalia as a bride. Carlo's proposed alliance with Saxony, which would seal a peace with Austria, was well received by Clement. In 1738, he granted papal dispensation for the wedding as well as permission for the newlyweds to cross the papal states. He also finally recognized Carlo, "the first resident monarch following almost two and a half centuries of subalternity to foreign powers," as the rightful ruler of Naples by conferring on him the right of papal investiture on May 10, 1738.[3]

The river god in the Solimena painting, then, likely alludes to that most enduring symbol of papal rule, the *Fountain of the Four Rivers* by Gianlorenzo Bernini; the river god's inclusion serves as a reminder of Carlo's victory in the lengthy dispute with the Holy See. Commissioned by Pope Innocent X in 1648, the Bernini fountain trumpeted the global reach of papal authority, as personified by four male river gods. As Louise Arizzoli has suggested, the river god in Solimena's painting is most likely Tiber, which would guarantee Carlo's role as a Catholic monarch.[4] The grafting of a loaded allegorical reference to papal hegemony onto an established reference for secular authority cleverly celebrates the fledgling Neapolitan monarchy by positioning it, and Carlo as its head, at the center of the world. Expanding on the visual message strategically deployed in the decor of one of the king's most personal rooms, Cooper Hewitt's porcelain set pairing the four rivers gods with the four continents was most likely a royal commission. The implicit reference to Bernini's fountain makes it possible to identify the robustly molded river gods in the porcelain group: Europe's river god is most certainly the Tiber and not the Danube, and America's is the Río de la Plata (the latter corresponding with the personification in Bernini's fountain).

The rigid hierarchy of the continents found on the canvas, which reads as an apotheosis of Europe (with Europe receiving the papal tiara and keys of Saint Peter), also plays out clearly between the porcelain continents. Instead of relying on scale as the ordering principle, the designers of the sculpted ensemble depended mainly on sexuality to reinforce relative position. Europe, fully clothed, is the image of elegance. She is regal, matriarchal, and confident. Next in rank is Asia, elevated on a high pedestal. While she vies with Europe in her graceful poise and composure, her left breast is exposed. Africa, her right breast bare, is depicted as particularly nubile, her natural fruitfulness and fecundity emphasized by the overflowing cornucopia in her right arm. In contrast to Solimena's painting, in which America's humble status is connoted by her small stature and near invisibility, America's low status in the porcelain set is communicated by her availability. Whereas the other figures are richly attired in floor-length gowns and mostly clothed, she is nearly naked. Her place at bottom of the scale is further confirmed by the pose of her attendant river god, the Río de la Plata. His deep slumber, in contrast to the marked alertness of the Tiber at Europe's feet, reinforces her vulnerability. Of the four river gods, he is the only one who is uncrowned.

Solimena's ceiling painting was but one of many visual manifestations of the four continents "staged" to celebrate the strategic union of the House of Bourbon with that of Saxony. The subject was deployed repeatedly in the palace's refurbishment as well as the outdoor displays conceived for the wedding festivities. For the first antechamber (*sala diplomatica*) of the palace's ground floor (*piano nobile*), for which an allegory of the royal couple's virtues were painted on the ceiling by Francesco de Mura, the painter also executed four grisaille ovals representing allegories of the four continents. Carlo even commissioned a replica of De Mura's paintings to send to Madrid as a gift to his mother in September 1738—perhaps a nod to the four silver sculptures of the four continents by Neapolitan sculptor Lorenzo Vaccaro that were sent by Fernando de Benavides, count of Esteban, viceroy of Naples (1687–95), to King Charles II of Spain in 1695. In one of the ephemeral structures built outside for the joyous occasion, four wooden statues of the four parts of the world dressed in waterproof gilded cloth were placed at the four corners. The four continents was an obvious vehicle for Carlo to project power, fame, and supremacy, but it appears to have played an outsized role in his visual messaging and self-fashioning as the king of the Two Sicilies—making it a potent subject for his future artistic commissions.

Other Visual Sources: Antiquities in Eighteenth-Century Naples

As tempting as it may be to propose that Cooper Hewitt's set was commissioned to commemorate the 1738 Bourbon-Saxon alliance, the Capodimonte porcelain factory was not yet established at the time of that event. Based on the figures' poses and current understandings of the factory's history, the set was more likely made for Carlo di Borbone between 1757 and 1759. The gracious stances and anatomical modeling of the figures recall not only highly popular and winsome female figures painted at Pompeii that were closely identified with Carlo's reign but also other famed classical statues located in and outside Naples that were important in forging a Bourbon Neapolitan identity.

Of the many notable cultural achievements associated with Carlo's years in Naples, he is perhaps best known for his guarded ownership of the excavations at Herculaneum and Pompeii, begun respectively in 1738 and 1748. These discoveries, assiduously overseen by the king and his immediate advisers, put Naples on the map in the eighteenth century. Tourists, amateurs, and savants flocked to Naples—then the third-largest city in Europe after London and Paris—in pursuit of tangible evidence of the city's Grecian past, only to find visitation to the recently

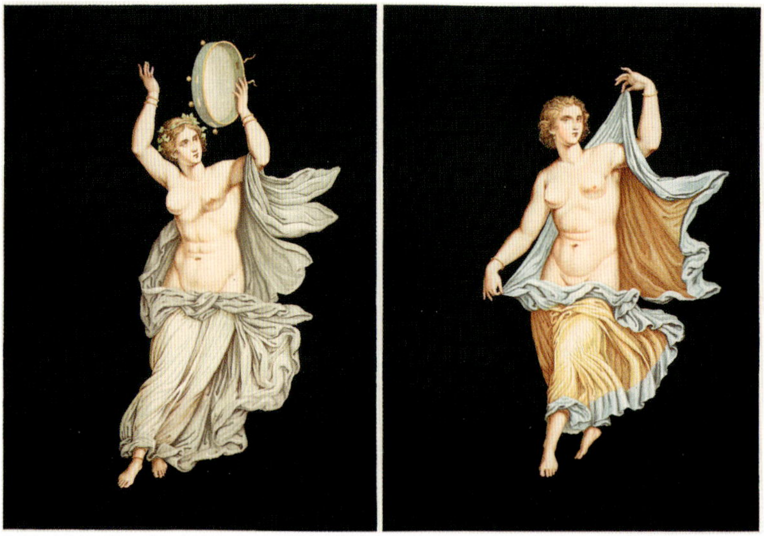

[FIG. 43]
Two dancing Maenads, Villa of Diomedes, Pompeii, Campania, Italy. Chromolithograph by C Weidenmuller from a drawing by Mollame, from *Le case ed i monumenti di Pompei* (*The houses and the monuments of Pompeii*), by Fausto and Felice Niccolini, volume II, plate 5, 1854, Naples.

excavated antiquities highly regulated. When granted access by royal consent, visitors were prohibited from making drawings of the artworks at Pompeii and Herculaneum. Carlo exercised rigorous control over the research, cataloging, and preserving of the finds too, all of which were finely engraved for reproduction in the *Antichità di Ercolano esposte* (1757–92) by the Accademia Ercolanese. The king himself determined who would receive copies of these publications.

The Cooper Hewitt set creatively channels the gaiety and graceful spirit of the *Herculaneum Dancers*, a set of wall painting fragments unearthed in the Villa of Cicero in Pompeii in 1749 [FIG. 43]. These panels, which were included in the first of nine volumes of the *Antichità di Ercolano esposte*, would prove to be transformative for Naples. Though small in scale—each panel was twenty-five centimeters tall on a black background—their discovery turned Herculaneum into a major tourist site in the south of Italy as well as forming a touchstone for a type of formal beauty that European artists were eager to reproduce. As Amelia Rauser has noted, the paintings of the *Herculaneum Dancers* were "copied and reproduced on objects from suites of furniture to porcelain vases to marquetry pianos, and . . . routinely invoked by writers and tourists as the gold standard of 'natural' female grace and beauty, free from fashion or modern artifice."[5]

Indeed, the triumphant arm of Europe in the Cooper Hewitt set directly recalls both the tambourine player in the *Herculaneum Dancers* and the dancer with swirling drapery—the most copied figures of the series. The disposition of Europe's upper limbs directly references the stance of the dancer arranging her fluttery drapery, while her uncrossed legs derive from the tambourine player. Asia's half-turned stance—her torso rotated to her right with her left arm facing the viewer—evokes the cymbals player. The athletic yet elegant bodies of the dancers, with their pronounced abdominal muscles, splayed but firm breasts, and forward tipping of the pelvis, would help explain the limber physiques of the porcelain continents, with their long slender necks. Their suppleness is further accentuated by the ways in which their gowns appear to cling to their bodies in lively folds while revealing the contours of the forms beneath, including erect nipples and perfect belly buttons. Indeed, like the painted and later engraved *Herculaneum Dancers*, the porcelain continents are the image of eighteenth-century Neapolitan feminine perfection.

It is possible that the grouping of the Cooper Hewitt's four continents set was made before the official public "debut" of the *Herculaneum Dancers* in 1757, but an earlier date does not correspond to the trajectory of the Capodimonte factory because of the issues with the paste used in the early years of the factory's production. Comparable monumental pieces, such as the chandelier for the Queen's Green Room (Naples, Museo Nazionale di San Martino), are dated to the mid-1750s. The technical complexity and size of the Cooper Hewitt ensemble, which test the limits of the factory's siliceous paste, argue for a later date.

Beyond the two-dimensional imagery of the *Herculaneum Dancers*, there were three-dimensional sculptural models available in Carlo's Naples that may have informed the poses and postures of the four continents set. The intriguing pose of Asia, with one leg prominently crossed over another, also draws on the local iconography of Naples by aping the stance of Apollo Pothos, a prominent classical sculpture in the Neapolitan urban landscape. Now grouped with the other pieces in the Farnese collection, the Apollo Pothos once stood on the top story of the facade of the customhouse (*Dogana*) in Avellino, the key hub of the city's trade during the eighteenth century. Most notably, the *Dogana* served as the backdrop for a small statue of Charles II, king of Spain from 1665 to 1700, which was set atop a pinnacle in the center of the square. Depicted with flipped yet similarly crossed legs—and few examples of classical statuary feature crossed legs—the figure of Asia deliberately gestures to a significant local marker of Spanish rule of Naples, past and present, that would have had specific resonance for Carlo.

Africa's open deportment also seems to derive from classical models of feminine ideals found further afield in Rome, but still bound up with Naples through the person of Carlo. As sole heir to the Farnese dynasty in Parma through his mother, the last duchess in the line of Parma and Piacenza, Carlo brought with him to Naples an immense artistic and archaeological heritage—although the process of moving the Farnese antiquities was only completed by his son Ferdinand IV starting in 1787. One of the prizes of the Farnese collection was the figure of Flora, whom Africa summons forth with her outstretched right hand. Though only sent to Naples in 1800, the fame of this sculpture was widespread from the 1500s onward. The sixteenth-century Netherlandish artist Maarten van Heemskerck drew the Farnese Flora at least three times during his sojourn in Rome, and it was prodigiously copied in the eighteenth century, often conceived of as a pair to the Farnese Hercules. This evocation of a celebrated statue from the Farnese collection in Rome would only be appropriate for a porcelain group made for the same owner.

Conclusion

The poses of the Cooper Hewitt's four continents ensemble, with their specific nods to classical monuments and wall paintings closely identified with Carlo's efforts to position the Spanish Bourbons as the enlightened and rightful rulers of Naples, lend further evidence to my working hypothesis that the impressive set was made at Capodimonte for the king of the Two Sicilies. Since the royal palace was under constant renovation, the subject of the four continents most likely continued to be relevant to the decor, each time updated slightly to reflect Carlo's latest accomplishments. One can imagine the Cooper Hewitt porcelain continents participating in the pageantry of Bourbon Naples at the same moment that the popularity of Herculaneum, which also served to trumpet the fame of Carlo, took hold of the rest of Europe.

Carlo's motivation for commissioning a set of the four continents in porcelain would be consistent with his deep embrace of the theme to promote his reign along with the medium itself. The desire to insert himself as an heir to the Saxon line was the overriding impetus for his establishing the first porcelain factory in Naples. As the daughter of Augustus the Strong, the founder of the first European factory to manufacture hard-paste porcelain, Maria Amalia's dowry included a significant amount of Saxon porcelain that would have decorated the royal couple's private apartments and elsewhere. Both she and Carlo were apprised of the latest models through the yearly shipments Augustus sent her, explaining in part the outsized influence Saxon models had over Capodimonte's production of both useful wares and sculpted figures.

No doubt Carlo and Maria Amalia were in possession of a Meissen set of four continents, and it is highly likely Carlo would have known about the great "Russian order" of Meissen porcelain of 1745, including its four continents figures. The Cooper Hewitt figures are even taller than the pieces made for Empress Elizabeth of Russia. Even the bright enamel colors, recalling the high-keyed palette of Carlo's favorite court painter, Anton Mengs, gesture toward the Saxon royal court. Trained in

Dresden, Mengs traveled from Rome to Naples in 1759 to paint a portrait of Ferdinand IV. The model of the four grisaille ovals painted by De Mura for the four corners of the *sala diplomatica* opens the intriguing possibility that Cooper Hewitt's four large porcelain figure groups may have occupied four corner niches in one of the rooms of the royal palace. In this context, they would have boldly signaled Carlo's modernity—his embrace of a quintessentially eighteenth-century model of artistry, the porcelain figurine—while also embodying his illustrious inheritances from the Farnese line, Spanish Bourbon dynasty, and House of Saxony that served to elevate Naples during his reign, thereby reaffirming the international prestige of Naples under Bourbon rule.

Too often eighteenth-century porcelain figurines such as these are not taken seriously in the field of art history. Frequently made in multiples and thus perceived as nonunique, they are easily written off as not worthy of sustained inquiry and analysis (as compared to paintings and sculpture). I hope to have demonstrated the value of these artworks, as well as the merit of marrying the tools of technical art history with those of traditional art history in this case study. The Cooper Hewitt set also posed another interesting problem insofar as the technical analysis of the set's material composition was surprisingly not definitive in shedding light on its history and geographic origins. I ultimately had to rely on the additional evidence of traditional art historical methods of visual and stylistic analysis to reveal the sociopolitical circumstances in which it most likely originated. This is rarely the case as technical analysis often helps to confirm when and how something was made, indicating that the field of ceramics is ripe for further investigation that takes into account equally an object's materiality, form, and design elements.

Remaking Porcelain: A Conservator's Perspective

Soon Kai Poh

As the other contributors to this volume attest, the grand narrative of ceramic never ceases to be retold, weaving together material, history, and technology, as they manifest in relationships and networks bridging peoples and cultures across time and in different places. Porcelain's physical presence in the world in the form of different objects that are exchanged as commodities, used in the household, displayed in institutional and private collections, or rediscovered on archaeological excavations and early shipwrecks, extends an invitation for people to connect with this material. The persistence of these narratives and the continued fascination with porcelain objects through time is certainly tied to their material qualities, not least that they have been preserved through the actions of menders and restorers. At times, the history of these actions are recorded and traceable through collection inventories or other forms of documentation, but this may not always be the case; such records themselves may not have survived to the present. For conservators, all of these trajectories coalesce in the quiet, unassuming forms of their charges, silently bearing the marks of their past. Ultimately, the physical reality of a ceramic item remains its own record and an outsized source of information that guides its future preservation.

A decagonal porcelain bowl with polychrome overglaze enamel decoration in the collection of the Cooper Hewitt, Smithsonian Design Museum, is an early example of porcelain produced by the Meissen Porcelain Manufactory (then the Royal Polish and Electoral Saxon Porcelain Manufactory) [FIG. 44]. Such porcelains were the product of technological discovery driven by royal and aristocratic desire in the seventeenth century, and precipitated by the luxury trade in Chinese and Japanese porcelains from Asia to Europe. The inscription on the underside of the bowl attributes it to the inventory committed to the unrealized Japanese Palace of Augustus the Strong, underscoring its place amid political maneuvers and imperial ambitions that sought to place East Asian and Meissen porcelain in direct competition, particularly highlighting the latter's superiority. Describing its present physical condition, I wrote the following report,

> The porcelain bowl is broken into eighteen fragments, and previously joined with an adhesive. The break pattern together with the predominance of fragments on one side of the bowl suggests that it may have broken on impact there. There are two areas of loss approximately 1 cm^2 as well as other smaller chip losses to the bowl that are now filled with a restoration material.
>
> An off-white overpaint covers the joins and the surfaces of the restoration material. In some areas of decoration, paint is present over both restoration material and the glazed ceramic surface, presumably once color-matched with the surrounding decoration.[1]

This clinical assessment represents only the beginning of a series of interpretative operations that I undertook in the conservation of this bowl. In this chapter, I trace the steps that I took to know and understand the Meissen porcelain bowl in order to conserve it through its remaking.

Knowing

My examination of the bowl in the conservation laboratory to learn more about it in the present is a reminder that it, too, is a form of material evidence of not only political circumstances but equally the historical and environmental contexts surrounding its making. Porcelains, like all ceramic items, are the embodiment of material transformation. In simple terms, they are made from clay dug from the earth, formed with water, and fired into being, traditionally using wood as fuel. This narrative of elemental material transformation is not coincidental; the discovery of porcelain manufacture at the Meissen Porcelain Manufactory is attributed in part to the work of an alchemist, Johann Friedrich Böttger, who was at the time interested in finding a substance that would turn base metals into gold. His interests and aptitude toward discovering such processes of transformation would inadvertently lead to his role in producing what is commonly acknowledged as one of the earliest instances of hard-paste or "true" porcelain in Europe at the time. Examining this bowl, I am reminded that I hold in my hands a memorial to this pivotal moment in the history of ceramic technology.

While the compositions of porcelain may change over time and no two porcelain items—even by the same maker—are truly identical in their makeup, at its core porcelain has a remarkably straightforward recipe. Porcelain is composed of a well-sorted (containing particles that are largely uniform in size), white kaolin-containing clay with the addition of

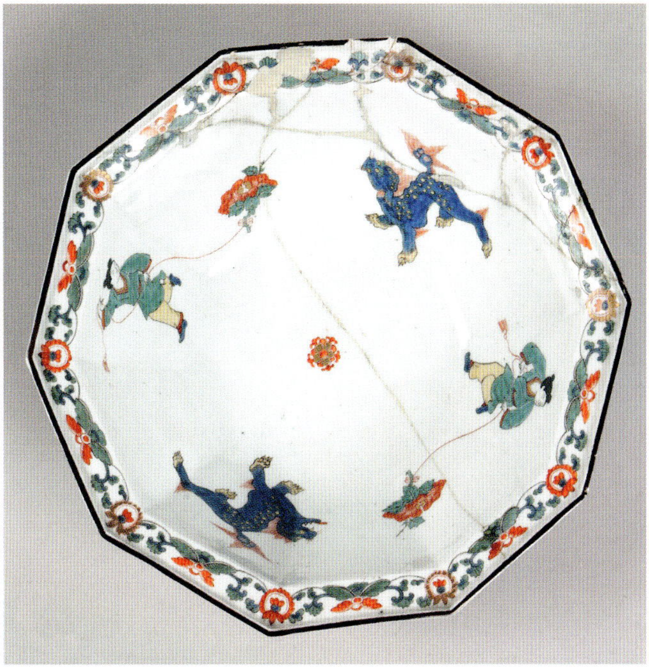

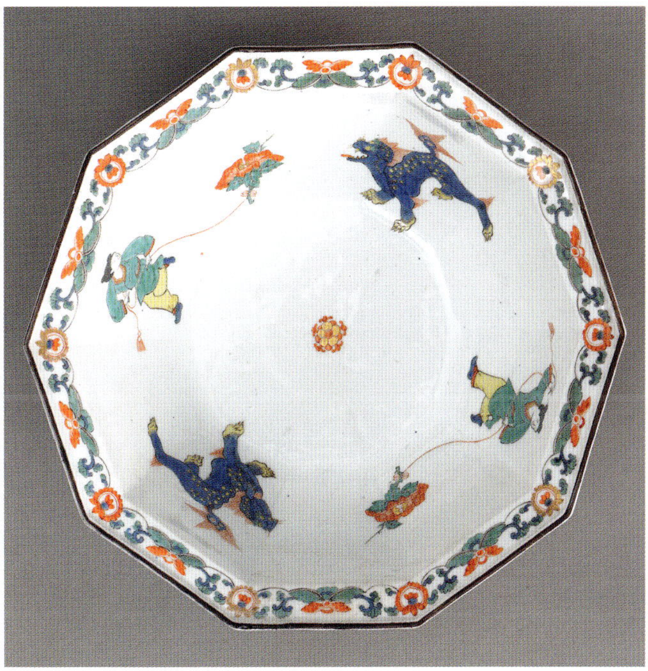

[FIG. 44]
A Meissen porcelain bowl before and after its 2019 conservation treatment. After treatment image by Matt Flynn. Decagonal slop bowl from the Royal Collections of Saxony, Japanese Palace, Dresden bowl. Manufactured by Meissen Porcelain Manufactory (Germany), ca. 1729–31. Hard-paste porcelain, vitreous enamel. 10.1 × 24.1 cm. Gift of Eleanor and Sarah Hewitt, Cooper Hewitt, Smithsonian Design Museum, 1923-22-55.

white quartz and feldspar-containing stone that serves as a flux. In China, this stone is the aptly named porcelain stone (瓷石, otherwise known as petuntse or 白墩子), a white stone sourced in the area of Jingdezhen, which is conventionally associated with the historical production of Chinese imperial porcelain. In the case of Meissen porcelain, a locally available stone with the addition of alabaster served a similar purpose. When finely ground and mixed, the clay and stone produce a clay body that is smooth to the touch and may be made incredibly thin, to the point of translucency. The firing of this same mixture requires relatively high kiln temperatures of twelve to fourteen hundred degrees Celsius, at which point the porcelain matures and vitrifies. Mullite crystals are formed from the kaolin-rich clay, embedded within a matrix of undissolved quartz and silica-rich liquid, that on cooling produce a fine, glassy, and nonporous microstructure. One may readily observe this when examining any fragment of porcelain: the break edges tend to be smooth, and any granular structure of the fired porcelain is not immediately discernible to the naked eye.

Within every fired ceramic item also lies the memorialization of its historical physical environment. The chemical composition of any clay body may be traced to the geological and hence geographic origin of its constituent materials. Impurities introduced during the processes of refining raw ingredients in the recipe, or even from the water used in making and forming items, may remain in the ceramic fabric. Depending on the elemental composition of the impurity, they may persist after firing and remain useful elemental markers for cultural heritage scientists today. Take, for example, this Meissen porcelain bowl. Nondestructive spot elemental analysis of the unglazed bottom of the foot ring shows a relatively elevated level of rubidium. This is a feature characteristic of Meissen wares from the years 1725–30, coincident with the items produced for the Japanese Palace. One might well imagine that the presence of this marker is due to the use of particular recipes and/or material sources during this period. Indeed, the higher levels of rubidium observed in this bowl in fact correlate to the Meissen manufactory's switch to a potassium feldspar-containing stone at this time, closer to that used in Chinese porcelain.

Furthermore, methods to ascertain the age of ceramics such as thermoluminescence dating rely on the fundamental idea that the occasion of their firing releases the accumulated radiation trapped within the crystalline structure of their component materials. Measuring the signal produced by the accumulated radiation since the item's making allows for the approximation of the time elapsed since its last firing. Time itself, and not just historical or environmental context, is captured within the ceramic material.

Understanding

All forms of conservation are a series of cumulative interventions on what may appear as a static object but that is nonetheless continually remade. The puzzle that faces the conservator seems deceptively simple in the case of a broken porcelain object such as this bowl: to take it apart (if it was previously restored) and put it back together. In her contribution to this volume, Vicki Parry discusses several examples of repairs performed on ceramic objects (including porcelain) that respond to this prompt: the Japanese practice of *kintsugi*, fired restorations, and the use of metal rivets and staples. As she describes, some of these repairs are valued today and are in fact preserved. In other instances, they may not be easily reversed (and hence will be left alone) or may leave traces that are difficult or impossible to completely remove, such as stains and residues from adhesive materials or the holes left behind from riveting or stapling. As I will show, attempting to undo prior restorations on porcelain is essential to the successful restoration of any porcelain piece because of the manner in which it breaks and the narrow scope one has to ensure that the constituent fragments fit together tightly. But undoing prior restoration is a consequential action that involves an erasure of the object's past. In modern practice, conservators come to terms with this erasure by recording the states of the objects through photographic and textual documentation. As long as these records remain external to the object itself, however, they are liable to be lost or disassociated, as is the case with many objects that lack documentary records of their past restoration history. In turn, their state of survival becomes their own best source of evidence.

The Meissen porcelain bowl was on at least one occasion joined back together from its broken fragments by an unknown individual(s); they additionally filled its missing areas and disguised them to match the remainder of the bowl. In fact, it was the discoloration of the overpaint applied to disguise these areas and the yellowing of the adhesive used to join the bowl that prompted its most recent campaign of conservation. These concerns are not solely aesthetic in nature; color changes in adhesives that were once clear are a result of changes to the chemical structure of the adhesive itself and may be a sign that the adhesive has begun to fail. Therefore, these disfiguring past interventions were failing in the objectives of both aesthetic appearance and structural compensation. The joins were additionally misaligned in places. Following discussions with the curator, we decided that these additions were not historically significant and hence not worth preserving in light of the possibility to address some of the structural and visual issues the present state of the bowl presented. And so I began to disassemble the bowl as a first step in remaking it.

Conservation is by nature an interpretative exercise that operates on multiple levels and builds on itself recursively; one might express this as a hermeneutic circle or spiral in time. Disassembling the bowl involved the use of chemical solvents known to dissolve or soften the adhesives or paint used; I selected these by iterative trial and error from a series of solvents specifically tested to be inert to such an object. The disfiguring overpaint was removed, and several joins and fills near the rim were undone with acetone. A closer examination under ultraviolet light of the residues left on the edges of fragments in these locations and in the fill material revealed a characteristic bright-orange fluorescence generally indicative of shellac. It is likely it was used both as an adhesive on its own and binder for the fill. More surprisingly, the remainder of the bowl did not respond to acetone, suggesting that this corner of the rim possibly constituted a more recent restoration than the other joins. Subsequent failed attempts at undoing these joins led me to suspect that the unknown adhesive could be animal glue, which softens with heat and moisture. After placing cotton poultices saturated with warm water over the joins, I applied gradual pressure to release the joins, which then finally came apart. I then reduced the adhesive residues and removed them to the greatest extent possible in preparation for the bowl's remaking.

This dry description of the conservation process fails to illustrate that however well intentioned, the disassembly of a previously mended item can be terrifying to attempt. It is an act of faith that the now-separated fragments can and will come together in a more satisfactory fashion than before, a judgment made on the basis of one's knowledge of and familiarity with the material as well as one's understanding of the particular item.

Remaking

The reality of conserving porcelain objects is to some degree commensurate with the level of refinement associated with their making. As previewed earlier, the challenge in so doing is prompted by the unique material affordances of porcelain. Since porcelain tends to break smoothly, much like glass, freshly broken fragments fit together with minimal room for error. This has direct implications for the suitability of different methods to join them.

Historically, menders have at times turned to using metal rivets or staples to hold fragments closely together, doing so at a distance, perpendicular to the break. Adhesives allow fragments to be joined without any further mechanical intrusion such as the drilling of holes necessary for stapling. Their material and working properties are crucial, especially since the bond line they form must be optimized for thinness without sacrificing strength, so that the tight fit between fragments is minimally affected. This is further amplified by the ever-present need to compensate for any spring that has resulted from breakage. Ceramics are held together by compressive forces on firing, and do not fit together unless that force can be approximated and sustained by the adhesive. The strength of any adhesive join is greatly improved when mechanical "keying" occurs; that is, when the microscopic surface roughness of a material aids the spatial registration of two fragments. For porcelain, the generally smooth break surfaces mean that there is a greater reliance on the strength of bonds between the adhesive and the bonding surface, or the constitutive strength of the adhesive itself, with the success of this join being primarily limited by the weaker of the two. Over time, adhesives have been developed to meet these requirements; the examples of animal glue and shellac found on the Meissen porcelain bowl are two of many types of adhesive encountered in old mends to porcelain objects. In some ways, the remaking that I undertook is no different from that which was previously performed on the bowl, albeit with materials that may have been developed since.

To remake the porcelain bowl, I used an epoxy resin that has excellent aging properties, Hxtal NYL-1. This resin has been formulated to retain its strength and will not discolor over time. Not by coincidence, this same resin was used in the well-publicized 1989 restoration of the Portland Vase at the British Museum, although the conservators, Nigel Williams and Sandra Smith, manipulated it differently then. Today, it remains in active use for the conservation of glass, in part owing to its refractive index that bears remarkable similarity to typical soda lime glasses. This means that light passes through the fully cured resin and these glasses at a similar speed, thereby rendering the boundaries between them less distinct to the eye and for the most part visually imperceptible. (A crack in glass, for example, is usually discernible because light passes through air in the crack at a different speed than the surrounding glass.) When one considers porcelain's vitreous characteristics, the success of this resin in the restoration of porcelain is unsurprising.

The working properties of Hxtal NYL-1 influence how it can be applied to the bowl. Hxtal NYL-1 can take up to a week to cure fully, and when freshly prepared, the resin has a low viscosity and flows easily. This allows for its introduction by capillary action into the tight joins between the porcelain fragments, which would form the thinnest continuous adhesive bond line possible. For this same reason, though, it inadvertently lubricates the join, and since it is not immediately tacky, the fragments have to be supported and held in place under tension while the resin cures, and ideally the entire item would be reconstructed in one go to minimize any dislocations.

Hence I fabricated a temporary armature to hold the bowl under tension while the resin cured; this involved metal staples secured by a solvent-removable adhesive applied to the surfaces of the fragments. This adhesive is removed after the joining is completed. The armature resembled the metal stapling employed by menders of the past, albeit now introduced as ephemeral tools, momentarily holding the bowl together in order to allow for the epoxy resin to be added to the joins. The resonances here between the mending techniques of the past and present remaking of the bowl are not merely coincidental or poetic; restorative actions to some degree reflect the different ways people have responded to the same affordances of the material over time, and recur as echoes of one another in material or application. Now, as the resin wicks in between the fragments, the join appears to dissolve away, its close refractive index rendering these joins practically indiscernible. Gradually, the Meissen bowl re-presents itself.

The filling of losses in porcelain follows this same theme. The translucent quality of porcelain poses a challenge to any attempt at producing a convincing substitute. The success of any fill for porcelain hinges on its color, texture, gloss, and translucency, among other material attributes. Today, a mixture of Hxtal NYL-1 resin and fumed silica added as a bulking agent and opacifier is a remarkably compelling solution. Fumed silica is chemically similar to quartz, the glass-forming component in porcelain, although in this form it exists as an amorphous instead of a crystalline substance. The resin and fumed quartz mixture is malleable like a soft putty, and can be colored with dry mineral pigments. By imitating the glassy attributes of porcelain using the same resin to join the bowl, and modifying its translucency, opacity, and color with these additions, one may have significant control over the credibility of the cured result.

In practice, I create a palette of these resin mixtures comprising the translucent base and a variety of colored mixtures. Slight adjustments to each application of the fill onto the porcelain bowl can be made to account for subtle variations. For example, owing to the presence of natural impurities from its material sources or processes of manufacture, porcelain is never truly white; this fine control of color is, on some level, an intuitive response to the localized nuances of the material. Using a silicone rubber mold of the underside of the bowl held in place with rare earth magnets, I gradually add this mixture to the area of loss, making adjustments where necessary to account for gloss and translucency, as on its topmost surfaces where a clear glaze is present [FIG. 44].

As with joining, time is a critical factor. The resin mixture resembles a soft paste when freshly prepared and similarly takes up to a week to fully cure. This mixture is intentionally left to cure partially in order to achieve a workable consistency and stored in a freezer when not in use to slow down the curing process. The remaking of the porcelain bowl involves the material manipulation of not just porcelain but also the materials of conservation themselves in time, on different timescales. When complete, the conserved Meissen porcelain bowl is yet again encountered largely absent of the echoes of restorers, restoration materials, and mending techniques of the past; it has been remade in the present.

Conserving

In the "Preface to the Third Edition: Acknowledgments" (2014–19) of his monumental series *Scratching on Things I Could Disavow*, artist Walid Raad describes a curious fictional incident where the "faces" of objects bound for the Louvre Abu Dhabi's 2017 opening were swapped with one another and lacked shadows on their arrival in the new museum. Raad astutely observes that the work of the "museum's conservator . . . to paint fake shadows next to each object . . . somehow brought forth the real ones. [But as] for the swapping of the objects' faces, it remains unsolved." Portraying these "fake shadows" as "prosthetic shadows," Raad displays them alongside these objects and their real shadows.

Raad's work is a particularly insightful depiction of what conservation typically entails: starting from a place of acceptance and respect for an item's past in that it is unalterable (the swapping of the objects' faces), conservators act to ensure that its existence may persist (by painting in fake shadows) and be recognized again by others (thus bringing forth real shadows). Various methods of mending ceramics mentioned in this chapter are evidence of these efforts, including those that I encountered in the Meissen porcelain bowl. The method of conserving the Meissen porcelain bowl described in this chapter, however, challenges Raad's metaphoric explanation of conservation. To remake the bowl, Hxtal NYL-1 was used for its optical properties, precisely to minimize the appearance of the "fake" and "prosthetic" shadows. The prostheses of the past—metal staples—were used in a transient manner and later removed. Might this be an instance where the curious incident of the "swapped faces" is resolved, or in other words, where the true item emerges, complete with its own real shadows? And so is it not more accurate to describe the conservation of the Meissen porcelain bowl in terms of its remaking? Furthermore, the process of its remaking, as outlined in this chapter, is reminiscent of Böttger's own experiments in the early eighteenth century to achieve a convincing imitation of Asian porcelain in Europe that eventually led to the creation of this bowl. In the continuous innovation of conservation materials and techniques, perhaps today's conservators find themselves in the company of makers and alchemists.

In this chapter, I dwelled on a particularly transformative moment in the trajectory of the Meissen porcelain bowl: its conservation. One commonly thinks of conserving porcelain as an act of recuperation and less so as a performative *remaking*, a term I have used extensively in this chapter and one that is borrowed from the vocabulary used by Williams and Smith when describing the conservation of the Portland Vase three decades ago. Although I have focused largely on the material qualities of porcelain and the affordances that conservators such as myself respond to, what becomes apparent in remaking such a bowl is that the cumulative record of the object lies not just in its material but also in the human effort that enables it to persist into the future even if this may not be immediately apparent when encountering the remade bowl. The hands and minds of others who have acted in the past—makers, menders, restorers, and conservators—are a reminder that I do not conserve alone. Crucially, the conservation of this bowl was completed by Sarah Barack owing to the circumstances of the COVID-19 pandemic. The knowledge and understanding of the materials, conservation methods, and techniques that I have described were transmitted to me through mentors and colleagues who have developed ways of working with porcelain over the course of their careers. The remade Meissen porcelain bowl is by extension an accumulation of their experiences too. In closing, I suggest that porcelain offers a unique proposition to the conservator—one that emerges from knowing and understanding its material affordances. We might consider these qualities of porcelain, the same ones that have assured our endless fascination with it, as those that extend a perpetual invitation to remake by conserving. The story of the Meissen porcelain bowl does not end here with its conservation; it begins anew.

Acknowledgments

I am deeply grateful to Vicki Parry and Ittai Weinryb for the generous invitation to contribute to this volume. The conservation of the Meissen porcelain bowl was overseen by Sarah Barack, to whom I owe the knowledge of working with Hxtal NYL-1 in this manner. I am additionally indebted to the guidance of mentors and colleagues who have informed my perspectives on working with porcelain as a maker and as a conservator: Kelly Connole, Lisa Bruno, Ellen Chase, Tina March, Chantal Stein, Donna Strahan, and Jessica Walthew.

Notes

Ceramics: The Art of Being Human

1. Letter from Gertrude Bell to her parents, dated December 21, 1917, Gertrude Bell Archive, University of Newcastle, http://gertrudebell.ncl.ac.uk/letter_details.php?letter_id=275.
2. Nigel Barley, *Smashing Pots: Feats of Clay from Africa* (London: British Museum Press, 1994), 140.
3. Bárbaro Martínez-Ruiz, "Funerary Pots of the Kongo in Central Africa," in *African Terra Cottas: A Millenary Heritage in the Barbier-Mueller Museum Collections*, eds. Floriane Morin and Boris Wastiau (Geneva: Barbier-Mueller Museum, 2008), 296.

Crazing, Shivering, Golden Cracks and Rivets

1. For general information and additional sources, please visit the American Ceramic Society, ceramics.org.

Animating the World

1. Jean Stillemans, *Las dimensiones del vacío. Vasijas y arquitecturas prehispánicas del Perú* (manuscript, n.d.).

Cycladic Bird Jug

1. Marina Panagiotaki, *The Central Palace Sanctuary at Knossos* (London: British School of Athens, 1999).

A Porcelain Set of Four Continents Fit for the King

1. Benjamin Schmidt, "The Rearing Horse and the Kneeling Camel: Continental Ceramics and Europe's Race to Modernity," in *Bodies and Maps: Early Modern Personifications of the Continents*, eds. Maryanne Cline Horowitz and Louise Arizzoli (Leiden: Brill Press, 2021), 316.
2. Thomas Lam, "Cross-sectional Electron Dispersive Spectroscopy Analyses of Capodimonte Porcelain," SEM Open Lab Report MCI#6575.13, internal use only.
3. Giovanni Salmeri, "Commentaries: II. The Italian and European Context of Neapolitan Eighteenth-Century Antiquarianism," *Journal of the History of Collections* 19 (2007): 263–67.
4. Louise Arizzoli, "The Golden Age of Allegories of the Four Continents: Francesco Solimena and the Wedding Celebrations of the King of Naples (1738)," *Italian Quarterly* 56 (2020).
5. Amelia Rauser, "Living Statues and Neoclassical Dress in Late Eighteenth-Century Naples," *Art History* 38 (June 2015): 462–87.

Remaking Porcelain: A Conservator's Perspective

1. Treatment report for decagonal slop bowl (unpublished manuscript, 1923-22-55, Cooper Hewitt, Smithsonian Design Museum).

Further Reading

"About the Museum." Smithsonian National Museum of the American Indian, 2021. https://americanindian.si.edu/about.

Adamson, Glenn. *Thinking through Craft.* Oxford: Berg, 2007.

Albert, Kasi. "Ceramic Rivet Repair: History, Technology, and Conservation Approaches." *Studies in Conservation* 57, supp. 1 (2012): S1–S8.

Andres-Acevedo, Sarah-Katherina (ed.). *The Prince Amyn Aga Khan Collection of Early Meissen Porcelain.* Munich: Röbbig, 2017.

Arizzoli, Louise. "James Hazen Hyde and the Allegory of the Four Continents: A Research Collection for an *Amateur* Art Historian." *Journal of the History of Collections* 25 (2013): 277–86.

———. "The Golden Age of Allegories of the Four Continents: Francesco Solimena and the Wedding Celebrations of the King of Naples (1738)." *Italian Quarterly* 56 (2020): 24–53.

———. "Collecting the Four Continents: James Hazen Hyde (1876–1959), an American in Paris." In *Bodies and Maps: Early Modern Personifications of the Continents,* edited by Maryanne Cline Horowitz and Louise Arizzoli, 343–75. Leiden: Brill, 2021.

———. "Dealing with Allegories of the Four Parts of the World. James Hazen Hyde (1876–1959) and His Network." In *Art Markets, Agents and Collectors: Collecting Strategies in Europe and the United States, 1550–1950,* edited by Adriana Turpin and Susan Bracken, 294–305. London: Bloomsbury, 2021.

Backlin, Hedy. "The Four Continents: An Allegory for Artists." In *The Four Continents from the Collection of James Hazen Hyde.* New York: Cooper Union, 1961.

Bailey, Douglass W. *Prehistoric Figurines: Representation and Corporeality in the Neolithic.* London: Routledge, 2005.

Baldwin, Cinda K. *Great and Noble Jar: Traditional Stoneware of South Carolina.* Athens: University of Georgia Press, 1993.

Barakat, Heba Nayel, and Zahra Khademi. *Qajar Ceramics: Bridging Tradition and Modernity.* Kuala Lumpur: Islamic Arts Museum Malaysia, 2019.

Barley, Nigel. *Smashing Pots: Feats of Clay from Africa.* London: British Museum Press, 1994.

Burger, Richard. "¿Reyes o Curacas? Las particularidades del ejercicio del poder en los Andes prehispánicos." In *Señores de los Reinos de la Luna.* Lima: Colección Arte y Tesoros del Perú, Banco de Crédito del Perú, 2008.

Caiger-Smith, Alan. *Lustre Pottery: Technique, Tradition and Innovation in Islam and the Western World.* London: Faber and Faber, 1985.

Cardew, Michael. *Pioneer Pottery.* New York: St. Martin's Press, 1971.

Carpio, Kelly. "El fruto decorado. Mates burilados del Valle del Mantaro, una aproximación a su origen." In *El Fruto Decorado. Mates burilados del Valle del Mantaro (siglos XVIII–XX).* Lima: Instituto Cultural Peruano Norteamericano, 2006.

Carswell, John. *Blue and White: Chinese Porcelain around the World.* London: British Museum Publications, 2000.

Carter, C. Barry, and M. Grant Norton. *Ceramic Materials: Science and Engineering.* New York: Springer Science+Business Media, 2013.

Cartwright, Mark. "Ancient Japanese and Chinese Relations." In *World History Encyclopedia,* June 27, 2017. https://www.worldhistory.org/article/1085/ancient-japanese--chinese-relations.

Cassidy-Geiger, Maureen. "Appendix: Archival Specifications for Gifts to and from the Saxon-Polish Court." In *Fragile Diplomacy: Meissen Porcelain for European Courts, c. 1710–63*, edited by Maureen Cassidy-Geiger. New Haven: Yale University Press, 2007.

"Ceramics in Mainland Southeast Asia." Freer Gallery of Art and Arthur M. Sackler Gallery, 2020. https://archive.asia.si.edu/publications/seaceramics/default.php.

Chaney, Michael A., ed. *Where Is All My Relations? The Poetics of Dave the Potter*. New York: Oxford University Press, 2018.

Chilton, Meredith. "The Spaghetti Eaters." *Metropolitan Museum Journal* 37 (2002): 223–29.

Christakis, Kostis S. "A Wine Offering to the Central Palace Sanctuary at Knossos: The Evidence from KN Zb 27." In *Cretan Offerings: Studies in Honour of Peter Warren*, edited by Olga Krzyszkowska, 49–56. London: British School at Athens Studies, 2010.

Ciarlo, Roberto, ed. *The Eternal Army: The Terracotta Soldiers of the First Emperor*. Vercelli, Italy: White Star Publishers, 2012.

Clark, Garth. *Garth Clark on Ceramic Art*. New York: Distributed Art Publications, 2003.

Clarkson, Thomas. *The History of the Rise, Progress, and Accomplishment of the Abolition of the African Slave-Trade by the British Parliament*. Cambridge: Cambridge University Press, 1808.

Clydesdale, Heather Colburn. "The Vibrant Role of *Mingqi* in Early Chinese Burials." Met, April 2009. https://www.metmuseum.org/toah/hd/mgqi/hd_mgqi.htm.

"Code of Ethics and Guidelines for Practice." American Institute for Conservation, 1994. https://www.culturalheritage.org/about-conservation/code-of-ethics.

"Conservation." Smithsonian National Museum of the American Indian, n.d. https://americanindian.si.edu/explore/collections/conservation.

Cook, Jill, ed. *Ice Age Art: Arrival of the Modern Mind*. London: British Museum Press, 2013.

Cooper Union Museum for the Arts of Decoration. *The Four Continents from the Collection of James Hazen Hyde*. New York: Cooper Union, 1961.

Cummins, Thomas. "Let Me See! Reading Is for Them: Colonial Andean Images and Objects 'como es costumbre tener los caciques Señores.'" In *Native Traditions in the Postconquest World*, edited by Elizabeth Hill Boone and Tom Cummins, 91–148. Washington, DC: Dumbarton Oaks Research Library and Collection, 1998.

Curtis, Julia B. *Trade Taste and Transformation: Jingdezhen Porcelain for Japan, 1620–1645*. New York: China Institute, 2006.

Day, Jane Stevenson, Kristi Butterwick, and Robert B. Pickering. "Archaeological Interpretations of West Mexican Ceramic Art from the Late Preclassic Period: Three Figurine Projects." *Ancient Mesoamerica* 7, no. 1 (Spring 1996): 149–61.

de Aza, Antonio, Angeles De la Torre, Miguel Aranda, et al. "Rietveld Quantitative Analysis of Buen Retiro Porcelains." *Journal of the American Ceramic Society* 87 (March 2004): 449–54.

de Bary, Wm. Theodore, Donald Keene, and Ryusaku Tsunoda. *Sources of Japanese Tradition, 1600 to 2000*. 2nd ed. New York: Columbia University Press, 2001.

de Waal, Edmund. *20th Century Ceramics*. New York: Thames and Hudson, 2003.

Dodds, Jerrilyn, ed. *Al-Andalus: The Art of Islamic Spain*. New York: Metropolitan Museum of Art, 1992.

Dodero, Eloisa. *Ancient Marbles in Naples in the Eighteenth Century: Findings, Collections, Dispersals*. Leiden: Brill Press, 2019.

Donnan, Christopher B. *Ceramics of Ancient Peru*. Los Angeles: Fowler Museum at UCLA, 1992.

Eliade, Mircea. *Symbolism, the Sacred, and the Arts*. Edited by Diane Apostolos-Cappadona. New York: Continuum, 1985.

Fabbri, Bruno, Sabrina Gualtieri and Francesca Amato. "Capodimonte

Porcelain: A Unique Manufacture." In *Craft and Science: International Perspectives on Archaeological Ceramics*, edited by M. Martinón-Torres, 117–24 (UCL Qatar Series in Archaeology and Cultural Heritage). Doha: Bloomsburg Qatar Foundation, 2014.

Ferguson, Patricia, ed. *Pots, Prints and Politics: Ceramics with an Agenda, from the 14th to the 20th Century*. London: British Museum Press, 2021.

Fittipaldi, Artura. "Museums, Safeguarding and Artistic Heritage in Naples in the Eighteenth Century: Some Reflections." *Journal of the History of Collections* 19 (2007): 191–202.

Gaimster, David R. M., and R. J. C. Hildyard. *German Stoneware, 1200–1900: Archaeology and Cultural History: Containing a Guide to the Collections of the British Museum, Victoria and Albert Museum, and Museum of London*. London: British Museum Publications, 1997.

Galanakis, Yannis, ed. *The Aegean World: A Guide to the Cycladic, Minoan, and Mycenaean Antiquities in the Ashmolean Museum*. Oxford: Ashmolean Museum, 2013.

Garachon, Isabelle. "From Mender to Restorer: Some Aspects of the History of Ceramic Repair." In *Glass and Ceramics Conservation, 2010: Interim Meeting of the ICOM-CC Working Group*, edited by Hannelore Römich, 22–31. Corning, NY: ICOM Committee for Conservation, 2010.

———. "Fired Infills and Replacement Parts to Ceramics in the Rijksmuseum." *Rijksmuseum Bulletin* 65, no. 4 (2017): 372–85.

Gerritson, Anne. *The City of Blue and White: Chinese Porcelain and the Early Modern World*. Cambridge: Cambridge University Press, 2020.

The Golden Age of Naples: Arts and Civilization Under the Bourbons. 2 vols. Detroit: Detroit Institute of Arts, 1981.

Golte, Jürgen. Formas básicas y formas combinadas en la cerámica mochica. *Túpac Yawri: Revista andina de estudios tradicionales* 2. Centro Andino de Estudios Tradicionales, Atoq Editores, Cuzco, 2011.

———. *Moche, cosmología y sociedad: una interpretación iconográfica*. Cuzco, Peru: Instituto de Estudios Andinos, 2009.

Gombrich, Ernst. *The Story of Art*. London: Phaidon, 1995.

Graves, Margaret S. *Arts of Allusion: Object, Ornament, and Architecture in Medieval Islam*. New York: Oxford University Press, 2018.

Greenhalgh, Paul. *Ceramic, Art and Civilisation*. London: Bloomsbury, 2020.

Hanson, Tony. *DigitalFire* (blog), n.d. https://digitalfire.com/.

Harrod, Tanya. *The Crafts in Britain in the 20th Century*. New Haven, CT: Yale University Press, 1999.

———. *The Last Sane Man: Michael Cardew: Modern Pots, Colonialism, and the Counterculture*. New Haven, CT: Yale University Press, 2013.

Hemingway, Séan. "Art of the Aegean Bronze Age." *Metropolitan Museum of Art Bulletin* 69, no. 4 (2012): 4–48.

Hur, Nam-lin. "Korean Tea Bowls (*Kōrai chawan*) and Japanese *Wabi-cha*: A Story of Acculturation in Premodern Northeast Asia." *Korean Studies* 39, no. 1 (2015): 1–22.

Jackson, Margaret. *Moche Art and Visual Culture in Ancient Peru*. Albuquerque: University of New Mexico Press, 2008.

Jesse, Friederike. "Early Pottery in Northern Africa—An Overview." *Journal of African Archaeology* 8, no. 2 (2010): 219–38.

Kana'an, Ruba. "The Carved-Stucco Mihrabs of Oman: Form, Style, and Influences." In *Islamic Art in Oman*, edited by Heinz Gaube, Lorenz Korn, Abdulrahman al-Salimi, Faysal al-Hafiyan, Ruba Kana'an, Seth M.N. Priestman, Birgit Mershen, et al., 230–59. Muscat, Oman: Al Roya Press and Publishing House, 2008.

Kaner, Simon, and Douglass W. Bailey, eds. *The Power of Dogu: Ceramic Figures from Ancient Japan*. London: British Museum Press, 2009.

Kerr, Rose. *Asian Ceramics in the Hallwyl Collection*. Stockholm: Hallwyl Museum, 2015.

Kerr, Rose, and Nigel Wood. *Science and Civilisation in China: Volume 55, Chemistry and Chemical Technology. Part 12, Ceramic Technology.* Cambridge: Cambridge University Press, 2004.

Kettering, Karen. "The Russian Porcelain Figure in the Eighteenth and Nineteenth Centuries." *Magazine Antiques*, March 2003, 114–19.

Keulemans, Guy. "The Geo-Cultural Conditions of *Kintsugi*." *Journal of Modern Craft* 9, no. 1 (2016): 15–34.

"Kintsugi: Ceramic Repair." Gen Saratani, n.d. https://www.urushi.info/kintsugi.

Koob, Stephen. "Obsolete Fill Materials Found on Ceramics." *Journal of the American Institute for Conservation* 37, no. 1 (Spring 1998): 49–67.

Krahl, Regina, John Guy, J. Keith Wilson, and Julian Raby, eds. *Shipwrecked: Tang Treasures and Monsoon Winds.* Washington, DC: Smithsonian Books, 2010.

Kuetter, Angelika R. "Simply Riveting: Broken and Mended Ceramics." Chipstone Foundation, 2016. http://www.chipstone.org/article.php/742/Ceramics-in-America-2016/Simply-Riveting:-Broken-and-Mended-Ceramics.

Lapérouse, Jean-François de, Karen Stamm, and Vicki Parry. "Re-Examination and Treatment of Mina'i Ceramics at the Metropolitan Museum of Art." In *Glass and Ceramics Conservation 2007: Preprints of the Interim Meeting of the ICOM-CC Working Group*, edited by Lisa Pilosi, 112–19. Nova Gorica, Slovenia: Goriški muzej, 2007.

Larco Hoyle, Rafael. *Las épocas peruanas.* Lima: Santigo Valverde, 1963.

Leach, Bernard. *A Potter's Book.* London: Faber and Faber, 1978.

———. *A Potter's Book.* London: Unicorn Press Ltd., 2015.

Le Corbeiller, Claire. "Miss America and Her Sisters: Personifications of the Four Parts of the World." *The Metropolitan Museum of Art Bulletin* 19 (April 1961): 209–23.

Lesser, Casey. "The Centuries-Old Japanese Tradition of Mending Broken Ceramics with Gold." Artsy, August 24, 2018. https://www.artsy.net/article/artsy-editorial-centuries-old-japanese-tradition-mending-broken-ceramics-gold.

Li, Zhiyan, Li He, and Virginia Bower. *Chinese Ceramics from the Paleolithic Period through the Qing Dynasty.* New Haven, CT: Yale University Press, 2010.

Li Ning Anticona, José. *El Gollete estribo de la cerámica precolombina peruana, interpretación estética.* Lima: Fondo Editorial UNMSM, 2000.

Lucas, Gavin, and John Robb. "The Terrain of Thingworlds: Central Objects and Asymmetry in Material Culture Systems." *Journal of Material Culture* 26, no. 2 (2021): 219–38.

Lynn, Martha Drexler. *Innovation and Identity, 1940 to 1979.* New Haven, CT: Yale University Press, 2015.

MacIntosh, D. *Chinese Blue and White Porcelain.* 3rd ed. Suffolk, UK: Antique Collector's Club, Ltd., 1994.

Makowski, Krzysztof. *La Arqueología y el estudio de las religiones andinas.* Lima: Colección Arte y Tesoros del Perú, Banco de Crédito del Perú, 2000.

Mañueco Santurtún, Maria del Carmen. "La porcelana del Buen Reitro. Investigaciones recientes." *Boletin de la Sociedad Española de Céramic y Vidrio* 38 (2011): 335–44.

Marchand, Suzanne. *Porcelain: A History from the Heart of Europe.* Princeton, NJ: Princeton University Press, 2020.

Martínez-Ruiz, Bárbaro. "Funerary Pots of the Kongo in Central Africa." In *African Terra Cottas: A Millenary Heritage in the Barbier-Mueller Museum Collections*, edited by Floriane Morin and Boris Wastiau, 288–311. Geneva: Barbier-Mueller Museum, 2008.

Maske, Andrew L. *Potters and Patrons in Edo Period Japan: Takatori Ware and the Kuroda Domain.* Abingdon, UK: Ashgate Publishing, 2011.

Mason, Robert, and Edward Keall. "The Abbasid Glazed Wares of Siraf and the Basra Connection: Petrographic Analysis." *Iran* 29 (1991): 51–66.

Mathews, Karen Rose. "Other People's Dishes: Islamic *Bacini* on Eleventh-Century Churches in Pisa." *Gesta* 53, no. 1 (2014): 5–23.

Mueller, Shirley. "Chinese Export Porcelain Curiosities." *Oriental Art* 46, no. 1 (2000): 16–27.

Munger, Jeffrey. *European Porcelain at the Metropolitan Museum*. New York: Metropolitan Museum of Art, 2018.

Nieuwenhuyse, Olivier, and Renske Dooijes. "Ancient Repairs: Techniques and Social Meaning." In *Konservieren oder restaurieren: die Restaurierung griechischer Vasen von der Antike bis heute*, edited by Martin Bentz and Ursula Kästner. Munich: C.H. Beck, 15–20.

———. "A New Life for Old Pots: Early Pottery Repairs from 7th Millennium Tell Sabi Abyad (Northern Syria)." Edited by Abraham van As. *Leiden Journal of Pottery Studies* 24 (2008): 159–70.

Nikolakopoulou, Irene. "Middle Cycladic Iconography: A Social Context for 'A New Chapter in Aegean Art.'" In *Cretan Offerings: Studies in Honour of Peter Warren*, edited by Olga Krzyszkowska, 213–22. London: British School at Athens Studies, 2010.

———. "Objects of Memory or Objects of Status? The Case of Cycladic Bichrome Ware Vases in Aegean Contexts." In *MNEME: Proceeding of the 17th International Aegean Conference Held in Venice and Udine, 17–21 April 2018*, edited by Elisabetta Borgna, Ilaria Caloi, Filippo M. Carinci, and Robert Laffineur, 455–61. Leuven, Belgium: Aegaeum 43, 2019.

Nollert, Angelika, ed. *African Ceramics: A Different Perspective*. Cologne: Walther König, 2020.

Odundo, Magdalene. *The Journey of Things*. London: InOtherWords, 2019.

Panagiotaki, Marina. *The Central Palace Sanctuary at Knossos*. London: British School of Athens, 1999.

Parry, Vicki. "Nishapur Ceramics in the Metropolitan Museum of Art: 70 Years of Restoration Techniques." In *Greater Khorasan: History, Geography, Archaeology and Material Culture*, edited by Rocco Rante, 151–60. Berlin: De Gruyter, 2015.

Pedley, John Griffiths. *Greek Art and Archaeology / John Griffiths Pedley*. 4th ed. Upper Saddle River, NJ: Pearson, 2007.

Peiro, Victoriano, and Charles P. Blanc. "Predicting the Spring Abundance Distribution of Red-Legged Partridge Populations in Agricultural Regions Using Environmental Models and an Application for Game Management." *Folia Zoologica* 60, no. 3 (2011): 203–13.

Petrie, Kevin, and Andrew Livingstone. *The Ceramics Reader*. London: Bloomsbury Academic, 2010.

Pierson, Stacey. *From Object to Concept: Global Consumption and the Transformation of Ming Porcelain*. Hong Kong: Hong Kong University Press, 2013.

Pietsch, Ulrich (ed.). *Meissen für die Zaren. Porzellan als Mittelsächsisch-russischer Politik im 18. Jahrhundert. Katalogbuch zur Ausstellung im Residenzschloss Dresden, 4. Juli—26. September 2004*. Munich: Hirmer, 2004.

Pradines, Stéphane. *Historic Mosques in Sub-Saharan Africa: From Timbuktu to Zanzibar*. Leiden: Brill, 2022.

Pye, E. "Writing Conservation." In *Writing as Material Practice: Substance, Surface and Medium*, edited by Kathryn E. Piquette and Ruth D. Whitehouse, 319–34. London: Ubiquity Press, 2013.

Quarcoopome, Nii O. "Akan Funerary Arts in Terra-cotta." *Bulletin of the Detroit Institute of Arts* 91, no. 1–4 (2017): 74–85.

Rafael, Johannes. "Zur 'Taxa Kaendler.'" *Keramos* 203/204 (2009), 25–67.

Rhodes, Daniel. *Clay and Glazes for the Potter*. Rev. ed. Radnor, PA: Chilton Book Company, 1973.

Ricciardi, Paola, Philippe Colomban and Véronique Milande. "Non-destructive Raman Characterization of Capodimonte and Buen Retiro Porcelain." *Journal of Raman Spectroscopy* 39 (2008): 1113–119.

Rice, Prudence M. *Pottery Analysis: A Sourcebook, Second Edition*. Chicago: University of Chicago Press, 2015.

Robson, Eleanor. *Ancient Knowledge Networks: A Social Geography of Cuneiform Scholarship in First-Millennium Assyria and Babylonia.* London: UCL Press, 2019.

Roosevelt, A. C., M. Lima da Costa, C. Lopes Machado, N. Mercier, H. Valladas, J. Feathers, W. Barnett, et al. "Paleoindian Cave Dwellers in the Amazon: The Peopling of the Americas." *Science* 272, no. 5260 (1996): 373–84.

Rosser-Owen, Mariam. *Islamic Arts from Spain*. London: Victoria and Albert Publishing, 2010.

Scott, Paul. "Tea Service: The Cockle Pickers Willow Pattern." http://cumbrianblues.com/wp-content/uploads/2017/05/12.CocklePickers.pdf.

Simmel, Georg. "Der Henkel." *Philosophie und Kultur*. 2nd ed. Leipzig, 1911.

Sorkin, Jenni. *Women, Ceramics, and Community*. Chicago: University of Chicago Press, 2016.

Stillemans, Jean. *Las dimensiones del vacío. Vasijas y arquitecturas prehispánicas del Perú*. Manuscript, n.d.

"Structure and Properties of Ceramics." American Ceramic Society, 2021. https://ceramics.org/about/what-are-engineered-ceramics-and-glass/structure-and-properties-of-ceramics.

Vandiver, Pamela B., Olga Soffer, Bohuslav Klima, and Jiři Svoboda, "The Origins of Ceramic Technology at Dolni Věstonice, Czechoslovakia." *Science* 246, no. 4933 (1989): 8.

Watanabe, Shinya. "La cerámica caolín en la cultura Cajamarca: el caso de la fase Cajamarca Media." *Bulletin de l'Institut Français d'Études Andines* 38, no. 2 (2009): 205–36.

Watanabe-O'Kelley, Helen. "Cultural Transfer and the Eighteenth-Century Queen Consort." *German History* 34 (2016): 279–92.

Watson, Oliver. *Ceramics from Islamic Lands*. London: Thames and Hudson, 2006.

Weintraub, Steven, Kanya Tsujimoto, and Sadae Y. Walters. "Urushi and Conservation: The Use of Japanese Lacquer in the Restoration of Japanese Art." *Ars Orientalis* 11 (1979): 39–62.

Welsh, Jorge, ed. *Ko-sometsuke: Chinese Porcelain for the Japanese Market*. London: Jorge Welsh Books, 2013.

Wen Wen. "Preconceptions of the Samarra Horizon, Green Splashed Ware and Blue Painted Ware Revisited through Chinese Ceramic Imports (Eighth to Tenth Centuries)." *Journal of Material Cultures in the Muslim World* 2 (2021): 150–83.

Wintle, Michael. "Gender and Race in the Personification of the Continents." In *Bodies and Maps: Early Modern Personifications of the Continents*, edited by Maryanne Cline Horowitz and Louise Arizzoli, 39–63. Leiden: Brill Press, 2021.

Witwer, Samuel. "*Liaisons Fragile*: Exchanges of Gifts Between Saxony and Prussia in the Early Eighteenth Century." In *Fragile Diplomacy: Meissen Porcelain for European Courts, c. 1710–63*, edited by Maureen Cassidy-Geiger, 87–110. New Haven: Yale University Press, 2007.

Wood, Nigel. *Chinese Glazes: Their Origins, Chemistry, and Recreation*. Philadelphia: University of Pennsylvania Press, 2011.

Wood, Nigel, Chris Doherty, and Mariam Rosser-Owen. "A Technological Study of Iraqi Copies of Chinese Changsha and Chinese Sancai Wares Found at Samarra." *Gu Taoci Kexue Jishu (Proceedings of the International Symposium on Ancient Ceramics)* 8 (2009): 154–80.

Wood, Nigel, and Michael Tite. "Blue and White—The Early Years: Tang China and Abbasid Iraq Compared." In *Transfer: The Influence of China on World Ceramics*, edited by Stacey Pierson, 21–45. London: University of London, 2009.

Wu, Xiaohong, Chi Zhang, Paul Goldberg, David Cohen, Yan Pan, Tri-na Arpin, and Ofer Bar-Yosef. "Early Pottery at 20,000 Years Ago in Xianrendong Cave, China." *Science* 336, no. 6089 (2012): 1696–700.

Zanardi, Tara. "Kingly Performance and Artful Innovation: Porcelain, Politics, and Identity at Charles III's Aranjuez." *West 86th: A Journal of Decorative Arts, Design History, and Material Culture* 25 (2018): 31–51.

Contributors

Caroline Fowler is the Starr Director of the Research and Academic Program at the Clark Art Institute in Williamstown, Massachusetts. She is the author of *Drawing and the Senses: An Early Modern History* (Brepols, 2017) and *The Art of Paper: From the Holy Land to the Americas* (Yale University Press, 2019). Her research has been supported by the Center for Advanced Study in the Visual Arts, Getty Research Institute, National Endowment for the Humanities, Historians of Netherlandish Art, and Renaissance Society of America.

Margaret S. Graves is an associate professor of art history at Indiana University. She works on the art of the medieval and modern Islamic world, with particular focus on the plastic arts of ceramics, metalwork, and stone carving as well as the histories of materials and making more broadly. She is the author of *Arts of Allusion: Object, Ornament, and Architecture in Medieval Islam* (Oxford University Press, 2018), and the winner of the International Center of Medieval Art annual book prize for 2019 and Medieval Academy of America's Karen Gould prize for 2021. Prior to receiving her PhD from the University of Edinburgh, she trained in studio art and art history.

Ulla Holmquist Pachas is the director of the Museo Larco in Lima, Peru. Previously, she was the director of the Inca Garcilaso Cultural Center of the Ministry of Foreign Affairs of Peru and the Museo Central of the Central Bank of Peru. She was also minister of culture of Peru, deputy director of the Museo Nacional de Arqueología, Antropología e Historia del Peru, and curator of pre-Columbian Art at the Museo de Arte de Lima. She is currently a professor in the MA program of museology at the Universidad Ricardo Palma and master's program of art history at the Pontificia Universidad Católica del Perú. Her research topics are Moche iconography and specifically the identification of the Moon Goddess in the northern coast pre-Columbian cultures of Peru.

Carl Knappett teaches in the Department of Art History at the University of Toronto, where he holds the Walter Graham / Homer Thompson chair in Aegean prehistory. He is a specialist in Bronze Age ceramics of the Aegean and east Mediterranean. He has published ceramic assemblages from sites on Crete such as Knossos, and has written on the production, exchange, and consumption of pottery from the Cyclades, Anatolia, and Cyprus. This ceramic focus has led him to explore the nature of materiality more broadly, as in his book *Thinking through Material Culture: An Interdisciplinary Perspective*. (University of Pennsylvania Press, 2005). A further interest is in connectivity and networks (see his *An Archaeology of Interaction: Network Perspectives on Material Culture and Society* [Oxford University Press, 2011]). His most recent volumes are *Aegean Bronze Age Art: Meaning in the Making* (Cambridge University Press, 2020) and a translation of Jean-Claude Poursat's *L'art égéen, The Art and Archaeology of the Aegean Bronze Age* (Cambridge University Press, 2022).

Sequoia Miller is a historian, curator, and studio potter. He is the chief curator at the Gardiner Museum of Ceramic Art in Toronto. Miller holds a PhD in the history of art from Yale University, an MA from the Bard Graduate Center for Decorative Arts, Design History, and Material Culture, and a BA in Russian from Brandeis University. Recent curatorial projects include RAW and Ai Weiwei: Unbroken at the Gardiner and The Ceramic Presence in Modern Art at the Yale University Art Gallery. Before reentering academia, Miller was a full-time studio potter based in the Pacific Northwest.

Magdalene Odundo, born in 1950, received her initial training as a graphic artist in her native Kenya. In 1971, she moved to the United Kingdom and enrolled in the foundation course at the Cambridge School of Art. In 1976, Odundo graduated in ceramics, photography, and printmaking from the University for the Creative Arts. Odundo completed her postgraduate studies at the Royal College of Art in 1982. In 2019, Odundo was appointed chancellor of the University for Creative Arts and was made a dame in the Queen's New Year Honours list 2020. Odundo's work is in the collections of many national and international museums, including the British Museum in London, Ashmolean Museum in Oxford, Victoria and Albert Museum in London, Fitzwilliam Museum in Cambridge, Metropolitan Museum of Art in New York City, Brooklyn Museum, National Museum of African Art at the Smithsonian Institution in Washington, DC, Los Angeles County Museum of Art, Gardiner Museum in Toronto, Stedelijk Museum Voor Hedendaagst Kunst in Hertogenbosh, Netherlands, Frankfurt Museum for Applied Arts, and Die Neue Sammlung (Design Museum) in Munich.

Vicki Parry, conservator of objects in the Department of Objects Conservation at the Metropolitan Museum of Art in New York City, conserves ceramic, stone, amber, bone, and ivory objects in the collection of the Met's Department of Asian Art. She has been involved in several major gallery renovations, special exhibitions, and projects as well as supervising conservation interns and fellows from the United States and several countries in Asia.

Soon Kai Poh is an objects conservator and postgraduate fellow at Bard Graduate Center. He received his undergraduate education at Carleton College majoring in studio art and chemistry, where he began working with porcelain in the studio. He is a graduate of the Conservation Center, Institute of Fine Arts, New York University, where he specialized in objects conservation with particular interests in Asian and Near Eastern works of art along with the interpretative and technological implications of transgeographic interactions for the understanding of material culture. At Bard Graduate Center as part of the Cultures of Conservation initiative, he cocurated Conserving Active Matter, an exhibition that presents and explores conservation as a process of inquiry, and with Peter Miller, coedited an accompanying eponymous volume of essays.

Ittai Weinryb is an associate professor at the Bard Graduate Center in New York. He teaches and writes on medieval art as well as material and visual culture from the greater Mediterranean to Eurasia and the Indian Ocean. He is the author of *The Bronze Object in the Middle Ages* (Cambridge University Press, 2016) and curator of the exhibition Agents of Faith: Votive Objects in Time and Place (2018).

Yao-Fen You is senior curator and head of the Product Design and Decorative Arts department at Cooper Hewitt, Smithsonian Design Museum. She joined the Smithsonian in 2019 following over ten years at the Detroit Institute of Arts, where she was associate curator of European sculpture and decorative arts. The author of *Coffee, Tea, and Chocolate: Consuming the World* (Detroit Institute of Arts/Yale University Press, 2016), she has published on a wide range of topics, from Netherlandish sculpture and painting of the sixteenth century to early twentieth-century design. A board member of the American Ceramic Circle and the Decorative Arts Trust, she is currently acting director of the Smithsonian Asian Pacific American Center.

Index

Note: Page numbers in italic type indicate illustrations.

Photography and Copyright Credits

© Ashmolean Museum: 38 (top right)

Ben Boswell: 31

© Clive Gracey (www.clivegracey.net): 9

© Fitzwilliam Museum, Cambridge: 30

Heraklion Archaeological Museum—Hellenic Ministry of Culture and Sports—Hellenic Organization of Cultural Resources Development (HOCRED): 38a

Icas94 / De Agostini via Getty Images: 43

Jens Mohr, The Hallwyl Museum/SHM (CC BY): 10

Courtesy of the artist and LGDR, New York © Takuro Kuwata: 3

© Metropolitan Museum of Art: 19, 20, 21, 22

Magdalene Odundo: 23, 24, 29, 31, 32

© Richard Wentworth: 7

© Victoria and Albert Museum, London: 8

ART/WORK

Caroline Fowler and Ittai Weinryb, Series Editors

Books in the ART/WORK series focus on specific media across time periods and cultures, collapsing longstanding asymmetries and bringing the specialist language of conservation to bear on the material history of art. The series presents accessible introductions to art history founded in collaboration, conversation, and an understanding of objects as they were formed through making, deterioration, care, and remaking.

Ceramic Art
Margaret S. Graves, Sequoia Miller, Magdalene Odundo, and Vicki Parry